In Dark Again in Wonder

In Dark Again in Wonder

The Poetry of René Char and George Oppen

Robert Baker

University of Notre Dame Press
Notre Dame, Indiana

Copyright © 2012 by the University of Notre Dame
Notre Dame, Indiana 46556
www.undpress.nd.edu

All Rights Reserved

The author is grateful for permission to reproduce poetry and other quotations from the following:

René Char, *Oeuvres complètes*, copyright © 1983 by Éditions Gallimard, Paris (encompassing all quoted poems by René Char published in separate editions listed in the Abbreviations, copyright © Éditions Gallimard). Reprinted by permission of Gallimard.

George Oppen, *New Collected Poems*, edited by Michael Davidson, copyright © 1960, 1961, 1962, 1963, 1964, 1965, 1967, 1968, 1969, 1970, 1971, 1972, 1973, 1974, 1975, 1976, 1977, 1978, 1981 by George Oppen; copyright © 1985, 2002, 2008 by Linda Oppen. Reprinted by permission of New Directions Publishing Corp. (World rights excluding U.K./Commonwealth)

George Oppen, *New Collected Poems*, edited by Michael Davidson. Reprinted by permission of Carcanet Press Limited. (U.K./Commonwealth rights)

Wallace Stevens, "Chocorua to its Neighbor" and "A Primitive like an Orb," from The *Collected Poems of Wallace Stevens*, copyright © 1954 by Wallace Stevens and renewed 1982 by Holly Stevens. Used by permission of Alfred A. Knopf, a division of Random House, Inc.

The Georgics by Virgil, translated with an introduction and notes by L. P. Wilkinson (Penguin Classics, 1982). Copyright © L. P. Wilkinson, 1982. Reproduced by permission of Penguin Books Ltd.

Elizabeth Bishop, "At the Fishhouses," from *The Complete Poems 1927–1979* by Elizabeth Bishop, copyright © 1979, 1983 by Alice Helen Methfessel. Reprinted by permission of Farrar, Straus and Giroux, LLC.

Louise Gluck, "On Impoverishment," in *Proofs and Theories: Essays on Poetry* by Louise Gluck, copyright © 1994 by Louise Gluck. Reprinted by permission of HarperCollins Publishers.

Library of Congress Cataloging-in-Publication Data

Baker, Robert, 1965–
In dark again in wonder : the poetry of René Char and George Oppen / Robert Baker.
    p. cm.
Includes bibliographical references and index.
ISBN 978-0-268-02229-7 (pbk. : alk. paper)
ISBN 0-268-02229-1 (pbk. : alk. paper)
 1. Char, René, 1907–1988—Criticism and interpretation. 2. Oppen, George—Criticism and interpretation. 3. Modernism (Literature) 4. Philosophy in literature.
I. Title.
PQ2605.H3345Z55 2012
843'.912—dc23
                          2012000247

∞ *The paper in this book meets the guidelines for permanence and durability of the Committee on Production Guidelines for Book Longevity of the Council on Library Resources.*

CONTENTS

Acknowledgments	vii
A Note on the Text	ix
Abbreviations	xi

Introduction: History and Metaphysics in the Poetry of René Char and George Oppen   1

CHAPTER ONE
René Char: Eros and Clairvoyance   15

CHAPTER TWO
George Oppen: Vision and Companionship   55
   A Note on Building and Seeing in Oppen   110
   A Note on Belief and Language in Oppen   117

Conclusion: Revisions of Axial Age Metaphysics in the Age of Modernity   121

Notes	175
Bibliography	209
Index	221

ACKNOWLEDGMENTS

Here at the University of Montana, my former dean, Gerald Fetz, and my former chair, Casey Charles, helped me to find the time to write this book. My current dean, Chris Comer, has been very supportive of my work as well. Chris Knight, the senior scholar in the Department of English here, took the time to read an earlier draft of this book with care. For years he has given his tremendous support to my teaching and writing. I'm very grateful to him for this. I've learned a great deal from my students who have engaged the work of René Char and George Oppen in classes I've taught over the years. It's a delight to thank them here. It's a delight to thank, too, Tom Seiler, a graduate student in our program, for having prepared the maps that appear on pages 76–77.

I wish to thank two anonymous readers who responded to this book for the University of Notre Dame Press. Their responses were expansive, insightful, and altogether constructive. My editors at the press, Harv Humphrey and Stephen Little, have been clear and helpful in everything. Margaret Hyre, a sharp copy editor, brought to the book a spirit of dialogue far beyond a copy editor's call of duty. I owe a special thanks to Rebecca DeBoer, my managing editor, for her help in guiding this book through the editorial process. Barbara Hanrahan, my former editor, first set the book on its ways to publication. My thanks to all these people.

Katie Baker and Kevin Tomlinson shared with me the quiet of their place in Portland at a moment when I needed quiet. I'm grateful to them for their generosity

Above all I want to thank a friend of mine, Melissa Kwasny, who read an earlier draft of this book with all her clarifying attention. For many years I've been reading Melissa's books and talking with her about Char, Oppen, and everything else, and I'm sure that a few of her words have found their way into this book (with inflections that are of course my responsibility), for a conversation is a gift and a voyage, taking us farther than we thought we were going, becoming a part of the way we see.

A NOTE ON THE TEXT

I've assumed that some readers of this book will know French well, that some will know French in part, and that some will not know French at all. And I would like this book to have the texture of four interconnected essays: a short introduction, a chapter on Char, a chapter on Oppen, and a long conclusion. Though it is of course ideal to include both the original text and the translation when one is working with a writer in a foreign language, and though one loses all sorts of nuances and ambiguities in not including the original, I wished to avoid here the sheer unwieldiness that all the double citations of every passage would involve, especially since I cite Char so frequently. Thus my citations of Char's poetry, for the most part, are given solely in English translations. The exceptions are four poems of Char's that I cite in their entirety: these I cite first in French, then in English. There are also a couple of extended passages, not complete poems, that I cite in both the French original and the English translation.

References to Char's poetry and prose are to the accessible Gallimard/Folio paperback editions of his books, or, on occasion, to the Pléiade edition of his *Oeuvres complètes*. These books—and the abbreviations with which I refer to them in the text—are listed in the abbreviations section. Usually I refer to poems by page number, but when citing the wartime sequence *Formal Share*, I refer to section numbers with Roman numerals. When citing the wartime journal *Leaves of Hypnos*, I refer to section numbers with Arabic numerals. The context should make these references clear, but because there are a few ambiguous places, I include the # sign in citing sections from *Leaves of Hypnos*.

In the abbreviations section I also provide the translations of titles of Char's books that I use throughout the book. Occasionally, as with *Le Poème pulvérisé*, I leave a title untranslated.

Translations of Char's poetry and prose in this book are mine. But, for interested readers, I've included a list of all the English-language translations of Char's poetry that I know of (p. xii).

*

Abbreviations for the works of Oppen's to which I most frequently refer are given in the abbreviations section.

References to Oppen's poetry are to the *New Collected Poems* edited by Michael Davidson. Usually I refer to poems by page number. But when discussing the long sequences "Of Being Numerous" and "Route," I refer to the section number of the sequence. The context should make this clear.

Oppen's essay "The Mind's Own Place," and the "daybooks" or "worksheets" of his that I cite, are listed in the Bibliography at the end of the book. I reference these in footnotes, not with abbreviations in the text.

*

I've included, in the abbreviations section, simple chronologies of Char's and Oppen's major publications.

ABBREVIATIONS

RENÉ CHAR

ES   *Éloge d'une Soupçonnée* précédé de *Fenêtres dormantes et porte sur le toit*, *Chants de la Balandrane*, *Les Voisinages de Van Gogh*. Paris: Gallimard/Folio, 1988.
      Translation: *In Praise of an Intuited Presence*

FH   *Feuillets d'Hypnos*. In *Fureur et mystère*.
      Translation: *Leaves of Hypnos*

FM   *Fureur et mystère*. Préface d'Yves Berger. Gallimard/Folio: Paris, 1967.
      Translation: *Fury and Mystery*

M   *Les Matinaux* suivi de *La Parole en archipel*. Gallimard/Folio: Paris, 1987.
      Translation: *The Dawnbreakers* or *The People of Dawn*

MM   *Le Marteau sans maître* suivi de *Moulin premier*. Ed. Marie-Claude Char. Postface d'Yves Battistini. Gallimard/Folio: Paris, 2002.
      Translation: *The Hammer without a Master* and *First Mill*

NP   *Le Nu perdu*. Gallimard/Folio: Paris, 1978.
      Translation: *Lost Nakedness*

OC   *Oeuvres complètes*. Ed. Jean Roudaut. Gallimard: Paris, 1983.

PA   *La Parole en archipel*. In *Les Matinaux* suivi de *La Parole en archipel*
      Translation: *The Word as Archipelago*

RBS   *Recherche de la base et du sommet*. Gallimard/Folio: Paris, 1971.
      Translation: *Search for the Base and the Summit*

English-Language Translations of Char's Work

The Brittle Age and *Returning Upland*. Trans. Gustaf Sobin, with a foreword by Mary Ann Caws. Denver, CO: Counterpath Press, 2009.
The Dawn Breakers. Trans. and with an introduction by Michael Worton. Newcastle upon Tyne: Bloodaxe Books, 1992.
Furor and Mystery. Trans. Mary Ann Caws and Nancy Kline. Boston: Black Widow Press, 2011.
Hypnos Waking. Ed. Jackson Mathews, trans. Jackson Mathews and others. New York: Random House, 1956.
Leaves of Hypnos. Trans. Cid Corman. New York: Grossman Publishers, 1973.
No Siege Is Absolute: Versions of René Char. Trans. Franz Wright. Providence, RI: Lost Roads Press, 1984.
Poems of René Char. Trans. Mary Ann Caws and Jonathan Griffin. Princeton: Princeton University Press, 1976.
Selected Poems. Ed. Mary Ann Caws and Tina Jolas, trans. Mary Ann Caws and others, with an introduction by Mary Ann Caws. New York: New Directions, 1992.
Stone Lyre: Poems of René Char. Trans. Nancy Naomi Carlson, with an introduction by Ilya Kaminsky. North Adams, MA: Tupelo Press, 2009.
This Smoke That Carried Us: Selected Poems. Trans. Susanne Dubroff, with an introduction by Christopher Merrill. Buffalo, NY: White Pine Press, 2004.
The Word as Archipelago. Trans. and with an introduction by Robert Baker. San Francisco: Omnidawn, 2012.

Simple Chronology of Major Works by Char

Le Marteau sans maître	1935
Moulin premier	1936
Placard pour un chemin des écoliers	1937
Dehors la nuit est gouvernée	1938
Fureur et mystère	1948
Seuls demeurent	w. 1938–44
Visage nuptial	w. 1938

Partage formel	w. 1942
Feuillets d'Hypnos	w. 1943–44
Loyaux adversaires	
Le poème pulvérisé	w. 1945–47
La fontaine narrative	w. 1947
Les Matinaux	1950
Recherche de la base et du sommet	1955
La Parole en archipel	1962
Le Nu perdu	1971
La nuit talismanique qui brillait dans son cercle	1972
Aromates chasseurs	1975
Chants de la Balandrane	1977
Fenêtres dormantes et porte sur le toit	1979
Les voisinages de Van Gogh	1985
Éloge d'une Soupçonnée	1988

GEORGE OPPEN

CP *New Collected Poems*. Ed. Michael Davidson, with a preface by Eliot Weinberger and an introduction by Michael Davidson. New York: New Directions, 2002.

IN "George Oppen." Interview with Louis Dembo. In *The Contemporary Writer*. Madison: University of Wisconsin Press, 1972. 172–90. Reprint of interview in *Contemporary Literature* 10.2 (1969): 159–77.

SL *Selected Letters*. Ed. and with an introduction and notes by Rachel Blau DuPlessis. Durham: Duke University Press, 1990.

SP *Selected Prose, Daybooks, and Papers*. Ed. and with an introduction and notes by Stephen Cope. Berkeley: University of California Press, 2007.

Simple Chronology of Major Works by Oppen

Discrete Series	1934
The Materials	1962

"The Mind's Own Place"	1963
This In Which	1965
Of Being Numerous	1968
"Interview" with Louis Dembo	1969
Seascape: Needle's Eye	1972
Myth of the Blaze	w. 1972–75
Primitive	1978

Introduction

History and Metaphysics in the Poetry of René Char and George Oppen

Merleau-Ponty is among those philosophers of the last century who have sought to reawaken the experience of wonder which the ancients thought to be the source of philosophy. At one point in his final book, *The Visible and the Invisible*, he cites a suggestive passage from Claudel's *Art Poétique*: "From time to time, a man lifts his head, sniffs, listens, considers, recognizes his position: he thinks, he sighs, and, drawing his watch from the pocket lodged against his chest, looks at the time. *Where am I*, and *what time is it*, such are the inexhaustible questions turning us to the world . . ." Such questions, Merleau-Ponty claims, are of a piece with the questions that philosophy takes up. "The questions are within our life," he says, "within our history: they are born there, they die there, if they have found a response, more often than not they are transformed there; in any case, it is a past of experience and of knowledge that one day ends up at this open wondering." This open wondering readily moves from questions like *what time is it?* and *where am I?* to questions like *who am I?*, and *what should I do?* or *how should I live?*, and *what is the whole that surrounds me and that I live within?* These are questions at the origins of philosophy. Perhaps it is worth stepping back from the terms in which metaphysics has so often been stigmatized in modern culture: as the search for a transcendent world behind the immanent world, or as the search for an ultimate foundation, the unconditioned ground from which everything conditioned derives, or as the search for a consoling presence. We might, rather, follow scholars of ancient philosophy and think of metaphysics as one dimension of a larger philosophical search: a search for an account of the whole, an account of the soul (or, if the language of a given time and place has changed, of the self or the person), and an account of the good. Stanley Rosen has underlined that, in order to provide an account of something, one has to have *seen*, or *glimpsed*, or, as the biblical tradition has it, *heard* the thing that one is trying to provide an account of, and it is not easy to see with clarity the whole, or the soul, or the good. So a measure of surmise will be inevitable. We live and think in a space of conjecture. Here poetry and philosophy cross through one another. If poetry doesn't come to life without an ear for the hidden turns, depths, and reaches of language, neither poetry nor philosophy comes to life without some sort of *vision*. Poetry, philosophy, and religion, in this sense at least, have deep affinities with one another.[1]

Where am I, who am I, how should I live?: questions like these are troubled and further perplexed in the modern world. There are of course many reasons why this is so. Not the least important is our distinctive modern sense not simply of taking place in history but also of making history, making our own history, defining and redefining ourselves in historical time, posing questions that have no need of natural or transcendent "ends," no need of farther "horizons" beyond those which we set for ourselves in freedom. The ancients did not lack an experience of historical difference in space and time, to be sure, but they did subordinate their sense of history to a larger religious or metaphysical comprehension of the whole, the good, and human life. This relationship between the historical and the metaphysical has been nearly inverted, or at least severely fractured, in the modern world. Indeed, a powerful thrust of modern culture, in particular from the French Revolution on, has been the repeated effort to debunk metaphysical questions as superstitions, errors, illusions, nostalgias, or masks of social power. Yet why has this effort had to be taken up again and again, with something like the urgency of an obsession? Perhaps because the questions of traditional philosophy, including the old metaphysical question *where am I in relation to the whole?*, do not simply go away even in an historicist epoch that tells us that, after all, we are in a particular time and place shaped by a particular if complex process of historical development. The recurrent renewal of metaphysical questions, in fact, turns out to be as pervasive in modern philosophy as the recurrent dismissal of these questions. It is as though modern philosophers, from Hegel on, were drawn again and again to the fissure between the historical and the metaphysical. This is perhaps nowhere more evident than in the existentialist tradition, in the broadest sense, taken here to include at least Kierkegaard, Nietzsche, Heidegger, and Sartre. I will set aside for a moment the tremendous differences among these thinkers. Each emphatically affirms decision, resolution, responsibility on the part of the individual; each, in an unmistakably romantic or modernist way, understands conventional social life to be often an obstacle to individual freedom, whether this obstacle then be called Christendom, the system, the herd, the they-self, or the network of social roles into which we are invited to step with all our fear of freedom, all our bad faith; each is suspicious of traditional metaphysics as yet another illusion, another threat to the difficult freedom of what Kierkegaard calls the concretely existing individual; and yet each, finally, comes to present a distinctive, highly conjectural vision of the whole in relation to which individual freedom is discovered and sustained, be this Kierkegaard's hyperbolic negative theology, Nietzsche's riddling account of power and flux at play in the eternal recurrence of the same, Heidegger's evocation of human being as the open in which Being comes to light (or, later, Being as the open in which human being comes to light), or Sartre's darker sketch of a restless consciousness at once trapped by and forever divided from a viscous materiality of pointless contingency. The metaphysical question of *where I am in relation to the whole*, if intently debunked in familiar versions, is brought back and lyrically unfolded in unfamiliar versions. It is as though there were a question here that we found at once impossible to retain and impossible to abandon, a question we could not quite fit into our historicist picture of ourselves without remainder, though we could not quite figure out, either, what to do with this remainder. Does it even make sense to speak of a remainder that, as it were, is what remains to our thought of the whole? How do we glimpse this? In fragments and indirections? What are we to call it? Nature? Being? Time? The Encompassing? The Mystery of Presence? The Open of Presencing? The Horizon of Faith after Faith?[2]

Existentialism, while it eventually becomes an important dimension of literary and philosophical modernism, emerges out of romanticism. The shared themes of existentialist philosophy and romantic and modernist poetry, in particular, are hard to miss: a concern with individual freedom, often understood in an agonistic sense, where solitude is conceived as a necessary moment of an authentic and free life; a distrust of traditional religious and metaphysical pictures of the world and the self; and, at the same time, a practice of vision, or a practice of surmise, evoking pictures of the whole that are precariously modern, or untimely, or even un-modern. This art of speculative vision is perhaps one reason why existentialist philosophy, in a broad sense, is sometimes said to be more literary than other types of philosophy. Another reason is that voices in this tradition, like voices in modern literature, tend to emphasize the connection between the basic existential concerns of the individual and an open horizon of metaphysical questioning. But, again, in the modern period any metaphysical horizon of this sort is left suspended, or made altogether uncertain, by an historical horizon of experience that over time becomes culturally dominant. We dwell in the rift between these two horizons, or, one might say, in the rift between these two ways of understanding where and who we are.

*

Sociology, social philosophy, philosophy of history, and empiricist historiography are the domains in which this modern historical horizon of experience has been given its clearest articulation. One could say, in shorthand, that existentialism and sociology represent a basic opposition in modern culture. From the 1840s on, existentialist philosophies, with their emphasis on individual freedom and an individual response to alienation or the loss of self, at once echo and contest liberal and radical social philosophies, with their emphasis on social freedom and a political response to alienation or the loss of self. It is true that one can locate the origins of these approaches to experience much further back in time (one could, for example, call Socrates and Jesus existentialists). It is also possible to trace these approaches back to important eighteenth-century voices. Or, too, one could simply observe that both approaches belong to the full unfolding of German idealist thought: the debate between existentialism and sociology can be seen as a variation on the Kant-Hegel debate or the slightly later Kierkegaard-Hegel debate. Yet the decade of the 1840s lends a kind of emblematic clarity to the tension between these two currents of thought. Kierkegaard, between 1844 and 1849, published the *Philosophical Fragments*, the *Concluding Unscientific Postscript*, *The Present Age*, and *The Sickness unto Death*, arguing that modern Europeans had forgotten what it meant to be an individual, had lost themselves in either an empty individualism or an equally empty obedience to social and cultural convention. In the same years, Marx and Engels developed the materialist philosophy of history that would come to be known as marxism: the so-called Paris Manuscripts were written in 1844, *The German Ideology* in 1845–46, and *The Communist Manifesto* in 1848. In 1848, revolutionary uprisings occurred throughout Europe, and if they failed, they also pointed to great changes to come, for workers' movements and nationalist movements would be tremendous forces throughout the modern world. After the events of 1848, further, the uneasy relationship between bourgeois social reality and bourgeois high culture became more sharply antagonistic. Kierkegaard and Marx gave voice to this altered climate as it came into being.

Kierkegaard and Marx were of course far from isolated voices. The context of the 1840s included liberal and conservative sociologies as well as Marx's radical sociology. It was between 1835 and 1840 that Tocqueville published *Democracy in America*, examining the forces of equality, self-government, and public opinion that, he said, were destined to shape the modern world. The context, too, included practical or moderate versions of individualism as well as Kierkegaard's provocative, nearly desperate version of religious inwardness. Mill's *On Liberty*, a spirited defense of individual freedom within a liberal framework, was published in 1859. Yet the stark opposition between the voices of Kierkegaard and Marx in the 1840s brings out an important tension that, usually in more ambiguous ways, runs through all of modern culture (a sharp polarity of this sort returns in the opposition between Heidegger and Lukács in the 1920s or between Camus and Sartre in the 1950s). Kierkegaard and Marx are both critics of Hegel. Kierkegaard criticizes Hegel in the name of the concretely existing individual irreducible to a moment of a social or a conceptual whole. At the same time he takes Hegel to be a symptom of a larger social tendency: the erosion of the inward life of the individual. Marx criticizes Hegel in the name of a revolutionary transformation of material social institutions that, he argues, still block the realization of freedom whose historical development Hegel claims to have comprehended. Marx, too, takes Hegel to be a symptom of a larger social process, namely, ideology, or the cultural disguising and rationalizing of social hierarchy and class conflict. Kierkegaard, concerned with spiritual life, wishes to rescue the concrete individual from the depersonalizing structures of modern society. Marx, concerned with substantive social freedom, wishes to rescue the concrete individual from the dehumanizing structures of the capitalist economy in particular. Marx, like all later sociologists, adopts Hegel's vision of social interdependence as the ground of existential independence. From this point of view, an existentialist critique of depersonalization is one-sided, blind to the modern reality of social atomization and the illusory promises of freedom it generates. Kierkegaard, like the whole existentialist tradition after him, expresses a romantic distrust of social routine, a romantic faith in an inward freedom discovered in relation to a metaphysical horizon transcending any given social world. From this point of view, a sociological critique of individualism is itself one-sided, ignoring the spiritual life of those who are to be free, and erasing the difference between the genuine individual, whose inwardness is concentrated and lived, and the aesthetic individual, whose sheer dispersal is a condition as alienated as any simple conformity. Kierkegaard sees his opponent as Hegel, not Marx, but the debate, however orchestrated, is an early phase of the long modern conflict between an historicist sociology and a romantic existentialism. This is a story I will engage in detail in my concluding chapter. Here I wish only to underline that the tension between an historical and a metaphysical horizon of experience is related to, though not the same as, the difference between a sociological and an existential way of seeing our lives. These two ways of seeing, at least implicitly, are always in conversation with each other. Often both are audible within the work of a single writer.[3]

René Char and George Oppen are two modernist poets in whose work, and in whose lives, a wrestling with the tension between the historical and the metaphysical comes to be sounded with all the resonance of a collision. Both are poets concerned with the abiding philosophical questions so often taken up in modern poetry and existentialist philosophy: the exploration of existential or spiritual freedom, the gathering of the self in relation to death, the meditation on the whole, the turn to Nature as the open space of the whole under the conditions of modernity, the clarification of the ground of vision in eros and love, the search for the good life. At the same time both are fully engaged with the crises and promises of the concrete historical worlds they inhabit, decisively responding, in particular, to the social upheavals of the thirties and forties in Europe and America. They express in their poems the tension between a metaphysical orientation of thought, grounded in basic existential concerns, and a political orientation of thought, alert to the social contexts in which they are situated. In this respect they are like a number of other major modernist poets, including Mandelstam, Akhmatova, Montale, Lorca, Hernández, Neruda, Vallejo, Rukeyser, Césaire, and Celan. These are all poets in whose work the tension between the historical and the metaphysical that I've just sketched is put under extreme pressure. My hope is that what I'm able to bring to light in my discussion of the work of Char and Oppen, then, will cast some light, too, on this broader field of modernist poetry and on this basic tension in modern culture at large.

The lives of Char (1907–88) and Oppen (1908–82) almost exactly overlap in the realm of chronology. Both belong to a generation of writers whom we might call the last modernists (the subtitle, in the singular, of Anthony Cronin's biography of Beckett). Probably it is first of all the differences or even the antitheses between these poets that are likely to capture one's attention: if Char in his youth embraces surrealism and a spirit of revolt, Oppen in his youth embraces objectivism and a spirit of attention; if Char is a visionary of the natural world, a writer of poems characterized by a quickened, at times abrupt movement, Oppen is a poet who practices a kind of existential phenomenology, a writer of poems that unfold with an uncommonly patient rhythm of disclosure; where Char is an anarchist by temperament, Oppen at times sounds like an almost reluctant solitary, mourning a missing social reconciliation that in his youth he had dreamed of finding. Char and Oppen, it is clear, are very different poets. Yet brief sketches of their lives and works, while bringing out these differences, should allow some important affinities to emerge as well.

"I was born with an aggressive breathing," Char writes in one of his aphoristic sequences (RBS, 145). Born and raised in L'Isle-sur-la-Sorgue, a small village in the Vaucluse, he left high school in his final year, after an argument with a teacher, and then spent a year in a business school in Marseilles. He had no further formal education. A young poet without a place or a direction, inspired by a contemporary poem he had come upon, he wrote a letter to Paul Éluard, as Rimbaud had once written a letter to an older Paul Verlaine. Éluard responded, and a short time later Char moved to Paris and became the youngest member of the surrealist group, participating in the movement from 1930 through 1935. Though he eventually went his own way, there is no doubt that the surrealist adventure provided him with an initiation into the alliance of revolt, eros, and imagination that would remain important to him all his life.

In the mid-thirties Char returned to L'Isle-sur-la-Sorgue, in part to sort out his differences with surrealism. As he watched the Spanish Republic collapse, the Popular Front fall apart in France, and the fascist nightmare (as he called it) descend on Europe, he began to sketch the lyrical, visionary, meditative, speculative path that he would follow in the decades ahead. In retrospect it almost seems as though he were preparing himself in solitude for a difficult trial to come. He served in the French army in 1939 and 1940, fighting in Alsace, until the defeat of France in the summer of 1940. He then returned home to a demoralized south of France under the Vichy regime. A year later, aware that he was under police surveillance, he moved to Céreste, a small mountain village not far from his home, and made contacts with other dissident spirits in the area. By 1942 he had become a leader in the Resistance, and by 1943 a commander in the Secret Army, in charge of the Lower Alps region, responsible for gathering munitions from parachute drops and carrying out preparations for the liberation. During the war years Char published nothing, choosing what his biographer calls a principled silence, yet he continued to write. He wrote all sorts of different texts, including verse and prose poems, a desperately defiant aphoristic sequence affirming the steep promise of poetry despite all, and an extraordinary notebook of observations and reflections composed during the last two years of his life in the Resistance. All these works were published after the war, and the wartime notebook, *Leaves of Hypnos*, would be considered one of the great works of literature to come out of the French Resistance. In the years just after the war, then, Char became a widely read poet in Europe. In these years he also formed or renewed friendships with a number of prominent writers and painters of the time, including Éluard, Camus, Braque, and de Staël.

Yet he hardly lost his independence. In the thirties, despite his hostility to capitalism, he had never had the faith in communism that some of his surrealist companions had, in part because he saw in communist politics an account of life too rationalist for his sensibility, or too corporatist for his defiant individualism (RBS, 38–39). Similarly, in the early postwar years, he kept a certain distance from the political sphere, though he expressed his vexation with the politically motivated myths of the Resistance that had begun to take shape almost from the day the war ended (RBS, 24–25). His concern in these years, it seems, was to recover that part of himself as open to the life of eros and encounter as Rimbaud had been to the life of fury and departure (RBS, 18). The book he published in 1948, *Le Poème pulvérisé*, consists largely of prose poems that are nearly Wordsworthian in their recollection of buried layers of experience, hidden depths of imaginative energy.

The élan of courage that Char found in the Resistance seems to have carried him through the late forties and early fifties. He wrote a great deal in these years. Yet eventually the damages and burdens of the war years made themselves felt. He went through a period of depression and insomnia in the fifties, and some of his major works of this decade, on occasion in a subterranean way, are crisis poems or sequences, writings whose animating force is a movement of recovery, of spirited pressing back against the pressure of reality, to borrow Stevens's phrase. Perhaps, as Char aged, the resonant luminous density of his earlier work became more difficult to renew again and again. Enthusiasm, as important to Char as exuberance was to Blake, is after all not inexhaustible. His individualist stance, his distrust of all mass movements, grew more pronounced in time. While in the mid-sixties he was active in an unsuccessful movement to keep nuclear missiles from being placed in Provence, he remained detached from both the crisis of the Algerian war for independence and the student movement of 1968. His later poems, as Paul Veyne has put it, are often given to an atheistic mysticism of space and the stars, of contemplative passage across the distances of night.

Oppen, again, is a very different sort of writer. He was born in New Rochelle, New York, and largely grew up in San Francisco, and, like Char, he had almost no formal education beyond high school. He left college after a single semester and, beginning his remarkably nomadic adult life, travelled across the country with the woman he would marry. Like Char, too, Oppen was still quite young when, in the late twenties, he found his way to a milieu of innovative modernist poets, in this case the force field of Williams, Pound, and Zukofsky. He was always inclined toward a certain empiricism, or a clear-eyed realism, though in his later work he would unfold this as a lyricism of reverent openness, a voicing of wonder in the presence of simple things taking place in the unfathomable whole. In any case he had little sympathy for prophetic, visionary, surrealist, or rhetorical poetic bearings. Char's work, then, represents many of the things that Oppen most distrusted in poetry.

And yet Oppen was a more romantic and agonistic individual than one might initially imagine him to have been. He was, in his quiet way, almost as defiant as Char. In fact, Char and Oppen—though the former was a spontaneous anarchist, the latter for a while an active communist—were both committed to the existentialist language of ungrounded choice, and both practiced what they preached, displaying an impressive independence throughout their lives. Oppen, like Char, found himself in a world of established modernist writers at a young age, and, like Char, he turned away from this world only a few years later, setting out to define his own path. Just here, however, there was also a major difference. In the mid-thirties Char withdrew to his native Provence to rethink his work in a measure of solitude. His political engagement in the Resistance would come a short time later. Oppen, in the winter of 1934–35, living in New York, seeing the misery of the Depression all around him, abandoned the writing of poetry and joined the Communist Party, helping to organize workers and to prevent evictions. One thing leads to another in a life. Oppen would not publish another poem for almost thirty years: he would not even write another poem for almost twenty-five years. During these years he worked as an organizer, made a particular effort to get drafted so that he could fight in the war (he fought and was seriously wounded in the Rhineland), returned to California after the war to re-begin a life with his wife and daughter, and then chose to live with his family in exile in Mexico for a decade rather than testify before the House Un-American Activities Committee. Only in the late fifties, near the end of his exile in Mexico, did he once again begin to write poetry. He returned to America with his family in 1960, living first in New York and then, from 1966 on, in San Francisco. Three decades earlier he had walked away from his wealthy family and his promising early work as a poet. His first book of poems, *Discrete Series*, had been published in 1934; his second book, *The Materials*, was published in 1962, after twenty-eight years during which he had had nothing to do with the world of poetry. He later made clear that in the thirties he simply felt that he ought not to fiddle while Rome was burning. He also, like Char, had no patience for didactic political poetry: poetry, he thought, had other tasks. Yet this is not to say that for him the tasks of poetry were unrelated to the hopes and predicaments of social and political life. Memories of the thirties, memories of the war, memories of the conflicts and the choices of those years, a concern with the social upheavals of the fifties and sixties: all these issues pervade Oppen's meditative poetry of the sixties and seventies. His poetry would not be what it is without his experience of those decades or his persistent thinking through of the significance of all he had lived through. In this respect, too, there is a parallel between Char and Oppen. Char wrote major sequences at the same time that he was fighting in the Resistance, while Oppen wrote major poems about the Great Depression and the Second World War at a remove of three decades or more. And yet in the poetry of both, the disasters of the thirties and forties, and the concrete demands that they felt these disasters placed on their lives, are seen in a clarifying depth of perspective.

There are other affinities between these poets. Both understand the open of poetry to have its ground in the life of encounter. Wonder, in particular wonder inseparable from anguish and the shadow of death, is an experience important in the work of both. A meditative practice, a thinking through of images and questions in a wide quietness of the mind, is essential to the searching poetry they both come to write. Audible in both is a demanding sense of vocation. In Oppen, I think, this is not attenuated but measured by his long silence.

"Belief? / What do we believe / To live with?" (CP, 52), Oppen asks in the first poem he wrote after a twenty-five-year break from poetry, and this question animates all his work from the late fifties on. He is a writer who brings the whole weight and scope of his experience to his writing. Char, too, approaches poetry in this way, finding in poetry a space in which to explore how to live, how to shape one's experience in relation to horizons of what matters. In a short essay on Camus, Char cites a statement of Nietzsche's that was as true for him as it was for Niezsche or Camus: "I've always put all my life and all my self into my writings. I know nothing of purely intellectual problems" (RBS, 93). "I am one of those," Oppen writes in a late poem, "who from nothing but man's way of thought and one of his dialects and what has happened to me / Have made poetry" (CP, 167). If Char began as a surrealist, and if Oppen began as an objectivist, both turned out to be idiosyncratic philosophical poets—even, in an untimely way, wisdom writers—who are difficult to place in any of the usual frames of our literary histories.

Stephen Fredman has addressed this issue in an essay in which he suggests that we might do well to think of writers like Oppen and Olson, or Char and Celan, as existentialists rather than as objectivists, or projectivists, or surrealists, or romantics, or modernists, and so forth. This seems to be meant not as a conclusion but as a point of departure, an unfamiliar way of thinking about these poets. The idea would be not that Char and Oppen are existentialists in some strict sense but that they are poets who explore existential questions in ways that recall writers in a broad existentialist tradition. Char and Oppen no doubt find echoes of their concerns in thinkers in this tradition. Nietzsche's heroic individualism, tragic vision of life, and affirmation of art as our last resource in the face of ruin are of great importance to Char. The existential phenomenologies of Heidegger and Merleau-Ponty are of great importance to Oppen. Both Char and Oppen, independent thinkers, are concerned with freedom, responsibility, the burdens of our decisions and engagements, the precarious or absent ground of our choices. Both understand their lives and commitments in relation to the social crises of their times. Though neither adopts Sartre's conception of engaged literature, an issue of such controversy from the thirties through the sixties and on, both are engaged individuals, deeply responsive in their lives and works to all that is happening in the social worlds around them. Both, further, are drawn again and again to what I've characterized as the tension in our culture between the historical and the metaphysical. A major question for both is the relationship between a concrete human life and the mystery of the whole in which any life takes place. One of Oppen's most memorable poems in which this question is unfolded—a poem that evokes at once the unending erosion of everything in time and the recurrent opening of a "there," a "miracle of place," that allows us to see where we are—turns out to be, at the same time, a love poem:

River of our substance
Flowing
With the rest. River of the substance
Of the earth's curve, river of the substance
Of the sunrise, river of silt, of erosion, flowing
To no imaginable sea. But the mind rises

Into happiness, rising

Into what is there. I know of no other happiness
Nor have I ever witnessed it . . . . Islands

To the north

In polar mist
In the rather shallow sea—
Nothing more

But the sense
Of where we are

Who are most northerly. The marvel of the wave
Even here is its noise seething
In the world; I thought that even if there were nothing

The possibility of being would exist;
I thought I had encountered

Permanence; thought leaped on us in that sea
For in that sea we breathe the open
Miracle

Of place, and speak
If we would rescue
Love to the ice-lit

Upper world a substantial language
Of clarity, and of respect.   (CP, 155–56)

Char's entire body of work is in some sense a long love poem. These two wisdom writers, for whom poetry is above all a site of disclosure and meditation, are love poets of great power. "Only my companion, she or he," Char writes, praising the power of both friendship and love, "can awaken me from my torpor, releasing poetry, launching me against the limits of the old desert so that I can overcome it. No other. Neither the heavens, nor a privileged place, nor the things by which we are shaken. / Torch, I dance only with a companion like this" (PA, 146). Or again, in the last stanza of "The Raised Scythe," a poem evoking the endangered hope that Char knew in the Resistance: "Fountain trembling in your austere redoubt, / You'll pour out what I've won to the thirsts of the fields. / From the humid fern to the feverish mimosa, / Between the old one gone and the new one come, / The pulse of love, descending, will say to you: / 'Save for here, no place, disgrace is everywhere'" (PA, 184). Eros and thought, vision and companionship, are at the core and far of these poets' journeys: journeys, one could say, in which the Socrates of *The Symposium*, with all his eros and concentration, is brought back to earth.[4]

CHAPTER ONE

René Char
Eros and Clairvoyance

"Fury and mystery by turns seduced and consumed him," Char writes in *Formal Share* (FM, 68), and the dialectical terms of this statement, *fureur et mystère*, form the title of the book that collects his major works from the late thirties through the late forties. *Mystère* for Char means all the horizons affirmed in poetry: the vast of earth and mountain, the open of air and light, the distances of night, the call of the Beloved, the transformative promise of Beauty, the spaces of the disclosive word, and many other things. In some important sense, too, it means life itself, "inexpressible life" (MM, 142), when life is found on the slope of poetry (RBS, 110). *Fureur* simply means rage, on one level, but the Latin *furor* and the old Italian *furore* echo in the word as well, suggesting enthusiasm, transport, or *l'amour fou*, to recall the title of Breton's 1937 book. This fury embraces the energy of social revolt, sexual desire, and existential longing in general. It is akin to Blake's devil, or the insurgent desire of Orc, and to Rimbaud's anarchist Prince, or the impulse to disorder, at the risk of chaos, all that is intolerably ordered. Blake and Char are able to gather this fire into the spaces of clarified vision. Rimbaud, in nearly all his poems, achieves this as well, in part by turning his wildness into a force of articulate compression, a lesson not lost on Char, a gifted writer of compressed parables and carved aphorisms. But Rimbaud nevertheless exhausted himself in furious rebellion. If we are to believe *A Season in Hell*, this was owing above all to a lack of love, and everything we know about his life would seem to confirm this diagnosis. Relationships of every sort were torment for him. Defiance in a life of isolation becomes despair, now a flailing, now a fatigue, blocking the way to genuine encounter, to the ardent patience Rimbaud came to long for. In Blake and Char, no less stubborn than Rimbaud, the fury of rebellion is brought into an alliance with the passion of eros and the clairvoyance of imaginative work. "The poem," Char writes, "is always married to someone" (FM, 69).

The energy of departure turns to the open, to a widened life. "Taken up by the abrupt swerve, poetry widens in a beyond without guardian" (OC, 783), we read in the fore-poem of one of Char's books. This linguistic turning corresponds to the existential turning that, in so many of his poems, is the first step in a movement of disclosure: "Camped on the hillsides around the village are fields of mimosa. In the season of gathering, it may happen that, at a distance from the fields, you encounter an extremely fragrant girl whose arms have been busy all day among the fragile branches. Like a lamp with a brightness of perfume, she steps away, her back turned to the setting sun" (FM, 20). An encounter that at once pierces, illumines, and calls further is everywhere in Char's work. This is an important surrealist theme to which he gives his own manifold inflections (RBS, 34–35). It is perhaps the life of the lyric itself. "Beauty, I go to your encounter in the solitude of the cold. Your lamp is rose, the wind is shining. The threshold of evening deepens" (FM, 32). There is a transparence in the evening dusk itself. Transparence is one of Char's figures for the space of immanent transcendence that he seeks in an always renewed quest.

*

A notable feature of Char's work is the resonance between his imaginative life and his understanding of concrete action in the Resistance. This is exemplified in "The Absent One" (FM, 39), a poem in which the poet and the partisan come together in a figure who hides, travels along "invisible paths," inhabits a threshold of the visible and the invisible, "sets his back against" the lies on all sides, is at once absent and present in the name of a hope and a unity to come. A poem that emerges out of a similar imaginative space, "The Crystal Wheat-Ear Sheds in the Grasses its Transparent Harvest" (FM, 40), gathers the energy of resistance, love, and departure in a single Orphic parable. The transparent harvest of this poem is part of a myth unfolded in many of Char's parables of freedom. The *Transparents* of the sequence by that name (M, 28–36) are akin to the *Matinaux*, or the people of dawn, of Char's book by that name. There is a fine aphoristic sequence, "Redness of the *Matinaux*" (M, 73–81), devoted to the awakenings of the latter. The former, the Transparents, seem to have been drawn from recollections of self-sufficient individuals whom Char knew as a child, eccentrics living on the margins of village life, whose spirited independence from ordinary habits of work Char would find again in some of his companions in the Resistance. "I am grateful for the good luck that has brought the poachers of Provence to fight on our side. Their deep memory of the forest, their aptitude for taking the measure of things, their keen intuition in any kind of weather—I would be surprised by failure on their part" (FH #79). The Transparents belong to a version of pastoral relatively widespread in modern literature, not idealized shepherds but compelling solitaries, at once part and not part of the social world, as though the ancient pastoral opposition of town and country had been recast as an opposition between the socialized and the not wholly socialized, the life of structured work and the life of far solitude or natural independence. Roguish and irreverent, at a distance from both Wordsworth's noble shepherds and Rimbaud's witches and outlaws, Char's Transparents dwell in the sun and the wind of a Rousseauian natural freedom. "Privileged are those whom the sun and the wind are sufficient to turn mad, to sweep through havoc" (M, 82). Earthy, unruly, spontaneous, they are threatened by the direction of modern history. "Man, like a sleepwalker, is marching toward deadly fields, led on by the singing of inventors" (FM, 118). In this way, of course, the life of the Transparents corresponds to the life of poetry as Char sees it.[1]

Thus is the life of the Transparents evoked in another of Char's poems, "From Moment to Moment," where it is suggested that one becomes a Transparent by virtue of participation in Transparence. In Stevens's "The River of Rivers in Connecticut" the town of Haddam begins to "shine" and "sway" in the light of the river of rivers running through things. The Transparents, too, approach a boundary where presence bends toward apparition:

Pourquoi ce chemin plutôt que cet autre? Où mène-t-il pour nous solliciter si fort? Quels arbres et quels amis sont vivants derrière l'horizon de ces pierres, dans le lointain miracle de la chaleur? Nous sommes venus jusqu'ici car là où nous étions ce n'était plus possible. On nous tourmentait et on allait nous asservir. Le monde, de nos jours, est hostile aux Transparents. Une fois de plus, il a fallu partir... Et ce chemin, qui ressemblait à un long squelette, nous a conduit à un pays qui n'avait que son souffle pour escalader l'avenir. Comment montrer, sans les trahir, les choses simples dessinées entre le crépuscule et le ciel? Par la vertu de la vie obstinée, dans la boucle du Temps artiste, entre la mort et la beauté. (OC, 803)

Why this road rather than that one? Where does it lead that it calls us with such force? What trees, what friends, are alive behind the horizon of these stones, in the distant miracle of heat? We have come this far because, in the place we were, nothing was possible any longer. They tormented us, they wanted to make us servile. The world, these days, is hostile to the Transparents. Once again we had to leave... And this road, which looked like a long skeleton, led us to a country that had only its breath with which to climb the future. How to show, without betraying them, the simple things sketched between twilight and sky? Through the virtue of stubborn life, in the circle of artist Time, between death and beauty.

"Once again we had to leave": thus the recurrent note of departure in Char's work. The *again* of *renewal* is sounded from one end to the other of his journey. The places we inhabit readily become places of torment; habit is menaced by inertia; the Transparents at our side, or within us, command us to leave. "Inner command? Summons from without?" Char asks in another poem (FM, 82). Perhaps both. The flight from conformity, in any case, is not simply an indeterminate negation, for the Transparents respond to presences in the distance, trees and friends "alive behind the horizon of these stones, in the distant miracle of heat." In "Threshold," too, the survivor standing on the edge of dawn, on the far side of the flood through which he has passed, speaks of friends who "are about to come" from behind the darkness of the horizon (FM, 181). There is in Char a sort of gnosis of expectation, a disclosive slope of premonition. In "From Moment to Moment" the Transparents reach this space by taking a road that along the way "resembled a long skeleton," a thinned road, suggesting that the passage toward encounter may initially require a dimension of asceticism, a willingness to relinquish the securities around which the familiar social world is organized. It is through this skeletal passage that one comes to a "country that [has] only its breath with which to climb the future." Climbing and ascending are perhaps the most basic of all the tropes in Char for the immanent transcendence of poetry. "The poem is furious ascent" (FH #56; cf. #162). "Poetry, unique ascent of ours, that the sun of the dead cannot darken in the perfect and ludicrous infinite" (PA, 195). The breath with which the Transparents climb here is at once their own spirit, the words with which they voice their journey, and the air in which they recover the fullness of a transparent harvest. It is a place akin to the invisible fullness of earth seen from the depths of failure in "Restore to Them" (FM, 165). It is a place akin to the region of song toward which the lovers, "preceding the country of their future," travel in "The Crystal Wheat-Ear" (FM, 40). The poetic task is "to show, without betraying them, the simple things sketched between twilight and sky," to disclose the hidden friends that these simple things bear in another dimension. Time is a source of the layering of depths and horizons, of the slopes between the given and the invisible, the immediate and the not yet. "Lend to the bud, in leaving it the future, all the brightness of the deep flower," Char writes in "Companions in the Garden" (PA, 152). Between twilight and sky, a threshold in time and an unlimited limit in space, things are "sketched" as if by a hidden designer, not God, not a rational structure transcendent to experience, but Time itself, an artist holding together chance and necessity, beauty and desolation. To undertake the journey of the Transparents is to enter the tragic miracle of disclosive Time. Dawn and dusk, hours of brightening and deepening at once, are privileged hours in Char.

*

What is it that Char hopes to see in his journey? How is this seeing to take place? All writers in the romantic tradition pose these questions in one way or another. We are as we see, and as we fail to see; at the same time, we see as we are, as we live, or as we fail to live.

Char's short poem "The Black Stags" sounds these questions with great clarity and power. This is such a suggestive poem, in fact, that I will take the risk of removing it from its context in the five-part "Lascaux" sequence of which it forms the second part (PA, 103–07). The cave paintings of Lascaux, discovered in 1940, were important to Char. He was always interested in origins. He had a fascination with caves and mountains, stirred in part by the landscape he was raised in, developed in part through his studies in the alchemical tradition. He had lived in hiding, amid caves and cellars and mountains, during his years in the Resistance: "LA FRANCE-DES-CAVERNES" is one of his names in *Leaves of Hypnos* for the France to which, he implies, he and his fellow *maquis* belong (FH #124). At times in his work he adopts a quasi-shamanistic sense of poetry. At times he alludes to a quasi-shamanistic sense of the mind itself: he was, according to Paul Veyne, intimate with the mind's capacity for reverie, for ecstatic meditation in the night. The theme of the hunt, finally, is nearly as essential to his work as the theme of encounter.[2]

"The Black Stags," in six lines, presents an intricate play of symmetries and antitheses:

> Les eaux parlaient à l'oreille du ciel.
> Cerfs, vous avez franchi l'espace millénaire,
> Des ténèbres du roc aux caresses de l'air.
>
> Le chasseur qui vous pousse, le génie qui vous voit,
> Que j'aime leur passion, de mon large rivage!
> Et si j'avais leurs yeux, dans l'instant où j'espère?

> The waters were speaking into the ear of the sky.
> Stags, you have swept across millennial space,
> From the rock's darkness to the air's caresses.
>
> The hunter who chases you, the genius who sees you,
> How I love their passion, from my ample shore!
> And if I had their eyes, in the moment when I hope?

The poem is formed of two exactly balanced parts. The first stanza, after an introductory line that places the poem in a cosmic context, describes the stags painted on the rock wall. The second stanza, whose concluding line is a sort of invocation that brings the poem back to the life of the poet composing it, imagines the activities of a hunter and a genius of sixteen thousand years ago, human actors beyond the boundaries of the painting itself, for they are not pictured there. The poem is at once apostrophic, invocatory, vivid in presentation, ranging in conjecture.

It is plausible to surmise that the poem is a response to the famous painting at Lascaux that scholars refer to as "the swimming stags." This expression refers to the way the stags, drawn in black from the neck up, their torsos faintly yet powerfully suggested in the volume of the rock they rise from, seem to be crossing a river. This may be an accident of the rock's shape and texture, of course, though the artists of the figures of Lascaux frequently made use of the volume, shape, and texture of the walls they painted on. As the stags appear now, at any rate, they seem to be fording a body of water, half-immersed, half-disclosed. They also seem to be gliding on the other side of, or emerging out of, a dark fissure in the wall. They have crossed millennial space, first of all, in the sense that they have traversed sixteen thousand years of hiddenness to become visible again to the eyes of the contemporary world. Yet they have also crossed a space "from the rock's darkness to the air's caresses," from the water glimpsed on a cave wall to another sky. "The waters were speaking into the ear of the sky." Where is this sky? In the figured world of the stags? In some lost shaman's journey? In the natural world of this poet and his readers? In all of these places? The stags of the painting appear with an extraordinary lightness, almost as though they were bodies of air embedded in rock, at once held there and touched by the evanescent. Char's poem, I think, is above all about this paradoxical impression.[3]

The stags are directly addressed from the second through the fifth line. Perhaps they are still addressed, implicitly, in the bold prayer of the last line. The hunter and the genius of the second stanza are described from within this arc of address. The hunter is said to *press* or *chase* the stags: the genius—presumably the artist of this painting—is said to *see* them. It is probably true, as Elizabeth Bosch has argued, that Char here adopts the view of those who take the hunt and the cave art of the people of Lascaux to be distinct activities, that is, the view of those who take the art to involve a ritual not directly linked to the hunt. Char would no doubt have been sympathetic to an emphasis on the visionary significance of these paintings. The poem, in any case, goes beyond this historical controversy. For the poet is ultimately concerned to bring together in his own activity the hunter and the genius whom he begins by distinguishing. Located on his "ample shore"—perhaps the shore of the present, perhaps the shore toward which the stags swim, perhaps the shore of the sky's ear into which the waters speak—he evokes *their* passion and *their* eyes. Both the hunter and the genius seek and see. They are dimensions of the full human being who is at once hunter and genius, Orc and Los, Prince and Génie, voice of fury and voice of mystery, the *maquisard* and the poet of premonition (FM, 19), the shark and the gull (FM, 190), or "the god that fights and the grace that meditates," as this is put in the fourth poem of the sequence (PA, 106). They are dialectical dimensions of the poet as Char understands him: a shaman-like figure, a visionary hunter, in a quest for a disclosive encounter, an ascending vision. This becomes clear in the question of the last line of the poem. "And if I had their eyes, in the moment when I hope?" The poet's eyes are now aligned with the eyes of the hunter and the genius: the *passion* of the hunter and the genius are now aligned with the poet's *hope*. The latter is a pervasive talismanic word in Char. It variously means resistance, freedom, premonition, and enthusiasm, the "demanding enthusiasm" that the bird-man of the first poem in this sequence, a shaman of some sort, is said to have felt before his death in an encounter with the now dying bison. The hope with which "The Black Stags" concludes bears a force of release, as though sheer longing could revive the vision manifest in the painting that the poem has called to mind. Yet the final question seems addressed not to the absent hunter and genius so much as to the stags that have been addressed from the second line of the poem on. It is their crossing of time and space to which Char turns in his invocation of inspired eyes.

Invocation approaches enactment by this point. The poem, in its saying, would accomplish what it sees. "Hear the word accomplish what you say. Feel the word, in its turn, come to be what you are" (NP, 67). What is said in this poem has to do with the mystery suggested in the second and third lines. "Stags, you have swept across millennial space, / From the rock's darkness to the air's caresses." Embedded in a rock wall, rising into air, the stags are not simply crossing the river in the represented space we see in the painting: they are crossing from darkness to radiance, from invisibility to visibility, from the hidden to the disclosed. They manifest in their appearance the force of manifestation itself. This is the inner lightness of their emergence, of what Rimbaud would call their *éclosion*, of what Heidegger would call their presencing, of what Char elsewhere calls a force of ascent. The stags, caressed by air, tremble with an inner force: the force of crossing implicit in their being. It is their dimension of emergence from rock and dark. What Char sees and voices in this poem is the scope of this force.

"Inner command? Summons from without?" (FM, 82). "We can only live in the half-opened," Char writes in "During the Journey," "exactly on the hermetic boundary between the shadow and the light. But we are irresistibly thrown ahead. Our whole being lends support and vertigo to this push" (PA, 196). This is the life of hope or enthusiasm that Char affirms in response to the world he encounters: it is a sort of inner command. Yet he also sees this as a dimension of the outer world itself. "An unspeakable meddling has taken from things, from circumstances, from lives, their brightening chance. There is no advent for us other than from this brightening. It does not bring invulnerability" (PA, 203). This brightening is the air the black stags enter. It is the place of their presence as advent. They glide and shudder there, as creatures and things tend to do in Char's poems, as the trout does, with greater force, in the second poem of the sequence immediately following the "Lascaux" sequence: "Grass, grass always unfolded, / Grass, grass never at rest, / What is it your creature becomes / In the transparent storms / Its heart hurled it into?" (PA, 109). An inward force and an outward force cross in a place of encounter: the place of a passage to air in all that comes to be. It is the implicit reach in things and lives. It is the trace of the river of rivers. It is an important part of what Char means by Beauty. The poet of "The Black Stags," standing with joy on his ample shore, conjures the space he would enter. The "demanding enthusiasm" required to go there, Char says, "does not bring invulnerability." It is as vulnerable as any genuine freedom, as any enthusiasm or love.

Enthusiasm is one of Char's names for eros. "The Black Stags" turns out to be another of his love poems. The hunter and the genius of the poem, brought together in the shaman-poet, are versions of the lover and the poet, and in Char the lover is typically a poet, the poet almost invariably a lover. The stags of the poem, in this light, are versions of the glimpsed and pursued beloved. The visionary hunter pursuing the disclosed stag is a version of the visionary bird-man who, in the first poem of the sequence, has hunted the bison with demanding enthusiasm. "There is no advent for us other than from this brightening. It does not bring invulnerability."[4]

Char is clearly a poet of the call of eros. "I only find my being, I only want to live, in the space and freedom of my love" (PA, 95). "Poetry is the realized love of desire still remaining desire" (FM, 73). His myth of eros, one could say, brings together Diotima's teaching of the transcendent élan of Eros in *The Symposium* and the romantic and surrealist celebration of revelatory encounter. He belongs to what Crane calls "the visionary company of love." He participates in what Éluard calls the life of "hands open / like eyes." A good many of Char's love poems take up the experiences typical of love poems—ardent encounter, spiritual expansion, tender recollection, anguished uncertainty—and erotic vertigo is clearly one of his versions of a transcendence embedded in earth and time. Enthusiasm, pursuit, praise, and reciprocal freedom are the song. Here the widened life is the generous life.[5]

The intimate alliance between eros and poetry comes out most clearly in Char's longer sequences that are less epiphanic testimonies than extended meditations on the place of eros in the work of poetry. "Lettera amorosa," perhaps the greatest of these, interweaves a version of pastoral retreat, a circulating address to an absently present beloved who appears multiple and on occasion arrives, and an elliptical meditation on the recovery of energy, perception, and concentration. "The heart suddenly bereft, the host of the desert becomes, almost legibly, the heart made fortunate, the widened art, the diadem" (PA, 91). The task is to find a path beyond the "ugly season where one regrets, where one plans, where in fact one grows weaker" (PA, 95). In this practice of faith, as it nearly appears to be, revived forces are found through memories, anticipations, visitations. "I've just returned. I walked a long time. You are the Continual. I make a fire. I sit in the healing chair. In the folds of the savage flames, my fatigue ascends in turn. Benevolent metamorphosis in alternation with the fatal one" (PA, 96; cf. FM, 191). In another poem, "Renewal," the recovering poet speaks of the effort "to cast off life's ugly accretions and find again the gaze that loved it enough in the beginning to display its foundation." This love, like Diotima's, comes from the deepest sources of a life. The love of this gaze is the passion of the eyes of the hunter and the genius in "The Black Stags." It is, as we have seen, the love that Char at times calls enthusiasm, the "demanding enthusiasm" felt by the dead bird-man in the painting at Lascaux, the "enthusiasm that lifts the weight of years" of which Char speaks in his war notebook (FM, 123), the "sun-mill" or wheel of light brought to the lover in "Enchantment in the Fox Den" (FM, 24). It is the capacity to lean into life again despite all. It is for Char one of the essential powers of Beauty. Beauty, in Stendhal's memorable erotic definition, is *la promesse du bonheur*, the promise of happiness. "Love," Shelley writes in his essay "On Love," "is the bond and the sanction which not only connects man with man, but with everything which exists. [...] So soon as this want or power is dead, man becomes the living sepulchre of himself, and what yet survives is the mere husk of what once he was." The sweep of Char's poems seems to come from a similar way of experiencing eros as a nearly transpersonal force. It is as though their author were given to responding to everything—wolf, wind, river, friend, beloved—under the aspect of romance. The life of poetry, for Char, is the life of these awakenings. It is, too, the continual search to revive a primary lyrical openness without which they are not possible, without which encounter and disclosure are not possible. "Through this cannon mouth it's snowing. It was hell in our head. At the same time it's spring at our fingertips. It's the long stride again allowed, the earth in love, the exuberant grass" (PA, 145).[6]

The types of images through which Char expresses his awakening are as manifold as his attention. At times, as in "The Crystal Wheat-Ear," his lovers enter a space of transparence. At times, as in "Enchantment in the Fox Den," they enter a space of sheer white light. At times, as in "So That Nothing Be Changed" or "The First Moments," they enter a space of wind and the open. All three of these types of images, significantly, are found just as frequently in Char's many poems of recovered innocence and elated perception. The ground of longing in youth, the quick of longing in perception, the depth of longing in love, the ascent of longing in poetry all come to rhyme with one another. In other poems, perhaps particularly in those of the war years and of Char's later years, a stark polarity of light and dark, at once intimate and cosmic, characterizes the space his lovers inhabit. In these poems variations on a figure-and-ground pattern are common: a gleam in the dark, a candle in the cave, a face in the void, a call in the distance, a trace of a being in flight, a passing apparition in the enduring texture of things. Beauty is there and elsewhere at once. This is the sort of space evoked in many of Char's parables of poetry that, presenting a mythopoetic vision of Eros and Beauty, draw on archetypal patterns of the lover and the beloved. "The poet is the genesis of a being that projects and a being that retains. From the lover he borrows the void, from the beloved, the light. This formal couple, this double sentinel, gives him his passionate voice" (FM, 77). "The poet is the one who Begins, the intransitive poet, commonplace in his intravenous splendors, drawing grief from his own abyss, with Woman at his side inquiring of the rarest grapes" (FM, 80; cf. FM, 58–60). For Char there is no seeing the advent and reach of things without the love which is the advent and reach of our own lives.[7]

Char, then, sees poetry under the aspect of love and love under the aspect of poetry. Or, put another way, Char—the spontaneous anarchist, the impatient critic of the intellect left to its own devices, the romantic for whom a generous enthusiasm is the essential teaching—is at the same time an altogether literary lover and poet. This paradox is as important to his work as the paradox of an emphasis on both the personal vitality of the poet and the impersonal scope of poetry. Perhaps this is one of the things that Geoffrey Hill and Laurence Greilsamer have in mind when they speak of the way Char echoes Petrarch. In Char's poems, as in a long tradition, the erotic or imaginative quest is imagined in the spirit of a serious game, conceived as a perpetually renewed hunt, a drama in which the hunter himself is likely to fall. It is in this "mass of legendary love," this geography of mythic and literary tradition, that our quests take place, as though they were at once ours and not ours, as is suggested in "Muttering":

> Pour ne pas me rendre et pour m'y retrouver, je t'offense, mais combien je suis épris de toi, loup, qu'on dit à tort funèbre, pétri des secrets de mon arrière-pays. C'est dans une masse d'amour légendaire que tu laisses la déchaussure vierge, pourchassée de ton ongle. Loup, je t'appelle, mais tu n'as pas de réalité nommable. De plus, tu es inintelligible. Non-comparant, compensateur, que sais-je? Derrière ta course sans crinière, je saigne, je pleure, je m'enserre de terreur, j'oublie, je ris sous les arbres. Traque impitoyable où l'on s'acharne, où tout est mis en action contre la double proie: toi invisible et moi vivace.
>
> Continue, va, nous durons ensemble; et ensemble, bien que séparés, nous bondissons par-dessus le frisson de la suprême déception pour briser la glace des eaux vives et se reconnaître là. (PA, 133)

> To persist unsurrendering, to find my way again, I offend you, but how in love with you I am, wolf, wrongly called mournful, steeped in the secrets of my back-country. It is in a mass of legendary love that you leave the virgin trace of your always pursued claw. Wolf, I call you, but you have no namable reality. What's more, you're unintelligible. Not appearing, compensatory, what could I know? Behind your maneless running I bleed, I cry, I shut myself in terror, I forget, I laugh under the trees. Pitiless, relentless chase where everything is put in action against the double prey: you invisible and I unwavering.
>
> Go on, run, we last together; and together, though separate, we leap over the shudder of pure disappointment to shatter the ice of living waters and recognize each other there.

The wolf is one of Char's many totemic animals. Here it figures a present absence, the trace of the slope of poetry. "Poetry," he writes elsewhere, "is the ripe fruit that we hold in our hands, with joy, at the same time as it appears, with an uncertain future, on the frost-covered stalk, in the flower's calyx" (PA, 194). "Not appearing, compensatory," unnamable, it is there and not there, or as Stevens says, "it is and it / Is not and, therefore, is." The *marmonnement* of the title presumably evokes not the sound of the fugitive wolf but the murmur of the desiring quester, drawn by a need of what is forever far in the near, "near invisible and so close to my fingers, oh my distant prey," as Char says in a later poem about the "permanent invisible" he seeks (NP, 79). The wolf is a wild creature of an outer country that is steeped in the obscure secrets of an inner back-country. The poet calls that which has called him, as the road leads the Transparents to the hidden friends that are the friends of their own imaginative back-country, for the horizon of their freedom is inseparable from the horizon of what they care for. If this presence that calls and is called has "no namable reality," if it remains "unintelligible," this is only insofar as the intelligible is taken to require clear concepts or empirical definitions. It can be shown in stories, parables, prayers, riddling aphorisms, unfolded figures. Intrinsic to the quest are joy and pain, laughter and tears, for it is moved by a freedom that is a passion, an activity that is a vulnerability, as the startling last line of the first paragraph suggests: in this unceasing quest, where the hunter is "unwavering" and the hunted "invisible," the hunter and the hunted alike are prey, the "double prey" against which "all is set in action." It is a quest in which approach is felt distance, as the lover and the being he longs for are "together though separate," as in poetry in general, Stevens says, we find "a tune beyond us yet ourselves." In Char's poem the space thereby opened promises a traversal of waters surpassing disappointment, an ultimate recognition in which hunter and hunted come together in the distances that eros holds open. Yet it is not in the place of arrival that one lives but in the space of this promise, on this slope of a gnosis of expectation. "We have within us immense expanses that we will never manage to cross," Char writes in another poem, "but they are helpful in the harshness of our climates, propitious to our awakening as well as our perditions" (M, 194).[8]

This returns us to the "double prey" of the poem. Perhaps they are the double prey, first, in the sense that the pursuit evoked here readily rebounds upon the pursuer, as is shown to happen in "The Fatal Partner" (FM, 123–24) or, in a different way, in the first poem of the "Lascaux" sequence. They are also the double prey in that, again, the hunter is seeking outside himself a dimension of his own back-country: the call and the caller are intimately if obscurely linked. Eros, or desire, or power (in the sense of capacity or élan), is at once that which moves and shapes and that which is moved and shaped by the presences it cares for, the horizons it turns toward. They are the double prey in at least one other sense: the drama of the hunt, or the quest, precedes and embraces them both. They participate in a pattern that exceeds them, as the lovers in "La passe de Lyon" (PA, 128) participate in a "flame" and a "work" that exceed them. The pattern of romance, the story of a quest for a renewal of love and vision, precedes us, calls us. At times, therefore, it can come to seem like a search not undertaken so much as undergone, less a promise than a desperation, a concern expressed by any number of poets, from Shelley and Rimbaud to Ashbery. Irony can then become the last god of our longing, an articulate shadow of desire knowing itself forever embarked and undone, left to make a reflective romance out of this condition itself, whether in a playful or a mournful spirit. This sort of irony is a pervasive stance in contemporary culture. It's what everyone is taught before anything else.

Char writes against the grain of any such irony. "An obsession with the harvest and an indifference to history are the two extremities of my arc. The most cunning enemy is contemporaneity" (RBS, 134). It is not, of course, that he is as indifferent to history as this polemical affirmation suggests. Nor is he unaware of the historicity of his art, his language, or the myths and patterns he draws on. The issue, as "Muttering" makes clear, is that he embraces the recurrence of these patterns with an awareness that is itself passionate, placing his hope in our capacity to renew an old story of erotic quest that adopts us as fully as we adopt it. The quest is as old as desire, as a passion is undergone rather more than it is chosen, and the hunter is left to choose how he will engage the wolf within and the wolf without, the promise that, neither simply outer nor simply inner, is the quick of life. Char fully embraces myths of departure, eros, and imaginative quest in part, it seems, because he sees in these myths themselves a basic pattern of returning to the fundamental and taking up anew the question of what matters. He sees eros in this sense as too basic to step beyond, as Nietzsche sees will to power as too basic to step beyond. It is for Char the force that finds its way to an elemental space of encounter, disclosure, decision.[9]

There is a passage in *Leaves of Hypnos* that brings this out with particular clarity. One tension in this notebook, as Jean-Claude Mathieu has underlined, is the oscillation between a sense that the extreme conditions of life in the Resistance place one in contact with the essential, with a bareness of earth and night and word that is almost lyrical, and a sense that those extreme conditions force one to construct walls between oneself and the essential, to turn oneself into a monster of violent defensiveness. Both points of view are registered at many points in the sequence. Near the end, however, it is a concern with a passage beyond the limits of the second of these stances that comes to the fore. Char at this point recalls the tenderness of love (#222); he celebrates the enchanting creatures of the prairie (#175); in one striking phrase, he says to himself, "suddenly you remember you have a face," an expressive presence beyond the hardened life of resistance and sheer survival (#219). It is in this spirit that he addresses to himself the following words (#195):

> Si j'en réchappe, je sais que je devrai rompre avec l'arôme de ces années essentielles, rejeter (non refouler) silencieusement loin de moi mon trésor, me reconduire jusqu'au principe du comportement le plus indigent comme au temps où je me cherchais sans jamais accéder à la prouesse, dans une insatisfaction nue, une connaissance à peine entrevue et une humilité questionneuse.

> If I come through this alive, I know I'll have to break with the aroma of these essential years, silently push away from myself (not repress) my treasure, take myself back to the beginning, to my most indigent bearing in those years when I was in search of myself, without claim to mastery, in naked unsatisfaction, with a barely glimpsed knowledge and a questioning humility.

It is clear that, on one level, he simply wants not to become the fixed portrait of the past that a war hero is readily turned into. "Take part in the leap, not in the banquet, its epilogue" (#197), he says a few sections later, recalling an imperative voiced earlier in the sequence: "Marry and do not marry your house" (#34; cf. #2). The passage I've cited above, further, might bring to mind the Stevensian demand that we ever return to our existential "poverty," ever find our way back to the bare condition of our vital encounter with what is there, with what Oppen calls "the miracle of place." *Pauvreté et privilège*, poverty and privilege, is the title of the first section of Char's *Search for the Base and the Summit*, and these words bear meanings in Char akin to those they bear in Stevens. Those who will "carry boughs," he says in "Lost Nakedness," are those who haven't lost the "nakedness" we are always at risk of losing (NP, 29). Above all, perhaps, the passage I've cited subtly recalls Plato's myth of Eros in *The Symposium*, according to which Eros, neither mortal nor immortal, at once a part of us and a part of what draws us beyond ourselves, child of poverty and resource, is left to wander barefoot and indigent, sleeping by the side of the road, in love with beauty, in search of beautiful bodies, beautiful words, beautiful cities, beautiful laws, beautiful ideas, and, in Char's lyrical version of all this, beautiful presences that in startling moments disclose the fuller life we are called to. All this is of course cast on a thoroughly immanent plane in Char. In the last aphorism of the notebook he writes: "In our darkness there is not a place for Beauty. Every place is for Beauty" (#237). The last aphorism establishes an analogy between the whole world—every place in the whole world—and the prison cell visited by a woman with a candle and a healing word in the painting by George de La Tour that Char describes earlier in the sequence: "This color print of 'The Prisoner' by Georges de La Tour, which I have pinned to the whitewashed wall of the room where I work, seems with time to have come to reflect the meaning of our condition. [...] For two years, there has not been a single partisan who, walking through the door of the room, has not felt his eyes burned by the meaning of this candle. The woman explains, the prisoner listens. The words that fall from this terrestrial silhouette of a red angel are essential words, words that immediately bring help" (#178). The feminine, the light, the word: three essential points of Char's vision of a beauty that calls to freedom, sustains hope.[10]

To remain receptive to this light, again, demands finding one's way to a primary indigence, an elemental lyrical openness. Images of this sort recur in Char's poetry. In the envoi-like poem at the end of *The Nuptial Face*, the poet evokes the "wearing away" of his own face in time as his "goings" unfold in the "air's astonishment" (FM, 62). In "The Effacement of the Poplar," the poplar tree speaks to the wind that strips it down, "sharpens its vigil," leaving it with prayers for a unity with the earth and a dwelling that is no more than, no less than, "a key" (NP, 15; cf. NP, 36). In

"I Inhabit Pain," the poet tells himself of a marriage to the wind possible once his house has lost its windows (FM, 178; cf. M, 204). In a hymn to *la fontaine de Vaucluse*, the speaker's discovery of an uncommon fullness for himself and his beloved, who are "adopted by the open," is inseparable from a force that "sands them down to the invisible" (FM, 213). On one level, as Mary Ann Caws has noted, all these passages are allusions to Char's métier, his practice of a compression that serves an expansion. The further suggestion, it would seem, is that transport in the open requires a shedding of our familiar forms of enclosure, a reduction to the invisible, a "going back to the beginning," to the place of an indigent bearing open to traces of beauty, hints of freedom. The wind-cut poplar discovers an abundant life. The thinned lovers are swept away in a fluent expansion. The skeletal road taken by the Transparents leads to a horizon of hidden friends. The youth of "The Struck Adolescent," having turned his suffering into a passage through "the noblest and most enduring things of the earth," returns to the social world "at once more vulnerable and more powerful" (M, 58). For Char it is this openness, this enthusiasm, that discovers the space of genuine encounter and the life of freedom (RBS, 50; ES, 177). This is the myth of eros and vision at work in "Muttering."

All of Char's poems are in some sense love poems. They are all responses to invitations, to talismans of the beautiful that speak of a farther slope, and at the same time intently composed invitations to others. As there is an eros of conversational quest in Plato, so there is an eros of lyrical dialogue in Char, made clear in the great sequences "The Library is on Fire" and "Companions in the Garden," as well as in the titles of two of his collections of essays on poets, painters, and philosophers, *Substantial Allies* and *The Sovereign Conversation*. The poem "Invitation" could serve as an epigraph to his entire body of work (PA, 141). There he "calls the loves" to a "soft perpetual insomnia," to "the pause in a dance that can be entered anywhere in the clouds crossing the sky." He says of his lyre that it makes a thousand years "weigh less than a dead man," for the song of eros is a song of levitation (FM, 40). "It's enthusiasm that lifts the weight of years" (FM, 123). He "calls the lovers" to a journey of open encounter, invites his readers to become allies in the erotic quest for the good life. Though they will make discoveries that are inevitably personal or particular (M, 73), they will be companions in what Northrop Frye calls the open community of vision. "The personal adventure, the miraculous adventure," Char says, "community of our dawns" (M, 78).[11]

*

If Char's poems are invitations, they are not simple invitations, for they are written indirections, as it were, and they make demands on the reader as steep as those they make on the poet. "May my presence, which causes you enigmatic unease, unrelenting hatred, be a meteor in your soul" (FM, 204). Yet they are nevertheless invitations: analogues in words of the invitations in the world to which the poet whom they alter responds. They invite one to take a path at a slant. They invite one to the life of enthusiasm, emanation, what Blake calls exuberance, what Whitman calls spending and scattering, what Stevens calls nobility, what the psalmist calls the overflowing of his cup. They invite one on a journey through the impersonal space that, for Char, poetry is meant to disclose. They are surely not mimetic representations of our lives, of course, nor is "the poet" so often named in Char's poems the same as Char or any reader. "The purpose of poetry being to make us sovereign by impersonalizing us, we touch, thanks to the poem, the fullness of that which was only suggested or deformed by the boastings of the individual" (PA, 118). Char's poems are fragments of this invisible presence, a sort of absent presence, which is the substance of his hope, his search for a wider life that we are always at risk of missing, that we so often lack the energy or freedom to turn toward. It is from this perspective that Char abruptly defines "the miracle of poetry" as "intelligence in life" (FM, 74). Paul Veyne has well characterized this simple yet exorbitant quality of Char's work as a whole:

> The work of René Char, or at least his poetic work, does not resemble that of most other poets. It is not a collection of pieces on diverse themes: it has a subject, beauty and poetry, or rather the place of beauty among basic human values and in human existence. Three quarters of his poems and aphoristic verses speak of nothing else: they speak of beauty or poetry as often as *The Song of the Cid* speaks of its hero. In short, this work is the poetic journal, the journal of meditations, of an atheistic mystic. The famous song of the *Sorgue*,

dedicated to Yvonne Zervos, sings of a river that hardly resembles the river by that name. However, what Char understands by Beauty involves much more than what an aesthete would understand by this word: his Beauty is above all love, freedom, truth, morality, and its true name would perhaps be happiness and the good.[12]

Veyne here brings out the hyperbole of Char's poetry. It is a poetry that, for all its hermetic qualities, has a vast candor, audacity, perseverance. One feels this in the force of its compressed language. It's as though all of Char's poems were turned toward some ever elusive space of *la vraie vie*, as though they were tracks or traces of a pursuit never completed, always renewed. Char's distinctive formal practice leads one into the substance of this adventure.

Char works in a diversity of forms: verse (both metrical verse and free verse), the prose poem, the aphoristic sequence, and the very short essay. The verse and prose poems are sometimes gathered in loose sequences or, in one of Char's figures, archipelagoes. The smaller collections or volumes within the larger books, often first published separately, are shaped similarly: they usually have a thematic horizon not unlike the shared horizon of the twenty-one poems gathered under the title *Le Poème pulvérisé*. No form seems particularly associated with a particular concern or perspective: there are poems of fury, departure, eros, quest, praise, loss, anguish, nature, and meditation in all of them. But I haven't the space here to look at all these forms. So I will leave aside the short essays, though they are not far from being prose poems themselves, and I will reluctantly pass by the verse poems, too, which tend to display a vertical, angular movement that places them somewhere between the prose poems and the aphoristic sequences. These latter two forms, in any case, lend a stylistic signature to Char's work.

Char writes in the romantic tradition, in a broad sense, and it is in this tradition that the prose poem emerges in French poetry, beginning with Chateaubriand's prose and Aloysius Bertrand's impressionistic prose poems. Rimbaud and to a lesser extent Mallarmé, not Baudelaire, have most influenced this form in France. This is to say that the prose poem in France since the second half of the nineteenth century, marked by an absence not only of meter and end-rhyme but of the line itself, tends nevertheless to be more lyrical than the lyric, as if it had been compensated for its losses through a heightening of other features that we associate with the lyric: compression, quickness of associative thought, a dense unfolding of imagistic and figurative language, and a decidedly expressive sound. Char belongs to this current, and Rimbaud is surely among the greatest influences on his work, and *a fortiori* on his prose poems. Many of these poems are testimonies: they bear witness to an encounter, a spirited movement of departure, an exaltation come and gone. They thus easily turn into two types of poem frequent in Rimbaud's *Illuminations*: the hymn, or the song of praise, and the portrait of the artist as variously enthusiastic, anguished, desperate, hopeful, serene, and as variously a quester, a seer, a wanderer, a rebel, a thinker, a writer. In Char, as I've underlined above, the portrait of the artist may just as easily be a portrait of the lover, these two roles being nearly inseparable for him. A good many of these prose poems, further, have something of the character of a parable: "The Absent One" "The Crystal Wheat-Ear," "Threshold," "The Shark and the Gull," "The Fatal Partner," and "Muttering," for example, are among Char's highly regarded prose poems that display this parabolic quality. In speaking of this I don't have in mind what is meant when it is said that Jesus speaks in parables, riddling sayings that *donnent à penser* and demand existential decision from their hearers, though the association is not irrelevant. I refer in part to an old gift of the lyric to condense and polish an anecdotal core into a resonantly concrete "emblem" or "story" of feeling and thought. As is often noted, Char's prose poems, like his aphoristic sequences, hold together the concrete and the abstract with remarkable force and range. While there is usually a dynamic first-person presence in these poems, they are rarely poems in what Charles Altieri has called the scenic mode, a mode in which the speaker is plausibly situated in a particular natural, urban, or domestic place in response to which the imaginative curve of the poem unfolds. Rather, the material in these parabolic poems, like the material in one of Yeats's poems, bears all the marks of a thing *worked* upon. It is as though they were at once notes written on the road and birds of hammered gold. One feels this in entering their paradoxically personal and impersonal space.[13]

Another important feature of Char's prose poems, to put it in plain terms, is their brevity: one great poem, "Lord," is two pages long; most of the prose poems are less than half a page long; a very high number of them are only three or four sentences, at times one or two sentences. A poem like "That Smoke Which Carried Us . . ." is not at all rare in Char. The poem, whose point of departure seems to be a memory of life in the Resistance, consists of two sentences: "That smoke which carried us was sister of the walking stick that unsettled the stone and the cloud that opened the sky. It had no scorn for us, it took us as we were, thin streams fed by disorientation and hope, with a lock in our jaw and a mountain in our eyes" (FM, 162). What should we call this? A prose poem? An aphorism? A lyrical note? A fragment of a larger poem on the horizon? From the other side, so to speak, many passages in the aphoristic sequences unfold into short prose poems. At one point in "The Library is on Fire," a three-page aphoristic sequence, we find a brief prose poem, a parable about poetry: "There's a curse unlike any other. It flutters about in a sort of laziness, has a welcoming nature, composes a face with reassuring features. But, after the feint, what power, what sudden flight to the goal! Probably, as the shadow where it builds is cunning, the region perfectly secret, it will elude a name, will always slip away in time. It sketches, in the veil of the sky of a few clairvoyants, quite frightening parabolas" (PA, 147). Eventually, I think, readers of Char come to see clearly what they probably intuit the moment they enter his work: the prose poems and the aphorisms are so closely connected with one another that they easily turn into one another. Striking aphorisms are embedded in the prose poems; short prose poems are embedded in the aphoristic sequences. It is as though the prose poem were an unfolded aphorism, the aphorism a pared down prose poem, the relationship between the two modulated by the rhythm of expansion and contraction that runs through all of Char's work. Here, too, one perhaps begins to see the place in his work of another sort of form: poems like "Long Live" (M, 42–43) and "Of an Unadorned Night" (PA, 168–69) might be described as either aphoristic sequences or long-legged free verse poems made up of discontinuous sentences. "My métier, at the cutting edge, is a métier of point," Char writes (PA, 147). The space-surrounded phrase is one of the essential elements of this body of work.[14]

Char wrote aphoristic sequences throughout his trajectory. The earliest, *First Mill*, marks his wrestling with the surrealist movement from which he was at the time breaking, and one might see the form as particularly appropriate to a project of sharp clarification. Two of the most ambitious of these sequences, *Formal Share* and *Leaves of Hypnos*, were written during the years of the war and his activity in the Resistance, and in this context there were clearly practical reasons of time and attention that might explain the choice of this form. And yet he continued to write these sequences in later years, from the fifties through the eighties, and indeed to such an extent that, again, one comes to see that the form is somehow essential to his gift, basic to his vision. Interestingly, Char himself, according to Jean-Claude Mathieu, did not like to speak of the "aphorisms" of his work; apparently he preferred the term "propositions." If I nonetheless use the familiar term "aphorism" here, as Mathieu does in his book, I mean to bear in mind that what Char hopes to achieve in this mode is not itself familiar. It is a question that his work poses for a reader. What are we to make of these well-spaced gatherings of carved phrasings that so concentrate image, feeling, intuition, thought?[15]

It is worth considering the sources that might have inspired Char to work in this form, or that in any case his work appears to recall and refract. First of all, one might think of Char's admiration for the pre-Socratics in general and Heraclitus in particular. Since Char takes "poetry and truth" to be "synonyms" (FM, 70), he naturally displays an acute interest in the philosophical aphorism, the speculative riddle. In a short essay on Heraclitus he writes: "With the exact word, both on the tip and in the wake of the arrow, the poetry [of Heraclitus] runs immediately upon the summits, for Heraclitus possesses that sovereign ascensional power whereby language, struck with openness, endowed with movement, is made to serve its own consummation" (RBS, 101). The whole essay bears echoes of Nietzsche, whose affirmatively tragic philosophy is everywhere in Char, whether by influence or shared intuition. Nietzsche is indeed a second possible source for Char's practice of the aphorism. "The will to a system is a lack of integrity," Nietzsche writes in *Twilight of the Idols*, adding a few pages later, "For me they were steps, I have climbed upon them—therefore I had to pass over them. But they thought I wanted to settle down on them . . . ." At one point, in a passage Mathieu cites, Zarathustra says: "In the mountains the shortest way is from peak to peak: but for that one must have long legs. Aphorisms should be peaks—and those who are addressed, tall and lofty." The art of the aphorism is then the art of thought in motion, of the life of the mind en route. "I loved you. I loved your face, like a storm-furrowed spring, and the enigma of your domain that enclosed my kiss. Some trust an entirely round imagination. For me going suffices" (FM, 22). Yet, despite the kinship, Nietzsche's aphorisms are on the whole very different from Char's, usually far more conceptually developed, often more psychologically probing, though Char is a fine psychologist himself. Char is seeking something else in his elliptical sequences. A third field of precursors that comes to mind in this context, however tenuous the connection might seem, is that of the French moralists of the seventeenth and eighteenth centuries (whose importance to Nietzsche has recently been emphasized by Robert Pippin). Char has something of La Rochefoucauld's poised pessimism concerning who we are, and something of the existential pathos and speculative scope of Pascal. "Man is only a reed, the weakest in all of nature; but a thinking reed." So begins one of Pascal's well-known aphorisms. This, one might say, is the *sort* of thing that Char is given to writing. "By turns abundant hillside, desolate rock, lightened shelter, such is man, beautiful and disconcerting man" (PA, 121). Char, to be sure, is as passionately anti-Christian as Pascal is passionately Christian. Yet both are spirits of metaphysical passion.[16]

There may well be echoes in Char's aphoristic practice of Heraclitus, of Nietzsche, of the French moralists, and, as Mathieu suggests, of Hugo. Yet there is another way of approaching this question that may be at least as illuminating as an effort to trace refractions of these sources. Northrop Frye, in a discussion of rhythm, observes that the associative rhythm of spoken language, so important to the texture of free verse, may enter prose and give rise to a texture of "discontinuous prose," a form favored by satirical writers, from Rabelais through Joyce. But, curiously, as a shift in perspective reveals, "the discontinuous aphoristic style has been in all ages and cultures the standard rhetoric of wisdom," too, as we recognize if we call to mind, say, the proverbs in the Bible, the sayings of Jesus, the writings of the pre-Socratics (at least in the dispersed citations in which they have come down to us), the sutras of the Koran, and many other texts of this sort. While this form of discontinuous prose is clearly a recollection of an oral tradition, Frye suggests one reason why writers might be inclined to reinvent it as a form of wisdom writing, whether in poetry or elsewhere. A piece of continuous prose, Frye notes, may initially appear dictatorial, but in fact it's a form that places the author and the reader on the same level, allowing them to work through an issue step by step. A writer of discontinuous prose has other concerns: "If a writer wishes to suggest that it is the reader's business to come to him and not his business to come to the reader; if he wishes to suggest that there are riches in his mind which his actual writing gives no more than a hint of, he will have to adopt a different kind of prose style. Such a style would be discontinuous, breaking up a straightforward exposition into a sequence of aphorisms, usually with typographical breaks in between. The use of discontinuous aphorisms suggests to the reader that here is something he must stop and meditate on, aphorism by aphorism, that he must enter into the writer's mind instead of merely following his discourse. What one says is surrounded by silence, as though a hidden context of mental activity lay behind every formulated sentence." "A poet," Char writes, "should leave traces of his passage, not proofs. Only traces stir our dreaming" (PA, 153). Frye goes on to note that "an important by-product" of this tradition "is a form of oracular writing which for some reason is more common in French and German literature than in English," as in writers like Perse and Char and, further back, Rimbaud at times. Probably something of this stance that Frye describes is at work in modernist poetry in general: the fragmentary or collagist text demands that the reader enter the "silent" spaces of its elliptical movement of thought, the "blank" spaces of its invisible transitions and hidden connections. These are the spaces of roving conjecture.[17]

In this larger modernist field, Char's practice of the aphorism nevertheless remains singular, in various ways. The first is simply the extremity to which he carries it in his incisive texts: he shapes his texts in such a way that they inevitably sound like a sort of wisdom writing, or quasi-religious writing, or existential literature of concern (to recall Frye's term). This is a risky stance on Char's part, no doubt, and the confidence with which he undertakes it is one sign of the urgency with which he writes, the ambition he brings to his art. It is a practice inseparable from the larger vision that all his resonant traces imply, or bear witness to, as Paul Veyne has underlined in the passage I cited above. "The high conception of creation to which Char adheres," Veyne writes in a commentary on

"I Inhabit Pain" (FM, 178–79), "means that he can leave behind only a fragmentary *oeuvre*." It is more true of Char than of most poets, that is, that all his poems are facets of a single poem about what Stevens calls the central poem hovering on the boundary of mind and air. This larger vision is as palpable in Char's work as is its absence: it is there and not there, the impersonal space of poetry that Char takes to be neither simply empirical, nor simply transcendent, but a sort of approaching-and-departing presence that emerges on the slope of resistant hope, that emerges as we turn in freedom toward those dimensions of life that we care for. Vital encounter discloses this first of all: words are to take us there as well. Char invents a range of figures for the relationship between this larger horizon of care and his aphoristic poems and sequences, including, among others, the pulverized poem (FM, 169–205); the word as archipelago (PA, 193); a route that is a shattered walking stick (RBS, 139); a springtime that is scattered across the seasons (RBS, 32); the splinters of a presence that flies into pieces when approached (RBS, 42); the well-spaced formal share that is the portion that one poet shapes out of a larger gift (FM, 63–82); the fragments of the long sentence of the sky that we read and speak as we walk along a road (NP, 66); and the brief flashes of *la vraie vie* that is at once *ailleurs* and *ici* (RBS, 110; NP, 79). The "transcendent presences" of poetry are at the same time "pilgrimaging storms" (FM, 75). The poem is at once a structure emanating freedom and a mere vapor in the air, a part and an opening onto a whole known only through experience, or the experience of poetry, not through detached reflection: "This fortress pouring freedom through every door, this fork of vapor that holds in the air a body of Promethenean scope, illuminated and unscathed by the lightning, is the poem with its exorbitant caprices, which in a moment takes us and is gone" (FM, 79–80). This is the sort of faith in the promise of poetry that we find in Blake, in Shelley, in Whitman, in Rimbaud at times, in the exuberant early years of surrealism, in Rilke, in Montale in his poems of resistance and love of the thirties and forties. It perhaps has a more vivid concreteness in Char than in these other visionary writers. Stevens writes meditations on this fiction at various points, as in the haunting "Chocorua to its Neighbor," or in the more schematic "A Primitive like an Orb," where the promise is called a "giant, on the horizon, glistening" and at the same time a "giant of nothingness." The "central poem" takes us, widens us, then vanishes, as the fork of vapor does in the passage from Char just cited:

> We do not prove the existence of the poem.
> It is something seen and known in lesser poems.
> It is the huge, high harmony that sounds
> A little and a little, suddenly,
> By means of a separate sense. It is and it
> Is not and, therefore, is. In the instant of speech,
> The breath of an accelerando moves,
> Captives the being, widens—and was there.

Stevens's "necessary angel of earth," though a local apparition rather than a giant on the horizon, comes and goes in the same way. "The huge high harmony that sounds a little and a little": another figure for the relation between the wider horizon of life that Char seeks and the poems that he writes. According to Jean-Claude Mathieu, Char once said that the landscapes of Provence were themselves aphoristic. His aphorisms, discontinuous inscriptions from a bewildering multiplicity of perspectives, are like the accidentally coherent contours of a landscape that speaks of depth and horizon. They are interanimating traces of a single sustained quest: a quest for a transparent harvest, a spaciousness that, owing to our love of the wrong things, we are always missing. Char, it is true, demands more of poetry than Stevens.[18]

*

Char, in his essay on Rimbaud, evokes what poetry may have meant for Rimbaud and surely means for Char himself: "Every movement of his work and every moment of his life participated in an undertaking guided to perfection, one might say, by Apollo and Pluto: poetic revelation, the least veiled of revelations, which as law evades us, but which as noble phenomenon haunts us almost familiarly. We are advised: outside of poetry, between our foot and the stone it presses, between our look and the field it surveys, the world is null. The true life, the indisputable colossus, takes shape only on the slopes of poetry" (RBS, 110). The expression "noble phenomenon" is significant. Poetry is "noble" in a sense that the term has in Nietzsche: poetry is an event, or a space, that Char associates with vital freedom, affirmative power, large-spirited generosity, expansive gratitude, *amor fati*. That Apollo and Pluto have replaced Nietzsche's familiar pair of Apollo and Dionysus is a subtle revision. For it is a certain tragic bearing without Nietzsche's theatrics, with a greater meditative poise, that Char affirms here and elsewhere in his work. It is a vision of our ambiguous life in time as at once profoundly bleak and yet traversed by promise. The passage from which I've just cited continues: "But we haven't the sovereignty (or haven't anymore, or haven't yet) to dispose at our discretion of this true life, to quicken ourselves there, except in brief flashes akin to orgasms. And in the darkness that follows these flashes, thanks to the knowledge they have brought, Time—between the horrible void it secretes and a hope-presentiment that arises solely from us (and is but the next condition of sheer poetry and vision announcing itself)—Time distributes itself, flows away, but to our gain, half orchard, half waste." Thus does Char evoke a dialectic of moment and journey, of epiphany and quest, in erotic and visionary terms. I've described Char's aphoristic work as a vast sequence composed of the testimonial and meditative fragments of this quest, a quest variously animated by fury, resistance, encounter, meditative voyage, the whole range of turnings toward this absent presence that Char calls poetry, or the poem, or beauty. At times he calls the animating passion of this quest "hope": "Every one of the letters that composes your name, oh Beauty, on the honor roll of suffering, embraces the level simplicity of the sun, inscribes itself in the giant phrase that cuts across the sky, allies itself with man, who is bent on trumping his destiny through its indomitable opposite: hope" (FM, 150).[19]

If Char often affirms "hope," he rarely draws on the word "faith," a decision that signals his emphatically anti-Christian stance. Yet there is clearly an analogue of faith, a kind of faith, implicit in the passage I've cited above and in the whole arc of Char's quest, at least if faith refers to a daily practice of attention and virtue, a daily shaping of habits of response, a daily directing of heart and mind, for the sake of a deepening of a life in relation to a transcendent presence whose sheer power is felt only in rare and privileged moments. This is an immanent transcendence in Char, of course, and one finds this analogue of faith in many other romantic, modernist, and existentialist writers, though not always quite as intensely or as pervasively as in Char. It has to do with the slope of poetry as Char and those in his tradition understand it. "The vitality of the poet is not a vitality of the beyond but a diamond-cut *actuality* of transcendent presences and pilgrimaging storms" (FM, 75). "To make a poem is to seize a nuptial beyond that's found well within this life, intimately connected to it, yet close to the urns of death" (PA, 193). As with any faith, if we do not turn to the promise, we will not hear what is said. One can look at this in the light of Nietzsche's paradoxical journey. Paul Veyne has clearly underlined the Nietzschean dimension of Char's thought:

> Thus, already at the age of twenty-five, Char's philosophy: the tragic, a conservation of elements across time, and a fatal error of humanity in turning away from the tragic. He placed these ideas under the patronage of Heraclitus, whose doctrine, he thought, could be held in two points: pessimism is the sole certainty we possess; the truth is noble "and the image that reveals it is tragedy." Pessimism: there is no meaning or end to human history, but only cycles of eternal return (and eternal departure). Noble truth: the depth of man is a noble reality, a "typic" essence, formed of energy and freedom, which subsists as potential across the cycles of history, despite the oppressions, despite the conformist "tenderness," despite the individual "distinctions," despite the fear of tomorrow. Tragedy is a way of living consonant with this essence; but the pre-Socratic age is no more; its truth has become a reality of exception. These are the only certitudes we have, or at least the only things it is important for us to know, and which suffice. The history of humankind is a succession of evils and changes so distressing that they seem repetitions of themselves. Subsisting there, nevertheless, visible in places, is an unbreakable ground of nobility. This involves a certain way of bearing oneself in relation to time.

What does this relation to time involve? It involves inhabiting a contradiction that Nietzsche pushes to an extreme. Nietzsche sets out to dismantle dualist metaphysics in any form, religious or philosophical, and to affirm a naturalism of time, chance, history, will to power. At the same time, however, he places himself in opposition to the dominant trends of the modern world that would seem to be allies of this project, notably empiricism, historicism, and a generally materialist stance. Nietzsche shapes his project through an opposition to both traditional metaphysics and the familiar modern destruction of metaphysics. It is as though he were searching for a philosophical perspective that would run at a slant or slope between these two perspectives. The major figures and concepts with which he imagines this slope are well known: gay knowledge, tragic wisdom, love of fate, creative will to power, a nobility that is first of all spiritual or existential. Some of these things, as Veyne makes clear, are relevant to Char's quest. Here the point I want to underline is that Char, like Nietzsche, like so many other post-romantic and existentialist writers, is in search of a paradoxical or contradictory perspective akin in its angle, at least, to the sort of perspective that Nietzsche is in search of. Char's "Threshold" (FM, 181) and "Restore to Them" (FM, 165) are among his most resonant parables of this search.[20]

Char has many ways of sounding the depths and distances of this space. At times he draws on a light mysticism that roams through all sorts of religious and philosophical traditions. At times he speaks of *le mystère*, the mystery, or *l'ouvert*, the open, or *l'inconnu*, the unknown, or *le sommet*, the summit, or *l'amont*, the upstream. At times he speaks of friends or gods that approach from obscure horizons. At times he turns the figures of light inside out and evokes a meditative voyage through the clarities of night. Often he speaks of expansion, of the vast of wind and wing, of a call from a distance, of the "spacious force" against which he has "leaned his days" (FM, 26). Stevens, in the opening lines of "Chocorua to its Neighbor," says, "To speak quietly at such a distance, to speak / And to be heard is to be large in space, / That, like your own, is large, hence, to be part / Of sky, of sea, large earth, large air," and though this is a rhythm never found in Char, it is the sort of space Char discloses in his poems, the space of a mountain speaking quietly to a mountain in the hour of pre-dawn. If it is possible to capture the gist of a poet in a couple of sentences, Mary Ann Caws has come close for Char, writing that in his work "the element of spaciousness is always predominant, along with that of freedom. That space is to be energized, impassioned by love and struggle together. . . ." "Calendar," a poem that seems to express Char's turn from the "violence" of his surrealist adventure, begins: "I've bound my convictions to one another and enlarged your Presence. I've granted my days a new course by leaning them against this spacious force. I've dismissed the violence that limited my ascendant. Quietly I've taken the wrist of the equinox. The oracle no longer subjugates me. I enter: to experience grace or not" (FM, 26). Every reader of Char is drawn into this spaciousness: the *elsewhere here* of his poetry.[21]

Eric Marty has brought to light one of Char's hermetic parables for this space of widened life. In "Notwithstanding," the second section of the late sequence "Everyone Gone," Char writes: "For a long time I've been a tenant of the fifth arch of the Saint-Bénezet bridge. I know everything about the vanished one, and she everything about me. From our dejections, our gaiety, to my writing" (ES, 58). Marty comments: "This fragment remains incomprehensible if one is unaware that this bridge Saint-Bénezet is the bridge of Avignon, a shattered bridge and, since the seventeenth century, a bridge broken from the fourth arch on. [...] The fifth arch of the bridge, where the poet resides and recognizes himself, is precisely the arch absent from the bridge, that which the text here designates as the site of writing, the missing arch." The missing arch where one can dwell. This is the place of crossing. It is the present absence that invites us to a spaciousness of life. It is found only through an existential turning, a passionate going, yet at the same time, however deep our intuitions, it is only fully disclosed in words. Earlier I spoke of an analogy with faith: an inwardness of spirit, inseparable from words to think upon, found in relation to an outward transcendence. Here I would draw a perhaps more apt analogy with Platonic philosophy and its ancient tributary streams: an inwardness of the soul, inseparable from eros and thought and discourse, found in relation to a transcendent space of ideas visible in the light of the good. It is this space, from which transcendent Forms and a transcendent God have now vanished, that remains the open toward which Char's poetry of eros reaches.[22]

If we pursue the Platonic analogy a little further, we will recall that a discovery of the space of transcendence requires a turning away from the shadows on the wall of the cave, and an ascending departure for the outer light. This twofold movement is animated by both disillusionment with what is given and erotic longing for what is hidden, invisible. Char,

I suggested earlier, can be understood to reimagine this Platonic teaching of visionary eros as a teaching of a transcendence in this world. The accents of abrupt rebellion or quiet departure in his work are efforts to find his way to some domain of genuine encounter, the domain where calls of a further life are heard, where disclosures take place. Blake finds in the prophetic demand that we abandon idols an analogous teaching. For Blake, in an eccentric Christian mode, and Char, in an anti-Christian mode, our existence is in-caverned, for which reason we fail to discover the space of giant forms (in Blake) or the spaciousness of vital promise (in Char). "Outside is where the mind resides," C.D. Wright says, but the walls are multiple, everywhere, both within and without: they are part of our condition, part of our individual psychic histories, part of the built social worlds we inhabit. How will we find our way to the wider life? How, Blake asks, will we "fallen fallen light renew"?[23]

*

Char's writings of the war years, notably the long sequences *Formal Share* and *Leaves of Hypnos*, give one a clear sense of the expansive scope of his vision. To no small extent this has to do with the historical context in which these sequences were written. It was in these years that, in Char's life and work, there occurred a collision between his existential and metaphysical stance, on the one hand, and an extreme historical actuality, on the other. This could be seen as Char's version of the tension between the metaphysical and the historical running through all of modern culture. If the prose poems of *They Alone Remain*, written between 1938 and 1944, hold together a decisive lyrical bearing and a furious political bearing, the two long sequences of 1942 to 1944, in particular, form a riven-and-connected testimony to this tension. They convey the full range of Char's journey.

The first of these, *Formal Share*, is a sequence of aphorisms written in 1942, the year in which Char entered the Resistance and began to make clandestine connections, though there was little action to be taken at the time. The second of them, *Leaves of Hypnos*, is a sequence of aphorisms written in 1943–44, the years in which Char was a leader, *capitaine Alexandre*, in the Secret Army, in charge of storing munitions and gathering information throughout the Lower Alps region. If ultimately these sequences are complementary, held together by deep affinities, one is likely to be struck first of all by their differences. *Formal Share* presents what can only be called a metaphysical vision of poetry: it is sweepingly figurative, pitched in ambition, at once desperate and affirmative in tone, and pervasively metapoetic in its angle of reflection. Well over half the aphorisms include the words "poète," "poème," or "poésie," and those that don't are clearly moving in the same orbit. The first fragment, with its definition of the work of the imagination and its confident appropriation of religious language, sets the tone of the whole: "The imagination works by expelling from reality several incomplete persons, setting in motion the magic and subversive powers of desire, in order to bring about their return in the form of a wholly satisfying presence. This is the inextinguishable increate real" (I). Or, again, near the end of the sequence: "To traverse with the poem the pastoral of deserts, the gift of oneself to the furies, the musty fire of tears. To run in its wake, to beg it, to curse it. To identify it as the expression of one's genius or even the crushed ovary of one's impoverishment. In order, at last, one night, to be launched into the wedding feast of the cosmic pomegranate" (XL). In this sequence the poet walks in the vast of the cosmos, evoking the confrontation of the human and the natural, the imagination and the void, in a drama from which concrete social or historical realities are almost entirely absent. The sequence as a whole reads like a last testament, a surprisingly affirmative message in a bottle tossed out on the sea of a world in ruins, a fascist-dominated Europe as it appeared before the holding of Stalingrad in the winter of 1942–43. The curious title perhaps refers to this forming into fragments of the poet's share of an imaginative gift that has sources beyond anything visible in the desolate landscape in which it emerges. *Leaves of Hypnos*, in an important sense, moves in a quite different direction. Hypnos, the brother of the Greek god of sleep, refers first of all to the hypnotic nightmare that has fallen on Europe in the form of fascism (cf. RBS, 80, 125). Yet at the same time Hypnos, a *nom de guerre* that Char adopted, a name with which a letter included in the notebook is signed (#87), is the figure of a descent to the hidden resources of a transformative resistance: "Hypnos seized winter and clothed it in granite. Winter changed into sleep and Hypnos became fire. The rest belongs to us" (FM,

84). Hypnos, then, is akin to the "absent one" of Char's poem by that title (FM, 39). The prefatory note to *Leaves of Hypnos*, marking the altered direction and tone of this notebook, concludes: "These notes register the resistance of a humanism aware of its duties, discreet in its virtues, wishing to save for *the inaccessible* a clear space for the fantasy of its suns, and committed to paying the price for this" (FM, 85). In the literature of the last century, as is well known, war has usually been represented in the sober light of disillusionment, in the bleak light of the loss of humanity. The myths have been shown to be false, hollow, destructive. The heroism, courage, camaraderie, and love of freedom once said to be the stuff of war have tended to be reaffirmed only in the literature of resistance and liberation movements. Char's *Leaves of Hypnos* surely belongs to this second type of war literature. Yet it has a fierce sobriety of its own. The lyrical élan of *Formal Share* is here brought back to the reality of life with others, life amid the forces of history, and held in tension with the tasks and demands of survival in the Resistance. The notebook is traversed by practical notes, accounts of specific missions and perilous close calls, ethical and political meditations on the larger historical context, and vivid sketches of particular individuals with whom Char lived and worked in these years. The political reflections tend to be pointed and severe. "To the Prudent: It's snowing on the maquis and there's a perpetual hunt for us. You whose house no longer weeps, where avarice flattens love in a succession of warm days, your fire is only a sick-nurse. Too late. Your cancer has spoken. Our native country has no more powers" (#22; cf. #7 and #8). The ethical reflections, including reflections on virtues discovered in this passage through adversity, are often attached to portraits of fellow *maquis*, of which there are some twenty-five or thirty in the sequence. "Archiduc confides to me that he found his truth when he joined the Resistance. Until then he was a hard, suspicious actor of his own life. Lack of sincerity poisoned him. Gradually a sterile sadness settled upon him. At present he *loves*, he spends himself, he is committed, he goes naked, he defies. I greatly appreciate this alchemist" (#30). "A few days before his execution, Roger Chaudon said to me: 'On this earth, one is occasionally up, for the most part down. The order of these periods cannot be altered. It is this, at bottom, that brings me calm, despite the joy in life that shakes me like thunder . . .'" (#231). Rage, fear, pride, freedom, quick-footed intelligence in action, concentrated perseverance, defiant hope, as well as this sort of joy in life itself and the pulse of friendship, are all bearings affirmed in this notebook. It surely has a complexity of texture and a breadth of engagement not found in the steeply lyrical *Formal Share*. Not the least fascinating thing about these two sequences is the way they nevertheless emerge, side by side, out of this three-year arc of historical darkness.

Indeed, despite all their differences, these two sequences are intimately connected in ways that go beyond the context of their composition. Earlier I noted the long-distance rhyme in *Leaves of Hynpos* between the concluding aphorism concerning the openness to beauty everywhere and the Georges de La Tour painting of the woman who, "like the terrestrial silhouette of a red angel," is talking to the prisoner while holding a candle. These are figures of the call of beauty and the inward freedom discovered through a response to this call. Georges de La Tour is praised early in *Formal Share*, too, alongside Heraclitus: "To Two of Value. — Heraclitus, Georges de La Tour, I am grateful to you for having, during long spells, dislodged from every fold of my singular body the lure of the incoherent human condition, for having brought the uncovered ring of woman into accordance with the human face, for having made my dispersion agile and receptive, for having devoted your forces to crowning this immeasurable consequence of the absolutely imperative light: action against the real, signified by tradition, reenactment and miniature" (IX). The absolutely imperative light, like the candle and the word the woman brings to the prisoner, inspires the creative action against the real that is the creative representation of the real, realm of desolation and promise. The miniature or compressed work discloses the light that might otherwise remain buried. It is what Char sees as the light of beauty and hope. It is the candle of the painting. It is also the inner angel, the "candle that leans to the north of the heart," in the sixteenth section of *Leaves of Hypnos*: "Relations with the angel: our primary concern. / (Angel, that which, in the interior of man, stands aside from religious compromise, word of the highest silence, whose significance is beyond measure. Tuner of lungs which are the fortified grapes of the impossible. Knows the blood, ignores the celestial. Angel: the candle that leans to the north of our heart)" (#16; cf. #112, #5). This is the inner light that is also a light in the distance. "The light has been chased from our eyes. It is buried somewhere in our bones.

We, in turn, search for it to restore its crown" (#111). "You hold a match to your lamp and that which is lit sheds no light. It is far, far from you, that the circle brightens" (#120). "It is the hour when windows escape from their houses to light up at the end of the world, where our world is going to dawn" (#180). The angel of inward freedom and the angel who comes as a woman to the prisoner turn toward one another in the dimension of spaciousness. It is this that permits us to be at once here and beyond ourselves. One could trace multiple similar connections between the two sequences: they echo one another in images, words, bearings, horizons.

There is of course an obvious way to characterize the difference-in-similarity between these two sequences. One could say that *Formal Share* is idealist, *Leaves of Hypnos* realist; *Formal Share* expresses resistance and hope in lyrical and metaphysical terms, *Leaves of Hypnos* in worldly and political terms; *Formal Share* is an expression of spiritual freedom, *Leaves of Hypnos* a notebook of a concrete struggle for freedom. This is surely true in an important sense; there is a sharp difference in what is shown in these two works. The latter is an account of a practical engagement that is not at all a necessary consequence of the spiritual orientation expressed in the former. To say this is, in part, simply to say that Char committed himself to a course of action that only a small number of people in France were clear or courageous enough to undertake in 1941 and 1942, or even as late as 1943 and 1944. One could add that what is at stake here is that Char actually takes the language of a text like *Formal Share* seriously.

It is worth pausing, then, to consider the way Char himself appears to see the relationship at work between these sequences. Vitorrio Sereni, Eric Marty, and Paul Veyne have all emphasized that for Char, whose vision of history was deeply pessimistic, fascism was not the inexplicable event that it might have been for others but rather a grimly unsurprising version of the devastating baseness always possible in human history. "Certain epochs of the human condition undergo the chilling assault of an evil that finds support in the most dishonorable aspects of human nature" (FM, 79; cf. RBS, 24). "This war will prolong itself beyond any platonic treaties. The establishment of political concepts will be pursued in a contradictory way, with convulsions, and under the cover of a hypocrisy sure of its rights. Don't smile. Set aside skepticism and resignation, and prepare your mortal soul to confront, *intramuros*, icy demons akin to microbial agents" (FH, #7). This is the way a moralist or a lyricist sees history, not the way an historian does. It is the poet's task, Char says in the same aphorism, to stand in the center of this storm and affirm the "eternal return" of justice. There is a certain existential dualism in Char: human life is seen as a continual struggle between baseness and nobility, subjugation and freedom, humiliation and dignity, airlessness and spaciousness. "Freedom is found in the heart of whoever hasn't ceased to want it, to dream it, to win it against crime" (NP, 88). "I came into the world amid the distortion of chains on everything. The two of us made ourselves free. I drew from a compatible ethic the faultless support" (FM, 42). "River with a heart never destroyed in this world mad for prisons, / Keep us violent and friends of the bees on the horizon" (FM, 210). Every place in the darkness is for beauty, he affirms in the last aphorism of *Leaves of Hypnos*, and all his poetry is testimony to this hope and the quest it involves. In a "world mad for prisons," every place is also a place of darkness, of the nihilism of the base and the airless, of walls and vices that shut us off from the far light, the sustaining presence, the disclosive word. Char has a vision that pierces through and clarifies the parallels among all the many walls that crush us. These can be the structures of plainly oppressive states as well as the forces of violent armies. These can be the illusions and evasions of orthodox religion and the rationalizations of political ideology. These can be the social conventions that have become routines of blindness, the conformist pressures that the Transparents flee for the open, the grids of method and technology that sap our river-life of dream. "Will our brain, filled to bursting with machines, still be able to save its slender stream of dream and evasion?" (FM, 118). These can be an obsession with wealth or an addiction to security that for Char are hardly less hopeless than many other clenchings against the life of genuine encounter (FM, 88, 92, 169). These can be all the internalizations of these maladies that lead to the erosion of instinct and intuition, or to the neurotic torments of "psychic man" (FM, 95–96). "Imitate men as little as possible in their enigmatic disease of tying knots" (M, 79). To see these ruinous forces as all the same, we say, is to lose proportion and lucidity. Char, though he has his own sense of measure, loses neither. To see them as intimately related to one another, nevertheless, is to see far, to see to the end of the fallen world, as it were, and above all to take responsibility for the way one lives, for the way one relates to the structures and habits of the world one inhabits. It is in this latter sense that there is a demanding *fureur* in Char, an extremism in his concern for a life lived in freedom, turned to *le mystère*. His action in the Resistance is a clear sign of his sense of proportion and feet-on-the-ground intelligence. The entire arc of his poetry bears witness to his demanding vision of a spaciousness related to and yet beyond the measured responses required by specific circumstances. It is from this wider perspective that *Formal Share* and *Leaves of Hypnos* appear not to diverge from one another so much as to embrace one another.[24]

I'm not sure what the best word for this way of seeing is. It is a perspective that perhaps has a place in all religious or philosophical teachings with an "existential" bent, with a concern to address the individual. At least such works invite wheeling allegorical responses on multiple levels. In the modern epoch it has deep roots in romantic humanism, in Schiller and Blake and Shelley (and, in a very different way, Hegel), writers particularly concerned to trace parallels or homologies among different levels of our lives: the psyche, the family, the state, the economy, custom, culture, religion, language. There are mind-forg'd manacles as well as state-forg'd manacles. In Blake, as in Char, despite all their differences, there is a similar intensity and scope of vision of this sort which might be called *clairvoyance*. Here the word is meant to suggest not only a visionary quality—a capacity to see depths and distances invisible to eyes fixed on familiar boundaries—but also a deep sanity manifest as an "eccentric" insistence on taking our thousand daily compromises as seriously as everything else. We are ourselves as mad for prisons and as fearful of freedom, these writers teach, as are the gods, generals, priests, and plutocrats who have forever ruled us. We are ill and in need of recovery. "This failing of man dying at the center of the creation because the creation has dismissed him: how long will this last?" (FM, 195). Char's biographer tells a story that is of interest in this regard. In early December of 1935, Char published an open letter to Benjamin Péret, in which he made explicit and definitive his break with the surrealist movement. He then had this letter printed in the form of small notices which he posted in various places around L'Isle-sur-la-Sorgue (the village of his childhood to which he often returned when needing to take his bearings). It is fair to guess that Char's neighbors had no interest in this literary decision of his. Nor was this the first time that Char had declared his literary intentions in this way. "Once again," Greilsamer writes, "Char takes his neighbors as witnesses, neglecting the gap between their centers of interest and the quarrels of surrealism. He gives formal notice, displays a confident trust, makes a mockery of propriety, common sense, logic . . ." This is the same man who would later be praised for his unfailing steadiness of leadership in the Resistance. If this is an act of surrealist humor, it is also an act that calls to mind Blake. In Char, as in Blake, there is a visionary picture of our larger human predicament and our larger human promise, a penetrating insight into all our psychic demons that so readily align themselves with destructive social practices, and a comic when not nearly absurd disregard for the common sense of ordinary social life.[25]

This clairvoyance is like a lamp of spiritual freedom. Char, unlike Blake, is not a system-maker, not even a counter-system-maker. He is not a mythopoetic Christian humanist. He is a visionary existentialist, one with a pastoral bent, at least in the sense this term has had since Rousseau and Wordsworth and Thoreau and (in Char's eyes) Rimbaud, involving a faith in the formative power of an encounter with a natural world seen as both "half waste" and "half orchard" (RBS, 110), as both an abyssal ruin, an "external crematorium," and a sustaining ground, calling us "to roam generously over the seasons of the shell, while the almond at the core beats, free" (FM, 101). No doubt Char has an ample measure of Blake's or Rimbaud's confidence in the independence of the imagination: "action against the real, signified by tradition, at once reenactment and miniature" (FM, 67). Yet at the same time the imagination as he conceives it is always called by a slightly more than natural promise—beauty, the beloved, *l'Amie*, the flame, the brightness of an advent, as he variously calls this—found only through encounters with natural and human presences. It is inseparable from, it is the horizon brought to disclosure by, the saying of our erotic turning and going. "Inner command? Summons from without?" It is, finally, a certain pessimistic but resistant humanism, understood as a quest for the fully human, the bearing laconically affirmed in the prefatory note to *Leaves of Hypnos* cited above, defiantly affirmed in another passage near the middle of the sequence:

> I love these individuals so taken with what their hearts imagine freedom to be that they sacrifice themselves to save what little freedom there is from dying. Marvelous virtue of the people. (Free will

might not exist. The individual could be defined in terms of his cells, of his heredity, of the brief or prolonged course of his fate ... Nevertheless, between *all that* and Man, there is an enclave of unforeseen events and metamorphoses, our access to which must be defended and held to.)   (FH #155)

CHAPTER TWO

George Oppen

Vision and Companionship

Oppen began as a poet in the objectivist weather of modernism, influenced by Pound, Williams, and Zukofsky. In letters and interviews he often clarified that what this influence meant for him was not an epistemological stance but a formal practice. In an interview with Louis Dembo, he says: "There's been tremendous misunderstanding about that [what 'objectivist' really means]. People assume it means the psychologically objective in attitude. It actually means the objectification of the poem, the making of an object of the poem" (IN, 173; cf. SL, 139). One understands the point of the correction, especially when made by a poet like Oppen, whose sparely constructed poems explore so many concerns that go beyond the boundaries of any familiar empiricist position. Yet it is also true that the objectivist tradition has always involved a distrust of excessive subjectivity and a heightened attention to the things that present themselves around us, and so at least in this sense an empiricist or realist bent. "Of Being Numerous" begins, "There are things / We live among 'and to see them / Is to know ourselves'" (CP, 163). To call to mind an objectivist tradition in twentieth-century poetry is to call to mind at once a certain empiricist bent and a certain constructivist aesthetic. One might say that a strong interest in the series or sequence, in the long poem circling through a multiplicity of perspectives, is also a marked feature of this tradition, yet in fact this is a feature of twentieth-century poetry as a whole, and arguably of modern English-language poetry as a whole.[1]

When Oppen returned to writing poetry in the late fifties, in any case, he retained these objectivist bearings and at the same time moved far beyond them. He needed a widened poetic approach to address the issues of concern to him at this point in his life. In his poems and letters of these later years, it seems, three ways of thinking about poetry emerge as particularly important to him. One is the conviction that an accomplished poem is fundamentally *revelatory* or *disclosive*: it is to show what is there, to show the strangeness of what is there, to show the depth in which what is there appears. The poem "Psalm" exemplifies this concern (CP, 99). "The small nouns / Crying faith / In this in which the wild deer / Startle, and stare out," the poem concludes, evoking an encounter between the startled deer and a startled person, both caught up in the open. The poem brings to light the unfathomable relationship between the deer and the place where, "this in which," they appear, or, in Heideggerian terms, between these particular beings, the deer, and the Being that is the lighting or opening where they come to be. One might think of this as a sort of phenomenological deepening of the presentationalist poetic of Williams. "If, to speak of art, we will, as we should, use one word only, the word is disclosure."[2]

Of equal importance to Oppen's thinking in these years is an emphasis on the *meditative* dimension of poetry. Serious writing, he says, is "a process of thought" (SL, 99). The sequence "Route" begins, "Tell the beads of the chromosomes like a rosary, / Love in the genes, if it fails // We will produce no sane man again" (CP, 192), suggestive lines of a sort common in Oppen's work, lines in the life of thought that invite one to dwell with them, to turn them over and over in the mind as Oppen does. In a later poem he writes, "Prosody // Sings // In the stones // to entrust / To a poetry of statement // At close quarters // A living mind / 'and that one's own'" (CP, 228–29). "Still, the statement, what statement one can make," he says in a letter, "has value to me—O, has tremendous value, overwhelming value, as you know. There are things for each of us around which meaning gathers. The mission is to hold them, to be able to keep them in his mind, to try again and again to find the word, the syntax, the cadence of unfolding—I don't mean to promise redemption of course.

A matter of being able to say what one is and where one is. And what matters" (SL, 160). This reads like a description of the patiently unfolded thinking characteristic of Oppen's poems.

Oppen, further, conceives the movement of thought in his poems as a turn in a conversation with others. There is a *dialogical openness* to his poems. "I mean to be part of a conversation among honest people" (SL, 55). The last poem of *The Materials*, "Leviathan," begins, "Truth also is the pursuit of it: / Like happiness, and it will not stand," and, with echoes of Wordsworth's account of the poet as "a man speaking to men," concludes:

> How shall we say?
> In ordinary discourse—
>
> We must talk now. I am no longer sure of the words,
> The clockwork of the world. What is inexplicable
>
> Is the 'preponderance of objects.' The sky lights
> Daily with that predominance
>
> And we have become the present.
>
> We must talk now. Fear
> Is fear. But we abandon one another.   (CP, 89)

If Plato defined thinking as the soul's conversing with itself, he presented his thinking in the form of dialogical quests for the true and the good. Thinking is a conversation with oneself; conversation is a thinking with others. Oppen, in this sense as in many others, is a sort of existentialist Socrates. His poems gather allusions and citations to a greater extent than one might initially guess. They include, too, words of his wife and daughter, words of other writers and correspondents, and words that he had initially formulated in letters to friends. The clarity and respect of words in conversation is part of the work of "rescue" that love accomplishes (CP, 156). The distinctive sound of thought in Oppen's poetry is that of a back-and-forth between a mind in meditative solitude, brooding on things, and a mind in conversation with others, sorting things out in a space of shared concerns.[3]

Oppen, then, in the sixties and seventies, develops a disclosive, meditative, dialogical poetry. It bears a strong autobiographical dimension, for it is embedded in the distinctive curve of his experience, as well as a demanding horizon, a steep sense of the vocation of poetry. One could characterize this, I think, as a late romantic, existentialist poetry, one refracted by the objectivist emphases of a certain phase of modernism and by the phenomenological currents in modern philosophy. Though his bearings are always tested by a skeptical force, Oppen does hold to a romantic faith in the capacity of poetry both to diagnose our impasses and to disclose the sources and horizons of value in our lives. "It is difficult / to get the news from poems / yet men die miserably every day / for lack / of what is found there," Williams writes in "Asphodel." Oppen shares this conviction.

American romanticism is one of the deep sources of Oppen's meditative journey. It is a troubled inheritance, to be sure, but it is nonetheless there, a promise to be conjured with, a question to be wrestled with. Whitman is cited in the last section of "Of Being Numerous," and if he is not the presiding spirit of this sequence, he is at least a voice in its margins, lending a long perspective to Oppen's meditation on the solitary self and the self with others, or on being singular and being numerous, to recall the unfamiliar terms in which Oppen rethinks Whitman's song of myself and song of democracy. There is a poem in *The Materials* titled "Myself I Sing" (CP, 56–57). The poem begins with an ironic observation of the relationship between the man and his clothes, the person and his appearance, an important question in the romantic and the existentialist traditions. "Me! he says, hand on his chest. / Actually, his shirt. / And there, perhaps, / The question." The speaker of the poem seems to be passing through a trailer park. The major turn in the poem begins with the question: "And I / Here talking to the man?" This leads to a twofold statement of belief, followed by a concluding evocation of a world of night and rocks beyond the provisional safety of the city. The first part of the statement has to do with the formation of the self through its relation to what it sees: "The sky // that dawned along the road / And all I've been / Is not myself? I think myself / Is what I've seen and not myself." The second part of the statement, taking up the theme of "rescue" that traverses all of Oppen's work, has to do with the formation of the self through its relation with other people: "A man marooned / No longer looks for ships, imagines / anything on the horizon. On the beach / The ocean ends in water. Finds a dune. / And on the beach sits near it. Two. / He finds himself by two. / Or more." Oppen would come to call these two lines of orientation, respectively, the vertical concern and the horizontal concern. In one of his daybooks he writes:

> In This In Which is a poem with the line: We want to be here. I meant the following book to begin from that line.
>
> I found myself at once a double consciousness   I knew that I could not reconcile perfectly the doubleness of the vertical and the horizontal concern   the vertical and the horizontal sense of the redemption of life or of the value of life — — I tried again to come to terms with that doubleness in Of Being Numerous.
>
> The next book will say again simply: We want to be here.[4]

The shipwrecked sailor, deserted and in need of rescue, is one of Oppen's recurrent figures for the isolated self at the basis of society. There is a measure of traditional liberal political theory at work in this thinking, with its picture of a society composed of isolated selves, though this is also the point of view of just about every major existentialist thinker. Freedom begins in ontological solitude. At the same time, for all his skepticism, for all his alienation from postwar American social life, Oppen never abandons a basic Whitmanian conviction that the genuine self is discovered only through meaningful relationships with others. Substantive freedom, in this sense, comes from being found and rescued by another, finding and rescuing another. Oppen's political faith in this promise, it is true, wavers and ultimately wanes; by the late sixties, it seems, he is able to affirm the reality of this reciprocity of care only at the level of marriage, family, and friendship, in a conversation unfolded with those close to him.

The vertical horizon of concern, the characteristic emphasis of a long American romantic tradition, is of importance to Whitman, to the solitary singer of so many of his great poems, but it surely has its source in Emerson. This orientation discovers sustaining value in the encounter of a solitary consciousness with the power of nature or of material presence. In Oppen, as elsewhere in this tradition, the encounter involves above all vision, a sort of seeing that is not simply an optical phenomenon but an emotional and imaginative rising into what is there (CP, 155). "The virtue of the mind // Is that emotion // Which causes / To see" (CP, 107). "The hand for holding, / Legs for walking, / The eye *sees!* It floods in on us from here to Jersey tangled in the grey bright air!" (CP, 70). This faith is affirmed at various points in *The Materials*. "What I've seen / Is all I've found: myself" (CP, 61), Oppen writes at the end of a well-made poem about well-made boats. In "The Hills," a short praise poem of vision and love, this faith is brought together with the horizontal faith in the poet's relationship with his wife across time:

> That this is I,
> Not mine, which wakes
> To where the present
> Sun pours in the present, to the air perhaps
> Of love and of
> Conviction.
>
>   As to know
> Who we shall be. I knew it then.
> You getting in
> The old car sat down close
> So close I turned and saw your eyes a woman's
> Eyes. The patent
> Latches on the windows
> And the long hills whoever else's
> Also ours.   (CP, 75)

The presence of things in the emanating present of time is given to us through our capacity to see, to respond to what is there. If there is a founding text of this American romantic faith, it is perhaps Emerson's early essay *Nature*. In the first chapter of this essay, a little before the famous passage in which a man walking across the bare commons becomes a transparent eyeball, Emerson speaks of the sort of "reverence" that would be so fundamental to Oppen's poetry, connecting it to the freedom of an open mind to partake of all that it sees. "The stars awaken a certain reverence, because though always present, they are inaccessible; but all natural objects make a kindred impression, when the mind is open to their influence." This thought leads to the passage echoed in the lines of Oppen that I've just been citing: "The charming landscape which I saw this morning, is indubitably made up of some twenty or thirty farms. Miller owns this field, Locke that, and Manning the woodland beyond. But none of them owns the landscape. There is a property in the horizon which no man has but he whose eye can integrate all the parts, that is, the poet. This is the best part of these men's farms. Yet to this their warranty-deeds give no title." "And the long hills whoever else's / Also ours." This seeing involves a sense of scope, or of what Oppen (like Olson in these years) sometimes calls "size," or of what Stevens calls "being large in space." We belong to a vastness at once frightening and inspiring, according to a familiar notion of the sublime, and for Oppen ultimately steadying as well.[5]

A great deal has been written in recent years about the destructive complicities of this Emersonian celebration of expansive vision: this way of seeing has been said to be a sublimated version of manifest destiny, nationalist expansion, the accumulation of capital, and so forth. All of these things are sharply relevant in the American context. At the same time a concern with expansive vision, or a concern with a vision of the whole, is never *simply reducible* to social practices of domination and appropriation. To think so would be to make thinking impossible. Oppen, in any case, revises Emerson's and Whitman's evocations of the whole in subtle and significant ways. One of these has to do with the changing relationship in time between nature and history, a change already marked at moments in Whitman. In Oppen there is a reverential opening toward the material thereness of the built world as well as the natural world: he is as likely to voice wonder in the presence of a brick or a bridge as in the presence of a hill or a river. It is nevertheless striking that the first poem of his first book after a twenty-five-year absence from poetry is titled "Eclogue" and evokes the difference between the built world, with its rooms of talking and planning, and the natural world, with its "quiet continent" of "flesh and rock and hunger" and "vegetative leaves and stems taking place" (CP,

39). Another reorientation undertaken by Oppen is expressed by his uncommonly understated language (an issue to which I will return further on). Perhaps the most significant reorientation is already implied in the recognition that, if Emerson writes in parallel with idealist philosophy, Oppen writes in parallel with existential phenomenology. He rethinks the place of the mind in relation to the world it encounters. This question is like a door into his entire journey.[6]

There are several closely related expressions to which Oppen returns again and again in his poems, letters, daybooks, and essays: "place of the mind and eye," "the mind's own place," "the life of the mind," "the power of the mind," "the miracle of place," and other like expressions. He is thinking something through in turning again and again to these expressions. In 1963 he published "The Mind's Own Place," one of only three essays he published in his entire life. A reader with some knowledge of Oppen might be surprised by a title that so clearly recalls the words with which Milton's Satan, affirming his independence of mind, embraces his fallen condition: "hail horrors, hail / Infernal world, and thou profoundest hell / Receive thy new possessor: one who brings / A mind not to be changed by place or time. / The mind is its own place, and in itself / Can make a heaven of hell, a hell of heaven" (I. 250–55). Oppen, though he has a measure of Satan's defiance, would presumably distrust his Promethean subjectivity. There is in fact a poem in Oppen's sequence "A Narrative" that borrows Satan's words in order to criticize a solipsistic subjectivity, a mind without stories:

Serpent, Ouroboros
Whose tail is in his mouth: he is the root
Of evil.
This ring worm, the devil's
Doctrine the blind man
Knew. His mind
Is its own place;
He has no story. Digested

And digesting—Fool object,
Dingy medallion

In the gutter
Of Atlantic Avenue!
Let it alone! It is deadly.
What breath there is
In the rib cage we must draw
From the dimensions

Surrounding, whether or not we are lost
And choke on words.   (CP, 153)

What is surprising, perhaps, is that the expression "the mind's own place" in the title of the 1963 essay—an essay published two years before the publication of the book that includes "A Narrative"—does not appear to have any such negative connotation; it appears to be meant in a positive sense. The expression itself, it is true, does not occur in the body of the essay. While the essay is complex, one does not mischaracterize it by saying that it draws a basic distinction between the demands of politics, driven by the necessity to reduce suffering, and the demands of poetry, driven by the need to articulate a horizon of what is variously called happiness, the good life, and "the thing wanted for itself," which Oppen takes to be inseparable from an individual vision beyond political action. What "the mind's place" means in this essay would seem to be very close to what Oppen calls "the life of the mind" in his interview with Louis Dembo. Given the importance of what Oppen says here, it is worth citing the exchange at some length:

> GO: . . . I suppose what I'm saying is that there is no life for humanity except the life of the mind. I don't know whether it's useful to say that to anyone. Either people will have discovered it for themselves or else it won't be true for them.
>
> LD: Well, exactly what do you mean by "the life of the mind" in this sense?
>
> GO: I mean the awareness . . . I suppose it's nearly a sense of awe, simply to feel that the thing is there and that it's quite something to

see. It's an awareness of the world, a lyric reaction to the world. "Of Being Numerous" ends with the word "curious" partly as a joke on Whitman, but also because men are curious, and at the end of a very long poem, I couldn't find anything more positive to say than that.

LD: Then by "life of the mind" you mean something intuitive, not something analytical?

GO: Yes, or just my word "faith." I said life of the mind and perhaps I spoke a little carelessly. I was anticipating, as its opposite, all the struggles for happiness, all the search for a morality of altruism, all the dependence on the poor to confer value—and eventually the poor might one way or another disappear. I was anticipating the whole discussion of "the good," of an ethic, and leaping ahead. I don't mean that there isn't anything to do right now, but I was thinking about a justification of human life, eventually, in what I call the life of the mind.

LD: I don't quite follow you. Are you suggesting that "the life of the mind" replace social values?   (IN, 177; cf. 185–86)

Dembo is a little taken aback by this sort of language from a former communist. At this point the issues raised in the 1969 interview dovetail with the concerns addressed by Oppen in the 1963 essay. Oppen in fact is not speaking of a replacement of one thing by another. He is trying to clarify the far from simple relationship between the demands of political action and the demands of poetic thinking as he conceives it, or, put in looser terms, between the horizontal dimension of our lives and the vertical dimension of our lives, or, put even more broadly, between an historical way of thinking and a metaphysical way of thinking. He is concerned with the place in poetry of traditional metaphysical questions of the whole and the good.[7]

What happens in Oppen's understanding of understanding, so to speak, is that the life of the mind is taken to be an opening outward in the place where it finds itself, where it comes to encounter persons, other beings, and the depth of Being. The mind takes place in the taking place of the world in time. "Look / Anywhere to the sight's limit: space / Which is viviparous: // Place of the mind / And eye" (CP, 70). "What was there to be thought // comes by the road" (CP, 199). The seventh section of "A Narrative" is thus eccentric, not in its stance, but in its specific phrasing. For when Oppen speaks of the life of the mind, or even of the mind's own place, he is usually speaking of the mind drawn outward to the dimensions surrounding, the mind going out to encounter the world that comes to encounter it. The mind enters the event of disclosure. It is this movement that is so powerfully evoked in the last poem of "A Narrative" (a poem I cited in my introduction). "River of our substance / Flowing / With the rest," the poem begins, "River of the substance of the earth's curve, river of the substance / Of the sunrise, river of silt, of erosion, flowing / To no imaginable sea. But the mind rises / Into happiness, rising // Into what is there" (CP, 155). "The mind rises," Oppen says, echoing one of Stevens's privileged figures for the experience of consciousness awakening to its power, clarity, joy in expansion. The "there" into which it rises is called the "open miracle of place" in the concluding movement of the poem:

> The marvel of the wave
> Even here is its noise seething
> In the world. I thought that even if there were nothing
>
> The possibility of being would exist;
> I thought I had encountered
>
> Permanence; thought leaped on us in that sea
> For in that sea we breathe the open
> Miracle
>
> Of place, and speak
> If we would rescue
> Love to the ice-lit
>
> Upper World a substantial language
> Of clarity, and of respect.

For Oppen, the life of the mind, of course, does involve the inwardness of memory, reflection, meditation, and decision. All his poetry bears witness to these dimensions of our inwardness. And yet at times it may seem, nevertheless, as though for Oppen the deep basis of this inwardness were the "coming to mind" of the outward, of the outer world toward which the mind "opens" in wonder. To think is to walk abroad; to think is to enter the world further; in poetry, as elsewhere, Jane Hirshfield writes, "attentiveness only deepens what it regards." We belong to the world that astonishes us. "Thought leaped on us in that sea": the mind, taken by the world, takes it bearings on the world. There is surely an affinity between this romantic experience of an embodied, embedded, disclosive consciousness and the existential phenomenologies of Heidegger, Marcel, and Merleau-Ponty.[8]

The conclusion of the poem cited above, alluding to the descent of Orpheus to the underworld to rescue Eurydice, suggests that the rescue of the beloved from death is a daily work: the rescuing of another *from* the flowing away of ourselves in the river of time, the rescuing of another *for* our participation in the miracle of place perpetually opened in this river of time. The further suggestion, I think, is that there is a connection of some sort, however uncertain, between the rising of the mind into what is there and the rising of rescued love from the erosive pull of death. This would be to say that there are analogies between the way we relate with others and the way we turn toward the world at large. What is the place of mind? What is it to be a self in the world? What is it to be a self in society? What is the place and movement of love in our lives? What is a genuine conversation? How are we to speak of these things? These are questions that Oppen explores, in a language of clarity and respect, throughout *Of Being Numerous*.

In a sense they all emerge out of the simple question that Oppen poses in the first poem that he wrote when he returned to poetry after twenty-five years of doing other things: "What do we believe / To live with?" (CP, 52). Rachel Blau DuPlessis, in one of the finest essays I have read on Oppen's work, writes that one could see all of his work as an effort "to define and clarify problems of value." This way of putting it is illuminating, and it has the virtue of drawing attention to the connection between Oppen's poetic practice and his entire life, a connection of great importance to Oppen himself. Oppen provides other terms for the source of this lived philosophic quest, including desire, or Eros (perhaps in the later Freud's sense though, ultimately, I think, in Plato's full and resonant sense), or care, the root of the word "curious" on which "Of Being Numerous" ends, care for what matters, care for the soul and care for those at our side, care that unfolds into "vision" and "companionship" (CP, 129), the open of attention and the open of love. The major sequences of the late sixties and early seventies are those in which these questions are most fully explored in sustained meditative movements.[9]

There is a letter of Oppen's, written before he wrote "Of Being Numerous," which clearly sketches the terms in which he approached this sequence and, more generally, his search for sustaining horizons to live by:

> The book [*This In Which*] will open with these two poems ["Technologies" and "Armies of the Plain"]. Followed by Philai, followed by Psalm. Which makes a prelude, a statement of the metaphysical vision and the anthropocentric—the 'social' as they would say.
> Not so easy for me as for Eliot --- whose metaphysical standpoint is faith and whose anthropocentric standpoint is the Age of Faith. And therefore I haven't, I'm afraid, written a Wasteland, haven't written a decisive expression of a period. I meant not to try in this book. I mean to try in the next [which would be *Of Being Numerous*]. Probably can't ---- My god, you should see me in this patched-up work room talking like this!   (SL, 108)

At one point in the sequence there is a citation from *Spring and All* (25), and elsewhere a clear allusion to Book IV of *Paterson* (11), indicating that "Of Being Numerous" is in dialogue, too, with Williams's venture in the long "social" poem. A concern with a breakdown of language at the center of our social life is addressed by both Williams and Oppen. Yet the explicit reference to Eliot's *The Waste Land* in this letter, if initially surprising, is finally unsurprising. It is surprising, of course, because Eliot and Oppen write from such different perspectives. They are nearly antithetical in every way. It is unsurprising, nevertheless, in several respects. Oppen's sequence is closer to Eliot's than to Williams's in length: it is a poem that can be held in the mind as a whole more easily than can, say, *Paterson* or *The Cantos*. While there is no larger mythopoetic pattern shaping Oppen's poem as the grail myth shapes Eliot's, and while Oppen's poem does not have the polyvocal or dramatistic qualities of Eliot's, Oppen does share Eliot's concern to bring together a social axis of concern and a metaphysical axis of concern, to probe the connection between the human relationships in his society and the fundamental ways of seeing of his society, and he does intend to write "a decisive expression of a period," in this case the America of the sixties rather than the Europe of the twenties. The two poems also share a certain "crisis poem" shape: both engage in a diagnosis of social ills, including a falling away from sources of value, and then undertake a movement toward larger horizons of value, though in both poems this movement is shadowed by a severe skepticism and, in the end, left ambiguously wavering. The reference to Eliot in this letter also reminds one of the temporal complexity of Oppen's sequence. The crises explored in Eliot's poem emerge above all out of the First World War and the twenties. Oppen, a generation younger than Eliot, was fourteen years old when *The Waste Land* was first published. The crises that shaped his consciousness were those of the thirties and forties, then the McCarthyite America of the fifties that forced him into exile, then the volatile America of the sixties to which he returned. In "Of Being Numerous" Oppen is primarily engaged with the America of the sixties: with consumer culture, the war in Vietnam, and the counterculture (the civil rights movement, and the emergent women's movement, are largely absent from the poem). But the poem includes one clear recollection of his experience during the Second World War (14); much of "Route," a sort of extended coda to this poem, looks backward in time; and a reader has a distinct sense, I think, that "Of Being Numerous" is a poem filtered through a mind of long experience, a mind that brings with it layers of lived time from the twenties through the sixties. "The thirties. And / A spectre // In every street, / In all inexplicable crowds, what they did then / Is still their lives" (CP 52), Oppen writes in "Blood from the Stone," the poem of 1958 that marked his return to the writing of poetry, adding a few lines later, "still our lives." This depth of perspective is implicit in "Of Being Numerous."[10]

    The sequence has a clearer shape and movement than is always recognized. I would suggest that it falls into five major parts or movements—the lines between which are not stark but subtle—and an epilogue or afterword consisting of a citation from a letter of Whitman's written during the Civil War.

    The first eleven sections, a sort of roaming introduction, present the basic questions with which the poem as a whole wrestles. There is the presence of things against an unfathomable ground of miraculous presencing and ultimate ruin, a ground underlying and irreducible to the built world, here the built world of New York City, with its towers, buses, streets, apartments, docks, and bridges. There are the communities of people that "flow" through the city, forming or failing to form coherent relationships in place and time, finding or failing to find their generational and cross-generational bonds and covenants, caught up in the promise and the burden of being numerous: yet each member of this "populace" remains, in some part of the self, a solitary Crusoe, a singular individual who, like the poet of this sequence, is ambivalently drawn toward and withdrawn from others, wanting both relationship and independence. There is the question of language, of the language spoken or not spoken in this world, of the language required for this sober, meditative poem that at times seems shaped as much around pauses and silences as around statements and utterances. The question of our "rescue" from solitude is posed with conciseness in sections 6 and 7. "Crusoe // We say was / 'Rescued'. / So we have chosen." "Obsessed, bewildered // By the shipwreck / Of the singular // We have chosen the meaning / Of being numerous." The question of consciousness rising into what is there—coming to awareness of itself as it comes to awareness of things appearing in the impenetrable world beyond our built world—is evoked with enigmatic brevity in sections 1, 2, 5, and 8. "These are the things / We live among 'and to see them / Is to know ourselves'. // Occurrence, a part / Of an infinitie series, // The sad marvels" (1). And the ambiguous images of light and shipwreck, including "the bright light of shipwreck," emerge in sections 9, 10, and 11: "To dream of that beach / For the sake of an instant in the eyes, // The absolute singular // The unearthly bonds / Of the singular // Which is the bright light of shipwreck" (9).

    The figure of shipwreck of course rhymes with the figure of a shipwrecked and rescued Crusoe. Oppen loved to sail all his life. In "Guest Room" he says, with simple wonder, "'It has been good to us,' / However.

The nights // At sea, and what / We sailed in, the large / Loose sphere of it // Visible, the force in it / Moving the little boat" (CP, 112). And yet images of shipwreck haunt all of Oppen's work. The old metaphor of life as a journey at sea, a journey that will inevitably end badly in one or many senses (SL, 56), pervades Oppen's thinking. It is thus particularly poignant that the first appearance of shipwreck in his work, in "Image of the Engine," occurs alongside words that perhaps recall a note that his mother left her family when she committed suicide (Oppen was four years old at the time):

> What ends
> Is that.
>   Even companionship
> Ending.
>
> 'I want to ask if you remember
> When we were happy!' As tho all travels
>
> Ended untold, all embarkations
> Foundered.   (CP, 41)

Here, one imagines, Oppen is reflecting, too, on his own fear that his and Mary's travels will end "untold," "foundered" in despair and speechlessness. And yet it is this acute sense of risk, of failure, of mortality, he underlines, that is the immeasurable background of our acute sense of both presence and articulated value in our lives. This, he says in a letter, is the paradox evoked by the "bright light of shipwreck" in "Of Being Numerous":

> 'The shipwreck of the singular' I wrote. We *cannot* live without the concept of humanity, the end of one's own life is by no means equivalent to the end of the world, we would not bother to live out our lives if it were - - - -
> and yet we cannot escape this: that we *are* single. And face, therefore, shipwreck.
> And yet this, this tragic fact, is the brilliance of one's life, it is 'the bright light of shipwreck' which discloses - - - - - - 'all.'   (SL, 263)

This tragic affirmative bearing, or tragic optimism, as Camus puts it in an essay on Char, runs through the whole existentialist tradition, at least in its atheistic current, from Nietzsche through Camus. In this, at least, in the holding together of a lucid pessimism and a lyricism of wonder, generosity, and openness to the whole, Char and Oppen have deep affinities. And both celebrate, if in very different ways, the sustaining life of companionship. Though social hope does eventually wane in "Of Being Numerous," the sequence interweaves an existentialist emphasis on the way a solitary inwardness in freedom discovers a relation to the whole of Becoming and Fate (as in Nietzsche) and an historicist emphasis on the way a self is always social, always comes to a coherent sense of itself only through struggle with others (as in Hegel), work with others (as in Marx), dialogue with others (as in Habermas).[11]

Section 12, a nostalgic evocation of a once simple social word embedded in nature, begins an extended movement of the sequence in which primarily social and political issues are explored (12–25). The tension between Oppen's longing to be singular, independent, and his longing to partake of the numerous, to be interdependent, is sounded in all its ambivalence in this movement (13–16). The question is how to align oneself with a society driven by blind consumption (13, 23), insane war (18, 19, 20), and unconcern with clarity of attention and of speech (14, 17, 21, 22). There is a fear of an "unreal" quality settling over this world: unreality, it seems, is what characterizes a life without the rising of the mind into what is there, the rising of "rescued" love into vision and companionship, and the articulation of what matters in a language of clarity and respect. One of Williams's major themes in *Paterson*—the link between social alienation and the loss of a vital clarity of speech—is echoed at this point: "He wants to say / His life is real. / No one can say why // It is not easy to speak // A ferocious mumbling, in public / Of rootless speech" (17).[12]

Sections 26 through 28, anticipated by sections 21 and 22, form a transitional movement wherein the sequence shifts its attention from primarily social and political questions to primarily familial and ontological questions. Oppen pauses here, as it were, to reflect on what can and cannot be done in poetry under the circumstances in which he is writing. "It is difficult now to speak of poetry" (27). Section 26, complex, searching, ranging, is a pivotal section in more than one sense: it at once divides and precariously holds together the major movements of the sequence (it is a section to which I will return below). The five-line section 28 seems to voice a hope that the book in which this poem appears will embody and disclose something of the light of emergence, the miraculous light of the whole, that the author of this book so intently turns to again and again: "The light / Of the closed pages, tightly closed, packed against each other / Exposes the new day, / The narrow frightening light / Before a sunrise" (28).

The fourth movement of the poem, then, running from sections 29 through 37, undertakes a meditation that oscillates between a quiet, at times quietly ecstatic, celebration of intimate relationships—father and daughter, husband and wife—and a quiet celebration of the incredible presence of the world to which the mind opens in wonder. "Looking up she sees the blue bright sky / Above the branches. / If one had been born here / How could one believe it?" (30), the poet asks at one point, perhaps speaking of his daughter, slightly skewing an idiom, as he so often does. "How light the air is / And the earth" (34), he says a few sections later. The lightness, the "bright light" of being, is then discovered in the life of those he loves. Need and desire are affirmed as a dimension of the luminous disclosure of our lives. "And the beauty of women, the perfect tendons / Under the skin, the perfect life // That can twist in a flood / Of desire // Not truth but each other // The bright, bright skin, her hands wavering / In her incredible need" (32). Not truth but each other, not knowledge but care, is a hierarchy of value emphasized again at the end of the sequence (38–39). It is no accident that Kierkegaard is cited in an earlier section (16). Kierkegaard underlines, more persistently than any other philosopher, that if truth is not likely to be given to us in ultimate matters, truthfulness is a bearing that is ours to adopt if we decide to, if we pledge ourselves to its demands. Oppen begins another poem: "I am the father of no country / And can lie. // But whether mendacity / Is really the best policy. And whether // One is not afraid / To lie" (CP, 150). Truthfulness bears a light of its own; it is a clearing in our lives. In this movement of the sequence Oppen aligns the truthfulness without which existential coherence and sustaining relationship are impossible and the truthfulness of bearing witness to what is there. "Which is ours, which is ourselves," he says, speaking of the desire and need of himself and his wife, "This is our jubilation / Exalted and as old as that truthfulness / Which illumines speech" (33).[13]

Two very short sections (38–39) form the final movement of the sequence. They present an old man in a room being cared for by a nurse, and recall again the "sad marvels," the transient things of the world, with which the sequence begins. Human relationship, these poems quietly affirm, is grounded less in knowledge than in care, less in knowledge than in acknowledgment, as Stanley Cavell would say, less in knowledge than in perception and touch, as it is put here: "You are the last / Who will know him / Nurse. // Not know him. / He is an old man, / A patient, / How could one know him? // You are the last / Who will see him / Or touch him, / Nurse" (38). The poem, of a peculiar generic simplicity, hauntingly foretells the condition of Oppen years later, an old man struck by disease, cared for first by his wife, then by a nurse.

The last section of the sequence, which I have called its epilogue, consists of a citation from a letter that Whitman wrote to his mother in the spring of 1864. At the time Whitman had been visiting soldiers in hospitals. There is a wistful simplicity in the voice of the passage Oppen cites. Whitman speaks of a new statue on the capitol, "the Genius of Liberty I suppose," and the bright light that "shines" on it at sundown. "I love to go and look at it." Oppen, too, at the end of this poem, wonders if a meaningful freedom will come to be realized in American society or if it will remain a distant gleam of hope. Are genuine freedom and value only discoverable in this world from a place of relative solitude and withdrawal? Given the movement of this poem, and of Oppen's poetry of the sixties and seventies as a whole, one could gather that he does come to think so (though without the sort of reversal of political perspective that occasionally came over former radicals of his generation). Yet the sequence concludes—the passage from Whitman concludes—with the word "curious": "The sun when it is nearly down shines on the headpiece and it dazzles and glistens like a big star: it looks quite /// curious . . .'" (40). In his interview with Dembo, Oppen says that this word is meant to suggest some saving openness despite all, despite the pessimistic bent of his poems in general:

> I wouldn't, for instance, talk about death with any intensity unless
> I thought I was going to die. As close as I come to a philosophic

statement is in that poem ["World, World—"] in which I wrote, "we want to be here"—just to set the fact down because the poems do have a kind of pessimism; and I'm reminding myself that I do want to be here, that I would not lack the courage to cut my throat if I wanted to do so. I don't do so. In fact I enjoy life very, very much. I wrote that poem in case there was any misinterpretation of that. And I set myself again and again, not in the spirit of any medical pragmatism, any philosophy offering to cure everything, nor in any effort to improve anybody, but just to record the fact, to saying that I enjoy life very much and defining my feeling by the word "curious" or, as at the end of "A Narrative," "joy," joy in the fact that one confronts a thing so large, that one is part of it. That sense of awe, I suppose, is all I manage to talk about. I had written that "the virtue of the mind is that emotion which causes to see," and I think that perhaps that is the best statement of it. (IN, 185–86)

Here "curiosity" becomes a version of "awe," an elated openness to the finite beings that appear—transient, swept toward shipwreck, and so in this sense "sad marvels"—against the perpetual opening of a "there" in the infinite. Yet this openness is not only metaphysical: it is a dimension of our relationships with others as well. "Ballad," the last poem in *Of Being Numerous*, tells of the curiosity of a woman who, with her husband, has shown the poet and his wife the sights of Swan Island. "She took it that we came— / I don't know how to say, she said— // Not for anything we did, she said / Mildly, 'from God'. She said // What I like more than anything / Is to visit other islands" (CP, 208). There are surely echoes of Donne in this voice of curiosity, of openness. The root of the word "curiosity" is "cura," or care, which invites one to connect the care of the soul, whose phenomenological axis is the rising of the mind into what is there, with the care for others, the care of the nurse at the end of the sequence, the care of George and Mary for one another and their daughter, the care or eros that is the profound root of a coherent social community (CP, 42, 77, 120–21, 177–79). "Of Being Numerous," then, ends with a word that gathers, in what Gadamer would call the openness of a genuine question, the horizontal and the vertical dimensions of care, of a capacious search for sustaining sources and horizons to live by, which the sequence as a whole and all of Oppen's poetry explore.[14]

At this point a map of this larger search might be helpful. I will borrow from an ancient story of creation. In Genesis there are two creation stories, an earlier folkloric story, which comes second in the text, and a later priestly story, which comes first. In the opening story, the whole of creation is astonishingly spoken into being, and the movement of dividing and ordering, of establishing limits or boundaries, is paramount. The first act of this sort is the movement of divine spirit against primordial chaos, the speaking and bringing into being of light, and the separation of the light from the dark, the day from the night. The second act of this sort is the holding back of the waters of chaos through the formation of a dome or firmament. We plausibly think of this as the sky. And yet the bounding appears to take place on all sides. In the story of the flood, it turns out, the destructive waters are released not only from the sky, during forty days and forty nights of rain, but also from the ground, from "fountains of the deep broken up." According to this strand of the Hebrew Bible, as Richard Elliott Friedman shows, the creation is a sort of egg surrounded on all sides by the dark waters of chaos. The image has a particular resonance in our age, for we, unlike millennia of human generations, are able to see photographs of the earth as a whole, of the earth as it appears from outer space, and in fact it looks like a bright egg, blue and green and white, drifting through an infinite sea of dark. It is the precarious egg of creation (which I have sketched in Map 1). It is there, here, in fear and wonder, that we ask, with Oppen, what do we believe to live with? It is there, here, that we search for a sense of who and where we are, of what matters, of what we care for.

Lest the mythopoetic picture seem to absolve us from our freedom and our responsibility to shape our lives, to build a habitable shared world, this egg of creation should also be imagined as the upper half of a set of parallel vectors unfolding in time (which I have sketched in Map 2). For it is we, far more than the natural world, who bring chaos and ruin into our lives, as René Girard has said, as the whole socialist tradition has always said, as any spirited idealism has always said, as a visionary like Blake passionately declares. The ruin, the unreality, the pointlessness of our lives are consequences of our failures of eros, work, care, talk.[15]

One question raised by these maps is the question of the word with which one should designate the force or forces located at the angle where the lines emerge. These lines represent horizons of value, or, in the

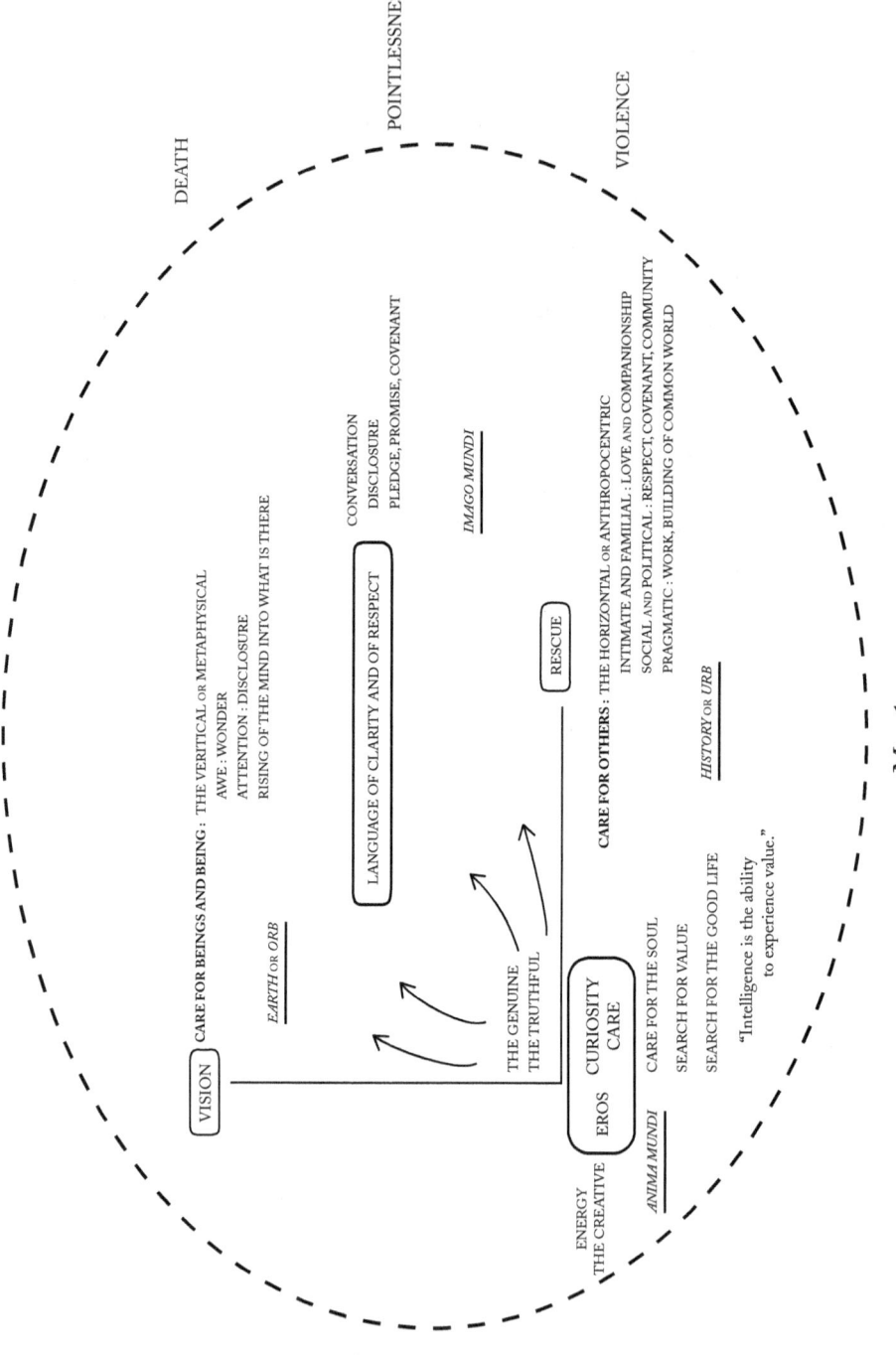

Map 1

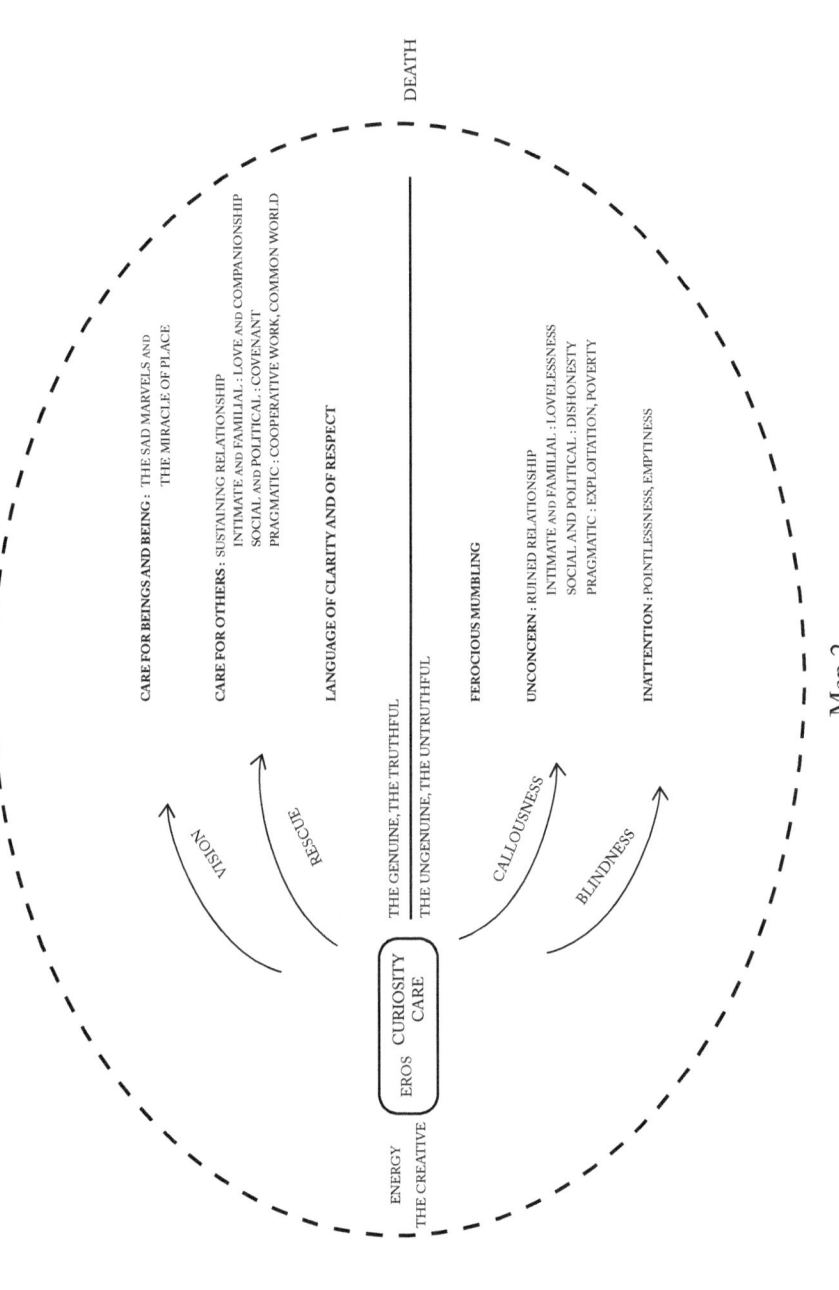

second map, horizons of both value and the betrayal and ruin of value. At their source, then, could be what Rachel Blau DuPlessis characterizes as a search for value tested by the weathers of experience and doubt. In contemporary culture, it would seem, "energy" is our most common name for this source beyond which we can go no further. The old biblical term for this source would be a creative "spirit" with a transcendent ground in the divine. The modern epoch as a whole—whose emblematic thinkers in this respect are Hobbes and Locke—tends to replace this with a natural "instinct of self-preservation" at the root. The dominant psychologies of our time, psychoanalytic or otherwise, are likely to place "desire" here. This would be compatible with Oppen's own existentialist emphasis throughout his work on "choice" as the human ground of ethical and political value (as distinct from, say, "perception" or "awareness" as the primary opening to a more elusive ontological significance). Contemporary liberal societies, as Alasdair MacIntrye has underlined, are pervaded by this basic way of thinking about ethical matters: we are "emotivist" in our ethical habits and vocabularies, MacIntrye says, whether we speak of decision (with the existentialists), desire (with the psychologists), power (with the Nietzscheans and the sociologists), preference (with the economists), or interest (with the political theorists). It is not easy to step outside this framework in contemporary culture, not least because it seems to be of a piece with consumer culture, with the logics of career and consumption that profoundly condition lives in a capitalist world-economy reaching everywhere. Oppen, however, does give intimations of another way of approaching these questions. "Eros—the will—drifts in the ontological," he writes in one of his daybooks (SP, 77). Eros is one of the terms he suggests for the searching energy at the source, as in the poem titled "Eros," which includes a reflection on the cemetery of Père-Lachaise:

Yet they come here too, the old,
Among the visitors, suffering
The rain

Here above Paris—

To the plaque of the ten thousand

Last men of the Commune
Shot at the wall

In the cemetery of Père-Lachaise, and the grave
Of Largo Caballero and the monuments to the Resistance—

A devoutness

Toward the future
Recorded in this city
Which taught my generation

Art
And the great paved places
Of the cities.   (CP, 120–21)

A "devoutness toward the future," a promise that holds across generations, is a "covenant," a concept of importance in Oppen's thought. The "paved places" or "bequeathed pavements" (CP, 53) of the built world, however "squalid" or "filthy" or "crumbling" they may become (CP, 42, 178, 200), are nevertheless emblems in Oppen's work of the shared project of constructing a habitable human world. The Eros of this poem, then, might be likened to the Eros of Freud's later works on civilization. In those works, Eros, now embracing the sexual instinct and the self-preservative instinct whose antagonism was at the center of Freud's early thought, is said to be the unifying force of civilization, a force set against natural limitation (which makes work a necessity), against death, and against a death-instinct that expresses itself primarily as aggression. The task of civilization, put simply, is to enforce renunciation or sublimation of those instincts which threaten to tear apart the sustaining activity of Eros in work, relationship, and culture. Writing in the twenties and thirties, watching Europe slide toward nihilism and fascism, Freud was pessimistic about the whole enterprise. Yet Oppen, for all his naturalism, for all his own pessimism, thinks of the energy of our search for value, our Eros at the root, in broader terms than Freud. One limitation of Freud's thought in the later works—surprising though it may sound to put it this way—is a thin picture of sublimation. Our turnings to horizons of value, for Freud, are always but substitutes and displacements to which we unhappily resign ourselves: they rest upon an explosive discontent. It is true that this point of view has the basic strength of disillusioned realism. But it is still too thin. Plato, like Freud, sees that Eros is deeply ambiguous: if it drives the tyrant's passions (in Book X of *The Republic*), it also animates the philosopher's love of beauty and ultimately of wisdom and virtue (in *The Symposium*). The question is the direction in which our Eros is turned, the way in which our Eros is unfolded. And Plato, too, sees a decisive measure of ascesis and sublimation in the turning of Eros to wider horizons of spiritual value: that is one thing that the mis-encounter between Alcibiades and Socrates is meant to show. But Plato does not see this as a path of either stoic resignation or repressed discontent: it is an enthusiasm, an elation of the mind rising into what is there. It is inseparable from our love of things and horizons beyond the self whose Eros turns to them. It is inseparable from what we care for. Socrates, drawn by Eros to horizons of care, becomes himself an embodiment of Eros that stirs the erotic curiosity of others. This is the full resonance of wonder, of curiosity: the openness of Eros longing to discover what matters, searching for sources and horizons to live by. "The girl who walked / Indian style—straight-toed— / With her blond hair / Thru the forests // Of Oregon / Has changed the aspect / Of things," Oppen writes in one of his great love poems:

> everything is pierced
> By her presence tho we have wanted
> Not comforts
>
> But vision
> Whatever terrors
> May have made us
> Companion
> To the earth, whatever terrors—   (CP, 129)

This is a joy in vision and companionship that is not clenched against either its own desires or the pressures of the real. There is sublimation here, if we wish to think of it that way, but it would require a broad, quasi-Platonic picture of sublimation. Freud's picture is true of our habitual vice, to borrow Emerson's expression, but not of the lives we genuinely *want* to live when our Eros, our enthusiasm, is genuinely awakened, genuinely turned and taken outward.[16]

Another question raised by the maps above is that of the relationship between vision and companionship, between the mind's rising into what is there and the heart's turning to others in concern, between the vertical and the horizontal dimensions of our lives. Oppen's response to this question is tentative and contradictory: he comes back to it again and again, turning it over in thought, turning it around on the page, without proposing to resolve it. In general Oppen holds to an existentialist position, itself an inflection of an older liberal position, according to which there is an unbridgeable divorce between fact and value, or between the realm of being and the realm of ethics, the latter having no ground outside of our desires and choices, outside of our establishing of ends for ourselves (if Hegelians, Marxists, and sociologists emphasize the social or collective basis of these ends, liberals, romantics, and existentialists emphasize their individual basis, and in this debate both sides have a serious portion of the truth). Thus in "Route," for instance, we read: "We are brothers, we are brothers?—these things are / composed of a moral substance only if they are untrue. If / these things are true they are perfectly simple, perfectly / impenetrable, those primary elements which can only be / named" (CP, 197; cf. 224). This awareness of a division between the thereness of being and the horizon of moral and political choice runs deep in Oppen. Yet this awareness is in tension with a part of him that, at the same time, wants to affirm *some sort of relationship* between his ethical bearing and his metaphysical bearing, between the range of his moral and political choices and his astonished openness to what is disclosed in the world around him. Thus in "Route," from which I have just cited, we also read: "To insist that what is true is good, no matter, no matter, a definition—?" (CP, 200). The repetition of "no matter," the sign of a conscience wrestling with itself, and the dash followed by a question mark, suggest that Oppen feels the pull of this sort of resolution but will not quite take the leap. In the last poem of "A Narrative," as we have seen, an affirmation of the rising of the mind into what is there is brought into the same space as an affirmation of the rescuing of love from the sheer flowing away of life. Two horizons of care are held together: to hold them together, to affirm them both, is not to ignore the difference between them.[17]

This question, explored throughout "Of Being Numerous," has a particularly acute place in the pivotal section 26, the longest poem in the sequence, and the place where there seems to occur a stepping back from the social realm and, in the rest of the sequence, a concentration on the life of a family. It is worth citing the whole poem here:

They carry nativeness
To a conclusion
In suicide.

We want to defend
Limitation
And do not know how.

Stupid to say merely
That poets should not lead their lives
Among poets,

They have lost the metaphysical sense
Of the future, they feel themselves
The end of a chain

Of lives, single lives
And we know that lives
Are single

And cannot defend
The metaphysic
On which rest

The boundaries
Of our distances.
We want to say

'Common sense'
And cannot. We stand on

That denial
Of death that paved the cities,
Paved the cities

Generation
For generation and the pavement

Is filthy as the corridors
Of the police.

How shall one know a generation, a new generation?
Not by the dew on them! Where the earth is most torn
And the wounds untended and the voices confused,
There is the head of the moving column

Who if they cannot find
Their generation
Wither in infirmaries

And the supply depots, supplying
Irrelevant objects.

Street lamps shine on the parked cars
Steadily in the clear night

It is true the great mineral silence
Vibrates, hums, a process
Completing itself

In which the windshield wipers
Of the cars are visible.

The power of the mind, the
Power and weight

Of the mind which
Is not enough, it is nothing
And does nothing

Against the natural world,
Behemoth, white whale, beast
They will say and less than beast,
The fatal rock

Which is the world—

O if the streets
Seem bright enough,
Fold within fold
Of residence . . .

Or see thru water
Clearly the pebbles
Of the beach
Thru the water, flowing
From the ripple, clear
As ever they have been

    The opening lines of the poem appear to allude to the "suicide poets" of the fifties and sixties, or to the weather of despair that these suicides expressed. More generally, the poem addresses a failure of the project of building a human world, a failure of the project of "rescue" in place and time, across the generations. "We want to defend limitation," Oppen says, voicing a substantive critical response to Emersonian and Whitmanian thought and, alas, American thought in general. A sense of limits—the limits that would shape a common sense and a common space of social life—has eroded in a society organized around the endless accumulation of wealth: an end that, as Jay Bernstein says, is not only without a further end but tends to make all other ends opaque. In "Blood from a Stone" Oppen speaks of "the bequeathed pavements, the inherited lit streets" (CP, 53); in "Eros" he speaks of the "great paved cities" as the material ground of the life of historical generations (CP, 120–21); in "Chartres" he evokes stones that "Stand where the masons locked them // Above the farmland / Above the will // Because a hundred generations / Back of them and to another people // The world cried out above the mountain" (77); in "The Book of Job and a Draft of a Poem to Praise the Paths of the Living," he calls the living, or perhaps the "children" who "rose in the dark / to their work," to "Pave / the world o pave / the world carve // thereon" (CP, 246); here, in "Of Being Numerous," the "denial / Of death that paved the cities, / Paved the cities // Generation / For generation" is the ground "we stand on." "Stand" is one of Oppen's talismanic words. In the last poem of *This In Which*, he writes, "The self is no mystery, the mystery is / That there is something for us to stand on" (CP, 159), evoking the bare earth on which our lives take place. Throughout his work, as I noted above, streets and pavements are usually emblems of the construction of a habitable world, the city of history built upon the ground of earth. This, of course, is potentially a good, a concrete dimension of the work of Eros in sustaining a shared life, a building of continuity in the face of death that Oppen affirms when he says, in "Image of the Engine," "I know that no one would live out / Thirty years, fifty years if the world were ending / With his life" (CP, 40–41). This is "the metaphysical sense of the future" that some of us are said to have lost. Something has gone wrong. The children in "Image of the Engine," "seeking love at last among each other," find only "squalid toys in the trash // Which is a grimy death of love," find themselves in a city where "every crevice [is] leaking rubble" (CP, 42). The roads are all "crumbling" in "Route." The pavement in the poem above "is filthy as corridors / Of the police." The young may not find themselves, may not "find their generation," and so may come to "Wither in the infirmaries / And the supply depots, supplying / Irrelevant objects," the squalid toys of a disoriented and loveless world, a world of imperialist war, state surveillance, and empty consumerism. This is a picture of our social life in the sixties clearly tilted toward despair.[18]

    At this point in the poem, after a moment of stillness, Oppen undertakes a twofold turn that marks a more general turn in his poetry of the sixties and seventies. One part of this turn occurs not in this poem, in fact, but in section 29 or in what I've characterized as the whole fourth movement of the sequence (29–37). There is a certain retreat from the social world and a heightened concentration on the intimate life of a family. This should not be overstated. Oppen's poetry continues to be formed by a troubled social conscience, it continues to wrestle with the events of a larger social world, but there does take place a shift in emphasis. The other part of this turn, marvelously evoked in the last several stanzas of section 26, is a deepening attention to what Oppen calls the vertical dimension of our lives. He sounds here the encounter of a solitary consciousness with the paradoxical opacity and clarity of what is, with the fatal otherness and the miraculous light of the outer world that appears to us. Recalling the Stevensian concern with "what will suffice," he emphasizes that the power of the mind "is not enough," does nothing against the natural world (which distinguishes the power of thought from the power of work that, earlier in the poem, is said to "deny death" through a practical transformation of the natural world that sustains generations). This is the world evoked as a perpetual opening in a river of endless erosion in the last poem of "A Narrative." Here it is evoked in figures drawn from Job (the Behemoth), Melville (the white whale), and Stevens (the fatal rock). These are figures of the chaos or death that the life of care holds at bay for a time, for our interval, the interval in which we draw on those resources the mind does have. The mind finds brightness in the streets, clarity in the night itself, clarity in the water and the pebbles of a beach. The fatal rock has been broken down, as it were, into minute particulars that allow us to see both the fatality and the miracle of the whole. "O if the streets / Seem bright enough, / Fold within fold / Of residence": the mind finds a residence, a meditative space, in a world that, the rest of the poem suggests, is increasingly a place of dispersal or alienation. The mind, folded back on itself in reflection, unfolds in the world at large. The repetitions here, as in the last stanza, as throughout the poem, as throughout the sequence, are marks of a circling process of thinking at work in this poem and in Oppen's poetry in general. In the last stanza the mind sees *clearly* (the adverb tells of the act of seeing) the pebbles that show themselves as *clear* (the adjective tells of the appearing of the pebbles) through the water. Clarity is at once a gift of the mind and a gift of being. "Clarity, clarity," Oppen writes in "Route," "surely clarity is the most beautiful thing in the world, / A limited, limiting clarity // I have not and never did have any motive of poetry / But to achieve clarity" (CP, 193). Where is this clarity? It would seem to be a quality of the mind and of language. In the next section of

"Route," however, it is said to be, also, a light of the world that comes to us. "There is a force of clarity, it is / Of what is not autonomous in us" (CP, 193). "Thought leaped on us in that sea." The place of the mind is at once an inward place and an outward place to which the mind opens in fear and wonder. This is Oppen's version of what Stevens calls "the poem of the mind in the act of finding / What will suffice." It is what romantics call the imagination. It is what Oppen often calls the life of the mind. At one point in his interview with Dembo, he cites his own statement, "the virtue of the emotion is that emotion which causes to see," and adds, "that's what I really mean by mind. If the virtue of the mind is missing, if somebody is 'wicked' in my sense, I have nothing to say to him and it is this fact that causes me to mourn, now and then, for large sections of humanity. I don't know whether I can tell a whole city or a whole college or a whole class full of people that their minds should possess that virtue. If they do not possess it, I really feel despair when I face them, and I do not know what to tell them" (IN, 186).[19]

Oppen, in this way, evokes what he takes to be one important "end" of the life of the mind, one dimension of a flourishing human life. This is for him inseparable from love and companionship, and in fact many of his most powerful disclosures of the miracle of place or the clearing of vision occur in poems that are at the same time love poems, as are "Of This All Things," the last poem of "A Narrative," "Anniversary Poem," "Disasters," and, in an important sense, both "Of Being Numerous" and "Route." Oppen, among other rare things he does, writes a quiet celebration of the life of a good marriage. At the same time, as the statement just cited makes clear, Oppen recognizes that his vision of the horizons of the good life cannot be grounded in universal concepts or unanswerably argued for in the framework of a liberal society. It is a vision of the good that emerges out of his own experience. It is a vision that he shows us and invites us to turn toward. He finds *a sort of connection* between the openness of vision and the openness of care. He belongs in this respect to a long romantic tradition. Wordsworth, anticipating the ecologists and ecocritics of our time, hoped to affirm a passage from "love of nature" to "love of humankind." That is probably not a promising way to think of it: the passage, as Oppen's work suggests, is more likely to go the other way. Blake affirmed an intimate connection beween the city of art, the expression of our freedom, and the city of love, our reconciliation with one another. Whitman prophesied a whole that would embrace both the dilated self of expansive perception and the sympathetic self of democratic community. Williams unfolds a similar speculative vision in the late, elegiac, luminous, occasionally desperate prayer and apology that "Asphodel" is, a poem that Oppen praises in his interview with Dembo. For "love and the imagination are of a piece, swift as the light to avoid destruction," Williams says at seventy-two, with Blakean defiance. Eros is at the root: vision and companionship are the leaf, the blossom, and the bole. "This is our jubilation / Exalted and as old as that truthfulness / Which illumines speech."[20]

*

A riddle of Oppen's poetry, notably of a sequence like "Of Being Numerous," is that it explores such a broad range of concerns in such a spare, fragmentary, at times nearly bare language. It is a poetry with a distinctive sort of meditative movement. "While rejecting a prior articulation of belief," DuPlessis says, "Oppen will not reject belief, or stop thinking about belief. So throughout his poetry, he meditates on value—what we can believe in, what facts or actions provide a meaningful ground. His themes and his structures both grow from such concerns. His poetry turns on and returns to such questions. And the meditative process by which he considers them creates his primal poetic structure."[21]

"What do we believe / To live with?" "I never did have any motive of poetry but to achieve clarity." "Looking up she sees the blue bright sky / Above the branches. / If one had been born here / How could one believe it?" This is a distinctive way of talking, of writing. Oppen occasionally alters the familiar order of words in speech ("blue bright sky") or bends an idiom ever so slightly ("if one *had* been born here / How could one believe it?"). In less deft hands, this could become a mannerism, but in Oppen it stays true to a course of puzzled and demandingly exact clarification. "Words, the words older // than I // clumsiest // of poets," Oppen says in the last poem of *Myth of the Blaze* (CP, 262), and one nods with recognition, for he is a poet who seems to move among words as among strange things, knotted pieces of wood that he picks up, turns around, puts down again in patterns that turn out to be revelatory. At one point he likens simple words to "handholds" and "footholds," the planks of a "substantial" language of clarity and of respect that hold firm in the sliding substance of time:

>   Who
> so poor the words
>
> *would   with   and*   take on substantial
>
> meaning   handholds   footholds
>
> to dig in one's heels   sliding
>
> hands and heels beyond the residential
> lots   the plots   it is a poem
>
> which may be sung
> may well be sung   (CP, 220)

The line in his poems seems to be considered and weighed in an analogous way. It becomes an element of syntax, rhythm, the taking place of thought, the unfolding of disclosure (SL, 141). Characteristically his lines reach backward and forward at the same time, as if measuring time and measuring thought. They mark, as Louise Glück observes, not the "scampering" quality of Williams's poems but a pausing-and-rebeginning quality, a rhythm of weighing and re-weighing:

> They have lost the metaphysical sense
> Of the future, they feel themselves
> The end of a chain
>
> Of lives, single lives
> And we know that lives
> Are single
>
> And cannot defend
> The metaphysic
> On which rest

> The boundaries
> Of our distances.
> We want to say
>
> 'Common sense'
> And cannot.   (CP, 178)

The line itself becomes, for a moment, an emblem of the marking of boundaries that connect.[22]

This patiently circling movement is also embodied in the practice of repetition pervasive in Oppen's work and carried to a subtle extreme in "Of Being Numerous." There is hardly a section in this sequence that does not include at least one repetition of a word. Many, like the poem of section 26 cited in its entirety above, include multiple repetitions (in this poem these would include, from the third short stanza on, at least the following: poets, poets; single lives, lives that are single; metaphysical sense of the future, metaphysic on which rest the boundaries of our distances; we want to defend, we want to say; paved the cities, paved the cities; generation for generation, how shall one know a generation, a new generation, who if they cannot find their generation; the supply depots, supplying irrelevant objects; the power of the mind, the power and weight of the mind; is nothing and does nothing; beast they will say and less than beast; fold within fold; see thru water clearly, thru the water clear as ever they have been). What is the meaning of this quiet folding and unfolding of echoing words and phrases? We tend to think of repetition in poetry—beginning with the recurrences of meter, alliteration, and rhyme—as a technique essential to the elevation, or intensity, or consolation, or concentration that poems so often express. Surely it is also an underlying dimension of the coherence of a poem, of an intuitive or felt unity within multeity, to recall Coleridge's expression. All of these things are variously at work in Oppen's repetitions—especially in his later poems, perhaps, where the syntactic breaks are moved internal to gliding run-on phrases, where the lines on occasion grow slightly longer, where punctuation largely vanishes, where the poems tend to become more aerated, expansive, incantatory, lyrical. Oppen's repetitions, further, mark and enable what DuPlessis has called the "turning and returning" movement of his thought. Repetition, indeed, seems to have an important place in a certain type of meditative poetry, in a poetry of "directly and indirectly getting at," as Stevens puts it. Stevens and Oppen form an interesting parallel and contrast in this regard. Both are meditative poets. Stevens is the preternaturally fluent poet, never at a loss for words, inventing one wheeling improvisation after another; Oppen is the clumsiest of poets, halting in his articulation, slowly stepping through words as through riddling shards of the world. Stevens risks the facile, the poem that is merely sonorous; Oppen risks the cramped, the poem that cannot find release. Yet both overcome their risks. Both are brooders and indeed a little obsessive. Both are searching for what will suffice, for what they can believe to live with, in response to the bare ground, the fatal rock, the blank that underlies the trials of device ("bare," in fact, is a talismanic word in both). At risk of simplifying, I would put one important difference this way: Stevens's improvisational repetitions and circlings are dimensions of a dialectic of thought, a working out of a larger picture of the polarities of our lives, where the real is itself always already mediated, always already drawn into what can be thought and said about it, and where the social and even other people, as everyone has noticed, are entirely absent (Stevens is the loneliest poet who ever wrote); Oppen's patient repetitions and circlings are dimensions of a dialectic of thought and actuality, where the testing of words against the concrete has a more emphatic and a more tactile place, and where the texture of the social world and of life with others is fully explored. It is almost as though the repetitions in "Of Being Numerous" were marking two moments of the mind at once, the attention to what is there *outside* thought and the working through of what is gathered there *in* thought ("Or see thru water / Clearly the pebbles / Of the beach / Thru the water, flowing / From the ripple, clear / As ever they have been"). This will all sound like a familiar distinction: Stevens is a romantic idealist, Oppen an objectivist with an empiricist bent, and there is the difference. But that is not what I mean to say. Stevens is a romantic idealist, to be sure, yet Oppen is also a meditative and in fact a ranging philosophical poet, concerned to write a complex "poetry of statement," and the languages of empiricist philosophy and objectivist poetics are not adequate to an understanding of what he is doing in his poetry from the late fifties on. Neither is the language of postmodern seriality. One has to find another approach to the sort of thinking he carries out in his work.[23]

The thinking unfolds in a curious way. There is the halting, searching path of articulation. There are the circling repetitions. There is the spare passage through hints, pieces, fragments of perception and thought that are sounded, set down, left for a time, returned to after a time, made to echo in long-distance rhymes of word, image, figure, thought. "Of Being Numerous" exemplifies all these features of Oppen's poetry. The sections of the sequence maintain a sort of resistant independence, as though each were a peculiar fragment, a firmly bound and yet porous place of vivid image and speculative statement, the relationships among the well-spaced sections only gradually emerging as the sequence unfolds. There is something in this of what Fredric Jameson, in a discussion of Williams's *Paterson*, has described as the characteristic modernist effort to deploy and at the same time block a larger narrative, conceptual, or metaphorical unity in a work: the unifying concepts or metaphors are meant to remain at once hinted at and hidden, dispersed across a texture of bewildering particulars that resist them. This sort of "nominalist" distrust of the concept, as Jameson puts it, is part of twentieth-century culture at large and is palpable in Oppen's sequences. Yet this sort of description still does not quite reach the sort of thinking unfolded in sequences like "Of Being Numerous" and "Route." They are not quite as nominalist as they initially appear. Their predominant movement is one of attention, statement, qualification, reorientation of attention, over and over, back and forth, in a spiralling movement that turns out to be a gradual widening of thought, a gradual deepening of disclosure.[24]

Oppen's letters and daybooks, in particular the latter, have a similar movement. One is not surprised to learn that Oppen, like Char, was interested in the pre-Socratics, or that, like Char, he was interested in a type of meditative practice. In one of his daybooks he writes: "I 'meditate' at least five hours every day   How else is poetry written." "There are certain things, appearances," he says in a letter, "around which the understanding gathers. They hold the meanings which make it possible to live, they are one's sense of reality and the possibility of meaning. They are there, in the mind, always. One can sit down anytime and sink into them – can work at them, they come into the mind, they fill the mind – anytime. One tries to pierce them" (SL, 123). It is of course true that the meditative movement in his work is unlike the movement of thinking typically demanded in philosophical or theoretical writing: in these domains the discursive—the organized presentation and elaboration of argument—carries the day. Yet at the same time the meditative movement in his poems is consonant with the patience, depth, and range of philosophical thought. Engaged readers of Oppen, I think, have a similar experience in this respect: puzzled at first, uncertain of the way, reaching for half-glimpsed bridges, they come to find that a wider, coherent, ranging space of thought does emerge as they return again and again to the journey of the poem, or the sequence, or the book, or the *oeuvre* as a whole. The poetry demands of readers the circling meditative patience that it practices. It demands of readers the immersion in a thinking across gaps, pauses, doubts, statements, and conjectures that it articulates. One could relevantly recall here the words of Frye's about modern recastings of wisdom literature that I cited in my discussion of Char. Oppen's sequences, too, in their way, are "archipelagoes" of fragments resonant with implication. The reader enters into the spaces between images and thoughts, the silences between statements, as much as into the images and thoughts and statements themselves. It is "difficult to know what one means / —to be serious and to know what one means" (CP, 208). The poem is a path of finding out. It requires attention, patience, humility, independence, wonder, curiosity. It requires dwelling in the poem's field of thought. It requires an ear for the unsaid, an openness to the silence on the edge of thought, within articulation itself, as Plato himself teaches when at the end of the *Phaedrus* he has Socrates underline that the written word, including the written word of a Platonic dialogue (and surely including the spoken word as well, since the spoken word is said to be a generative seed, not an end point), always points beyond itself to a further journey of thought. All that we engage in thought exceeds all that we think. "Clarity / In the sense of *transparence*, / I don't mean that much can be explained. // Clarity in the sense of silence" (CP, 175). Or, again, in a later poem that recalls, as so many of Oppen's later poems do, words and phrases of his earlier poems:

> bright light of shipwreck beautiful as the sea
> and the islands I don't know how to say it
> needing a word with no sound

> but the pebbles shifting on the beach the sense
> of the thing, everything, rises in the mind the
> venture   adventure
>
> say as much as I dare, as much as I can
> sustain I don't know how to say it
>
> I say all that I can   What one would tell
> would be the scene   (CP, 261)[25]

This passage displays the more expansive lyricism found in Oppen's last three books. There is a sort of luminous clearing in these poems: "the language 'rises' a little, etherealizes a little," as Oppen says in a letter (SL, 249). There are strong hints of this change, I think, in "Route," a sequence that further explores the concerns raised in "Of Being Numerous." The sections tend to be a little longer than those of "Of Being Numerous"; the line tends to grow longer, as well, often extending to the right margin; the spaces and spacings of the poem become roomier. It is almost as though Stevens and Oppen were approaching each other across a great distance. Stevens, in his youth the lyrical idealist and bright acrobat of sound, comes in old age to write lyrics of an uncommonly subdued clairvoyance, as if the bareness itself were becoming a disclosure of transparence. Oppen, in his youth a maker of fragments of angular perception and in his fifties a composer of spare meditative poems, comes in his last decade to write lyrics that often sound like articulations of air, of space. And yet there is a paradox in these later poems that already emerges in "Route." The expansiveness of Oppen's later work involves at the same time a deepened sounding of the tragic: of failure, guilt, fear, haunting memory, and the approach of death at the personal level, of extreme disillusion at the political level. Perhaps this is slightly to overstate the matter. Yet the ending of "Route" is apocalyptic.[26]

*

"Route" takes up again the concerns of "Of Being Numerous." It is shorter than the sequence it further unfolds, consisting of fourteen rather than forty sections, though the sections tend to be longer. It begins to tilt toward the looser form of Oppen's later work, but it includes a story told in prose, as well as lines that hover on the boundaries of verse and prose. The sequence is akin to "Of Being Numerous," too, in its meditative movement, a patient widening and deepening of perspective. The basic shape of the sequence is threefold: the first four sections address the themes at the center of "Of Being Numerous," the love that holds people together and the disclosive clarity of being and thought that allows us to encounter a world; the next three sections, moving backward in time, recall Oppen's experience in the Second World War, tell an extraordinary story of the threats to life and sanity that people under these circumstances had to wrestle with, and scrutinize ethical questions in existentialist terms; the last eight sections begin with a car wreck, turn to a disintegrating built world, reflect on the relationship between history and poetry, and ultimately descend five centuries back in time, evoking the first encounters between Europeans and Native Americans. This long movement of the poem is above all a weighing of the erosion of things in time and a measuring of the conflict between despair and hope, apocalyptic fear and presence of mind. I have addressed some of the concerns of the first two movements in my discussion of "Of Being Numerous." Here I wish to address, in particular, this last movement (sections 8–14), which approaches the relationship between the historical and the metaphysical dimensions of our lives in a different way, or with a different emphasis, than "Of Being Numerous" does.[27]

The sequence, like "Of Being Numerous," is set in the present of its writing, the America of the sixties, an America waging war in Vietnam. In the last part of the poem the moments from the past include the youth of Oppen and his wife (13), the years Oppen served as a soldier in the Second World War (11), the invasion and settling of North America (9), the journey of Cabeza de Vaca in the Americas (14), and the conquest of the Aztecs by the Spanish (14). The poem insistently evokes wrecks, crumbling roads, broken public works, curbs and culverts, ditches and weeds. Despair is a shadow that looms, held off through the power of companionship— "Love in the genes, if it fails / We will produce no sane man again" (1)— and through a saving attention to the miracle of presence, of disclosure, of "what was there to be thought" as "it comes by the road" (10).

The short section 8 affirms that poetry is not the evasion of wreck but a speaking from the place of wreck, not an evasion of despair but a passage through despair:

Cars on the highway filled with speech,
People talk, they talk to each other;

Imagine a man in the ditch,
The wheels of the overturned wreck
Still spinning—

I don't mean he despairs, I mean if he does not
He sees in the manner of poetry   (8)

The image of car wreck in this sequence is analogous to the image of shipwreck in "Of Being Numerous." In both cases a figure of failure or ruin is seen at the same time as a figure of our encounter with the strangeness of presence, the limits of experience (or what in the last poem are called the "limits of reason"), and dimensions of our lives that we are readily blind to, enclosed as we are in our routines, evasions, glass towers, speeding cars. Though car wreck and shipwreck are analogous figures in these sequences, cars and ships are not taken to be alike, for if Oppen loved boats, he seems to have had a certain antipathy to cars. At one point in his interview with Dembo, he says, "I have a very early poem [in *Discrete Series*] about a car closed in glass. I felt that somehow it was unreal and I said so—the light inside that car." He then reads the poem (CP, 13), and adds, "There is a feeling of something false in overprotection and over-luxury—my idea of categories of realism" (IN, 180–81). This unreality is evoked on a larger scale early in "Of Being Numerous": "A city of the corporations // Glassed / In dreams // And images" (2). To be "glassed in" is for Oppen what to be "closed up" is for Blake: to be trapped in unreality. It is necessary to "cleanse the doors of perception," to shake the mind into clarity, into the gift of presence and vision.[28]

The next five sections—passing through elegiac reflection, poised attention, anguished memory, bewildered solitude, profound gratitude—concentrate on roads, roadsides, ditches, margins, the rubble of things. It is a strange landscape that emerges at this point, in part a continent of highways seen as a built world going to pieces, in part a continent of ditches seen as a realm of revelation. "The cars run in a void of utensils / —the powerful tires— beyond / Happiness," we read in the first lines of the ninth section. Happiness is beyond the tires, beyond the void of utensils. This beyond, however, is first of all a place of exposure:

> Tough rubbery gear of invaders, of the descendents
> Of invaders, I begin to be aware of a countryside
> And the exposed weeds of a ditch
>
> The context is history
> Moving toward the light of the conscious
>
> And beyond, culvert, blind curb, there are also names
> For these things, language in the appalling fields   (9)

To see tires or cars as the "rubbery gear of invaders" is at once an odd and a literal point of view, and imperialist invasion is a question the poem returns to. The "appalling fields" here rhyme with the "appalling seas" of a later poem, "The Poem," where it is said that "in the appalling / seas language // lives and wakes us together / out of sleep" (CP, 270). The appalling is the fatal rock of the world, where we are shipwrecked and where we may see the miracle of things. Beyond the crumbling road is a space beyond our usual roads, a location where we are exposed, in danger, but a location where perhaps we open our eyes as well (cf. CP, 226). The next section begins with the turning of this perspective into a sort of indicative imperative: "Not the symbol but the scene this pavement leads / To roadsides—the finite // Losing its purposes / Is estranged" (10). The scene is that which is seen to the side of the road. "If having come so far we shall have / Song // Let it be small enough. // Virgin / what was there to be thought // comes by the road." The last lines here are a transposition of the mystical language of St. John of the Cross. Yet the next section returns to this language in a mood not of discovery but of anguish: "Tell the life of the mind, the mind creates the finite. // All punishes him, I stumble over these stories—Progeny, the possibility of progeny, continuity / Or love that tempted him // He is punished by place, by scene, by all that holds / all he has found, this pavement, the silent symbols" (11). The scene and the symbol, it turns out, have a more complex relationship than was suggested at the opening of the previous section. Indeed, as begins to become clear, these scenes, these cars and roads and ditches, are emblems of a larger social erosion. The pressure of time is quietly and powerfully evoked in the next section, "haunting the people in the automobiles," leaving the author of this sequence, once again, acutely aware of his solitude, of the uncertain address and destination of his words:

Time remains what it was

Oddly, oddly insistent

haunting the people in the automobiles,

shining on the sheetmetal,

open and present, unmarred by indifference,

wheeled traffic, indifference,
the hard edge of concrete continually crumbling

into the gravel in the gravel of the shoulders,
Ditches of our own country

Whom shall I speak to   (12)

Again, as in "Of Being Numerous," there is a folding and unfolding of echoing words: cars, finite, symbol, scene, pavement, crumbling, oddly, indifference, ditches, gravel. The crumbling evoked here is at once ontological, the endless "erosion" of things in time that Oppen stares into in the last poem of "A Narrative" (CP, 155), or the "silting sand of events" that frightens him in another poem (CP, 138), and social, the wearing away of the built world and its promises.[29]

The penultimate poem of the sequence brings together three major concerns. One is the young George and Mary's spirited and fateful decision to abandon convention, to take to the open road. The second is a reflection on the collapse of public works, the erosion of a common social project, which turns into a reflection on catastrophe in the last poem of the sequence. The third is a romantic or quasi-Heideggerian meditation on the disclosive openness of being that is irreducible to our technological projects. As in Heidegger's *Being and Time* it is the broken hammer that turns attention to Being, so here it is the broken works of the "Department of Plants and Structures" that bear us into the incalculable. Are the disclosures found in the margins forced upon one by the course of history, then, or are they freely chosen by those with spirit, or both? How is the relationship between the vertical and the horizontal measured here? This is a question that this poem dwells within:

> Department of Plants and Structures—obsolete, the old name
> In this city, of the public works
>
> Tho we meant to entangle ourselves in the roots of the world
>
> An unexpected and forgotten spoor, all but indestructible shards
>
> To owe nothing to fortune, to chance, nor by the power of his heart
> Or her heart to have made these things sing
> But the benevolence of the real
>
> Tho there is no longer shelter in the earth, round helpless belly
> Or hope among the pipes and broken works
>
> 'Substance itself which is the subject of all our planning'
>
> And by this we are carried into the incalculable   (13)

One might have guessed that the life of adventure that the lovers chose in their youth would have involved a faith in "chance," or "fortune," a sort of Whitmanian version of what the surrealists called *le hasard objectif*. Yet at this moment of thought, at least, it is not so. For it is the "benevolence of the real" that is said to have gathered the two of them into the incalculable of freedom and encounter. "And by this we are carried into the incalculable": by the benevolence of the real, by the sheer exposure of a shelterless and hopeless condition, by substance itself, perhaps by all of these things. The movement here is akin to that evoked at the end of the last poem of "A Narrative." "Thought leaped on us in that sea / For in that sea we breathe the open / Miracle // Of place." The life of the mind, again, is the disclosive clarity that turns to the outward clarity of what Heidegger calls the gift of being, or what Marcel calls the mystery of being. The duality of the appalling fields and the benevolence of the real in this sequence corresponds to the duality of the fatal rock of the natural world and the clear pebbles of the beach in section 26 of "Of Being Numerous." If one could, as I've said, characterize this way of seeing as Heideggerian or Marcelian, one could also characterize it as Emersonian, Whitmanian, Stevensian. Our lives take place within this ultimately unfathomable whole, appalling and benevolent at once, perpetually erosive and perpetually disclosive at once.

To some extent, it would seem, Oppen voices in "Route" the sort of stepping back from a failed social world that he voices in "Of Being Numerous." "The country's crumbling, the world's crumbling," he says in a letter written five years later, "and somehow it's clearing the air: Can't remember such clear air in my life time" (SL, 271). The place in the margins of things, while it is a place of car wreck or exposure to mortality, is also a place of "what was there to be thought," a place where the "benevolence of the real" is perceived. Whitman's faith in the open road, as it were, has become a faith in the unprotected ditches to the side of the open road. This is a Thoreauvian bearing expressed throughout Oppen's work. In "Guest Room" he characterizes the "noise of wealth" as "the voice of Hell," affirms his belief that "the virtue of the mind is that emotion which causes to see," and concludes by likening himself and his companion to "leaves of the most recent weed" perched on a coast above the city and the sea, at a distance that permits them to see:

Of the dawn
Over Frisco
Lighting the large hills
And the very small coves
At their feet, and we

Perched in the dawn wind
Of that coast like leaves
Of the most recent weed—And yet the things

That happen! Signs,
Promises—we took it
As sign, as promise

Still, for nothing wavered,
Nothing begged or was unreal, the thing
Happening, filling our eyesight
Out to the horizon—I remember the sky
And the moving sea.   (CP, 110)

These weeds anticipate the "exposed weeds of a ditch" of "Route": the former are on a cliff, the latter beside a road, yet both are in places "beyond" the cities and the roads, places in this sense like the beach of section 26 in "Of Being Numerous," places where the "unreal" routines and enclosures of our lives are abandoned and the "things that happen" are seen in joy, seen as promise. In "World, World" (CP, 159), it is true, the ditch is said to be a place of failure where "too much" is seen, just as "too little" is seen from prominence (perhaps the prominence not of cliffs but of glass towers). Yet "The Impossible Poem," defining "sanity" as "the roadside weed," makes clear the line of thought connecting poems like "Guest Room" and "Route":

Streetcars
Rocked thru the city and the winds
Combed their clumsy sides

In clumsy times

Sierra withering
Behind the storefronts

And sanity the roadside weed
Dreams of sports and sportsmanship

> In the lucid towns paralyzed
> Under the truck tires
> Shall we relinquish
>
> Sanity to redeem
> Fragments and fragmentary
> Histories in the towns and the temperate streets
> Too shallow still to drown in or to mourn
> The courageous and precarious children   (CP, 231–32)

Here the towns are "paralyzed under the truck tires" and "sanity" is a "roadside weed." The question with which the poem ends (a question whose urgency for Oppen and his wife led to a twenty-eight-year silence in his poetry) is whether they should remain in this marginal place or return to a struggle in the towns and cities. It echoes the more direct and directly pained statement in the fourth section of "Route": "as for a long time we have abandoned those in extremity and find it unbearable that we should do so" (4). Existential sanity and the clarity of the life of the mind, Oppen here suggests, are found above all in the peripheries of the paralyzed built world. It is not that one finds any sort of simple paradise in these peripheries. The tragic is there, too, car wreck, ruin, punishing memories, the erosion of things. But there the tragic is inseparable from the dawn wind of vision, the deer in the woods, the miracle of place, the pebbles seen through the water clearly, the beautiful tendons on the beach, the benevolence of the real, the thing that comes by the road to be thought. It is there that patience, care, and the life of the mind are possible. It is there that an openness to the disclosure of the whole happens. It is there, as the last lines of "Giovanni's *Rape of the Sabine Women* at Wildenstein's" suggest, that one can sustain or at least invoke a desperate faith in "the whole thing" (CP, 112–13). The fragmented towns and the glassy cities threaten all this. It is not that the miracle is invisible in the towns and cities: it can be glimpsed in a brick, a yard, a bridge, the Hudson River, the inherited lit street, the spot of light on a curb, the bright streets and folds of residence, the young sycamore that Williams saw rising between the wet pavement and the gutter (cf. CP, 149), and many other things. Oppen lived almost his entire life in large vital cities,

New York and San Francisco, and this whole meditation on vision in the margins is above all figurative, involving a reorientation of the spirit, not a counsel of flight. The side of the road, after all, is not the wilderness: it is a space of altered attention. Yet Oppen, one of the last romantics of the fifties and sixties, does come to believe that our failed social life brings with it large risks of a loss of self, dispersal, conformist inattention, rootless speech, impatience, carelessness. Oppen is in some sense the "meditative man" who "fails" in section 10 of "Of Being Numerous": he may no longer have a place in the world emerging around him. What he calls the vertical concern, a concern with perceptual awakening and metaphysical meditation, now exerts a stronger pull on him than the horizontal concern in its social sense (as distinct from its familial sense). But if this is a quietist stance, painfully come to by Oppen if by anybody, it is not held without severe tension.

Indeed this tension is far more complex in "Route" than I've so far suggested. We can approach this complexity first of all by asking again just what Oppen is showing us in this sequence. "The hard edge of concrete," he says, is "continually crumbling." There is no longer "hope among the pipes and broken works." The "Department of Plants and Structures" is "obsolete." It is "the old name / In this city, of the public works." What is falling apart? It is certainly not the case, of course, that in the America of the fifties and sixties the highways and roads, or the built world as a whole, were crumbling. General Motors had in the forties energetically worked to destroy public transportation in order to accelerate the age of the automobile. The government supported a massive expansion of the interstate highway system. Strong unions and Keynesian spending led to three postwar decades of historically unprecedented economic growth that transformed the entire built world of America. This built world was anything but broken in the years in which Oppen was writing *Of Being Numerous*. The images of crumbling in this sequence, then, are figures of a social and a political crumbling that Oppen sees taking place at the time. He speaks of the old name of the *public works*. It is the *public thing* that he has in mind. My sense is that he is evoking a falling apart of society, thinking through the failure of his own political hopes, the political hopes of the Old Left, to be sure, but also the political hopes of the New Left. At the end of a long letter to his sister in August 1967, he writes:

One sees that the Old Left was at no time totally without point, tho it deservedly or even fortunately collapsed. The continuation of the war is the collapse of the New Left. The truth that it is -- not paradoxically inhuman like the Old Left -- but, as we knew, ineffective, absolutely useless, therefore cynical, a game, a fashion, a form of self-display or of keeping oneself occupied or of asserting everyone else's failure and one's own innocence --

The left is at all times -- even when it is ineffective -- an attempt to take seriously the declared purposes of a society. It is always a matter of radical methods, radical means, rather than radical thinking, radical philosophy: its collapse is therefore no joke for anyone

one can of course declare his own purposes, his own, that is to say, morality.

or can one?

of course one cannot. Or only within the situation of the 'vertical consciousness' of oneself and god. Which of course would permit everyone else to be wrong and lost;   there is still what 'is right.' A simple matter requiring only an epiphany. in the absence of which one may prefer chocolate to vanilla, or, obviously: Money, praise, temperate climate, three hundred horsepower, twenty five rooms, hundred foot boats, electric everything – a matter of taste, of each one's goo. But why poetry? or anything of the sort, unless as a choice between flavors?

The poetry, the four books, Discrete Series, Materials, This In Which, Numerous -- proposed the awareness of the world as purpose. Nothing else essentially. Not, perhaps enough -- ? But the search for power is the attempt to *hide* the world from oneself; it is fatal;   Johnson, the Johnsons, fatal. They may in all literalness prove so   (SL, 164–65)

There is much in this letter that would require pages to sort through. I will briefly address only a few issues. One is that Oppen, here as throughout his work, is preoccupied with the "purpose" of life, of a singular life and a collective life, with what we loosely call the "meaning" or the "significance" of life, with what hermeneutic thinkers call a horizon of concern. Oppen again draws a distinction between a horizontal or social sense of purpose and a vertical or individual sense of purpose. The latter is here called "moral" and clearly linked to a religious or a metaphysical horizon. It is what in this chapter I have called an existential point of view. A question probably as old as society itself and certainly as old as Axial Age religion could be put in these plain terms: is it possible to live a good and meaningful life in a bad and meaningless society? "Wrong life cannot be lived rightly," Adorno answers in *Minima Moralia*, a book written in the years just after the Second World War. Axial Age religion has always responded to this question by saying, yes, it is unquestionably our vocation to do so. Oppen, too, answers affirmatively, though he is as aware as Adorno of the pressure of social context. He also recognizes that in a liberal society his bearing is likely to be seen as a choice essentially no different from the choice of a flavor of ice cream. On this level, it would seem, one can only keep talking, pointing, showing in speech, showing by example in life. His work is a practice of what Albert Borgmann calls "deictic discourse," a discourse of showing and witnessing, as distinct from scientific (deductive-nomological) or paradigmatic (subsumptive) discourse. It is a disclosure of what matters in the mode of testimony.[30]

The left, however, has traditionally argued that a good life in a bad society could only be a life actively engaged in a struggle for social transformation: anything less would be an evasion. Oppen's "of course one cannot" shows that this thought bears down on his conscience. A third issue raised in the letter cited above, which takes us back to "Route," is in fact the fate of the left in the twentieth century. Oppen's skepticism about the New Left is in part an expression of the conflict between the ascetic Old Left and the exuberant New Left, a well-known drama of these years. Yet there is more at stake here. The Old Left collapsed, he says, "deservedly" or "fortunately," for where it didn't fail it became a terrible travesty of its dreams. His judgment of the failure of the New Left, he makes clear, is based above all on the continuation of the war in Vietnam. His concern with a "moral" life, grounded in an "awareness" of the whole, discovered in the exposed places beyond the conventions of power and wealth and prestige and protected blindness, is embedded in this "insane and criminal" event of history. The last poem of "Route" sets this in a long perspective:

There was no other guarantee

Ours aren't the only madmen tho they have burned thousands
of men and women alive, perhaps no madder than most

Strange to be here, strange for them also, insane and criminal,
who hasn't noticed that, strange to be man, we have come
rather far

We are at the beginning of a radical depopulation of the earth

Cataclysm . . . cataclysm of the plains, jungles, the cities

Something in the soil exposed between two oceans

As Cabeza de Vaca found a continent of spiritual despair
in campsites

His miracles among the Indians heralding cataclysm

Even Cortés greeted as revelation . . . No I'd not emigrate,
I'd not live in a ship's bar wherever we may be headed

These things at the limits of reason, nothing at the limits
of dream, the dream merely ends, by this we know it is the real

That we confront   (14)

    It is a powerful poem, Oppen's version, one might say, of the sort of poem that Yeats was writing in the twenties. The first line, "there was no other guarantee," extends the last line of the previous section, "and by this we are carried into the incalculable," for there is no other "guarantee" than this movement into the "incalculable," this journey into the groundless ground of what is there, what is happening, in the impenetrable and erosive whole and in the inventions and destructions of history. The six lines after this first line address the war in Vietnam. These lines are startling in their dryness, their dry statement of what is obvious to those who haven't taken the rationalization of criminal violence to the point of insanity. The lines dryly assert, too, that of this sort of madness we can say both that it is not new in history—it has a vast history behind it—and that it may have reached a distinctively catastrophic point in our epoch of high-tech war: "strange to be man, we have come rather far." In an earlier poem, "The Crowded Countries of the Bomb," Oppen wonders, "What is the name of that place / We have entered: / Despair? Ourselves? // That we can destroy ourselves / Now" (CP, 78). There is an apocalyptic turn at this point in "Route": "Cataclysm . . . cataclysm of the plains, jungles, the cities // Something in the soil exposed between two oceans." Is the "soil" exposed or is "something in the soil" exposed? Perhaps both. This ambiguous image recalls the "exposed weeds of a ditch" earlier in the sequence. The ditch, I have suggested, is the place where disclosure happens, for those who open themselves to the whole, who entangle themselves in the benevolence of the real; it is also, this line suggests, the violent space of history, the place where suffering happens, for those who find themselves exposed to powers they cannot hide from, vulnerable to the malevolence of the real (cf. CP, 240, 247). There is existential despair, like that felt and overcome by a car-wrecked man who sees in the manner of poetry, and there is historically conditioned despair, like that felt by those whom Cabeza de Vaca encountered in campsites and in a different way by the author of this poem. Perhaps these dimensions cannot be as clearly distinguished as they seem to be—or as I have suggested they are—in "Of Being Numerous." The poem then turns from the contemporary imperialist war in Vietnam to the adventures of Cabeza de Vaca in North America and the conquest of Mexico City by Cortés. One thinks of a book that Chomsky published in 1993, *Year 501: The Conquest Continues*, for there is a similarly extended perspective at work in this poem. The history of violence and poverty is overwhelming; if one escapes these things, then one may be "glassed" in wealth and power, lost in an unreal life, trying "to hide oneself from the world"; if one gets past these things too, then one is, as Oppen repeatedly says he and Mary have been, lucky. "The bequeathed pavements, the inherited lit streets: / Among them we were lucky: strangest word" (CP, 53). Luck of this sort is of course scarred. It is as entangled in the roots and routes of history as it is in the roots and routes of the miraculous whole. Oppen, in this sequence, is holding these perspectives together in their difference, standing in a ditch, as it were, wrestling with despair in different dimensions, affirming the openness—curiosity, wonder, care—that is nonetheless a possible horizon of our lives for as long as we are here. "No, I'd not emigrate, / I'd not live in a ship's bar wherever we may be headed." He thus concludes the poem with an affirmation that is severe and prophetic. "These things at the limits of reason, nothing at the limits / of dream, the dream merely ends, by this we know it is the real // That we confront," he says, with no end stop. Just about every word in this statement is lucidly ambiguous. The "limits of reason," as Oppen notes in a letter (SL, 177), is a Kantian expression, though Oppen has inflected it in his own way, and by "real" he means something quite different from what Kant means. What is beyond the limits of reason here, in an important sense, is not the noumenal but the insanity and criminality of those directing the destruction of Vietnam. The real that we confront at the limits of reason, in this context, is first of all the violence of this war and, more generally, the unending violence and suffering of history. Yet it is also "what comes by the road" to be thought, or the astonishing "benevolence of the real," or the "countryside and the exposed weeds of a ditch" of which the speaker becomes "aware" when he turns his attention "beyond" the void of utensils and cars. The dream here is also ambiguous. It is first of all the nightmare of history from which Stephen Dedalus is trying to awake: the long bad dream of power, violence, dishonesty, and rationalization. Yet, too, at another level, as the letter from which I cited above indicates, it is the utopian dream of the Old Left and the New Left: the long good dream of justice, peace, integrity, and awareness. This dream, as Oppen sees things, is crumbling, and the world shown by its collapse is the world we have to confront with all the presence of mind we can gather. This, I take it, is what "reason" means in these concluding lines: lucidity, honesty, and, in Oppen's further sense, the life of the mind open to the whole, like a resilient weed in a ditch, like an unflinching Job standing in the whirlwind, with wonder seeing the whole of the world, with lucidity seeing the depth of injustice.[31]

"Route" may be Oppen's greatest poem. It draws everything in his work together. There is the halting, circling patience of the earlier poems and the incantatory, expansive lyricism of the later poems. There is the dismayed wrestling with a social world in crisis and the deep, steady, meditative affirmation of the unfolding of eros in vision and companionship. There is, as he puts it in the letter to his sister, a holding true to the moral life, to the vertical dimension of one's integrity, to a clearing of mind and an opening of care, to the life one does have to choose for oneself and with those whom one loves in the midst of history, as well as a holding true to the historical circumstances and pressures that deny so many this chance and hence scar this chance even where it is found and lived. The depth and intensity of wonder and gratitude voiced in the penultimate poem, a metaphysical expression of sheer love of life, is thoroughly weighed by the depth and intensity of sober acknowledgment in the last poem, a testimony to long historical disaster. In his Nobel Lecture, Seamus Heaney cites Yeats's "The Stare's Nest By My Window," and then says of the poem words that, I think, are relevant to Oppen's "Route" as well:

> I have heard this poem repeated often, in whole and in part, by people in Ireland over the past twenty-five years, and no wonder, for it is as tender-minded towards life itself as St Kevin was and as tough-minded about what happens in and to life as Homer. It knows that the massacre will happen again on the roadside, that the workers in the minibus are going to be lined up and shot down just after quitting time; but it also credits as a reality the squeeze of the hand, the actuality of sympathy and protectiveness between living creatures. It satisfies the contradictory needs which consciousness experiences at times of extreme crisis, the need on the one hand for a truth-telling that will be hard and retributive, and on the other hand the need not to harden the mind to a point where it denies its own yearnings for sweetness and trust. It is a proof that poetry can be equal to *and* true at the same time, which the Russian woman sought from Anna Akhmatova and which William Wordsworth produced at a corresponding moment of historical crisis and personal dismay almost exactly two hundred years ago.[32]

A Note on Building and Seeing in Oppen

A few stanzas in section 26 of "Of Being Numerous" read:

> We want to say
>
> 'Common sense'
> And cannot. We stand on
>
> That denial
> Of death that paved the cities,
> Paved the cities
>
> Generation
> For generation and the pavement
>
> Is filthy as the corridors
> Of the police.
>
> How shall one know a generation, a new generation?   (CP, 178)

As I said above (in note 18), my sense is that readers tend to take the lines concerning "that denial of death that paved the cities" as expressing a critical judgment. This, for example, is the way both Peter Nicholls (*George Oppen*, 87) and Michael Heller (*Speaking the Estranged*, 48) read them. Henry Weinfield, on the other hand, reads these ambiguous lines as ultimately affirming a denial of death whereby we ground a habitable human world (*Music of Thought*, 18, 84). Weinfield's reading of these lines is the sort of reading that I would like to unfold further here.

It makes sense, of course, that one would hear a criticism of "the denial of death" in these lines. The denial of anything, we tend to say, is not a good thing; to deny mortality would be unwise. Philosophy is the practice of dying, as Socrates said long ago, and as Heidegger said in a different but not unrelated way in *Being and Time*, and there are many passages in Oppen, notably the marvelous last poem of "A Narrative," in which a meditation on ruin or death is inseparable from an openness to the whole and a discovery of freedom. We take our fundamental bearings by sounding these questions. Denial can hardly be helpful in this respect.

Nevertheless. I take the lines addressing "that denial of death that paved the cities" to bear a positive implication. That the pavement is now "filthy as the corridors of the police" is, as I said above, a sign that something potentially good has gone bad, been damaged.

My reading of these lines as bearing a positive implication is based partly in the way they echo the other poems I've cited in my discussion of this section of the poem: "Blood from a Stone," "Eros," "Chartres," "The Book of Job and a Draft of a Poem to Praise the Paths of the Living" (CP, 53, 120–21, 77, 246). It is based partly in the talismanic value of the word "stand" throughout Oppen's work, an issue that Rachel Blau DuPlessis has illuminated in "George Oppen." And it is based partly in my broader sense that Oppen, even when he takes a romantic turn or a turn toward existential phenomenology in his work, retains his earlier political concern with the significance of the built world in which we live. The built world is part of what sustains, in the face of the death of every singular individual, a continuity of human life across the generations. The cultural world, of course, is another important part of this continuity. Above I cited from a letter of Oppen's written in 1973: "the 'Marxism' of Discrete Series," Oppen says, "is, was felt as, the struggle against the losts of the commonplace / can make a touch of Marxism out of this: Love is love of the future   Without which not" (SL, 254). "John," Open continues in the same letter, "your marxism is too 'scholarly'   Marx's books are Marx's books, but the Marxist political parties are ways to relieve the suffering,   and simple ways they are,   or they are abominations--- are or will become so – IF they are not, to get the dams built, to save the people --- / Marxists who don't get the dams built will sure as hell be lynched in a 'People's Republic'   Which means nothing at all about a new Socialist Man or a new art or anything of the sort, it means getting the dams built ---   and, no, don't want people to be hungry /

And then?" (SL, 255). Oppen, in this important sense, is decidedly not Heideggerian. He values the building of dams and the paving of cities. As Weinfield puts it, "the generations *stand* on the *pavement* (the image is concrete, literally as well as figuratively) that they themselves (as a result of the denial of death) have paved; the pavement is the 'ground' of historicity, that which allows the 'generations' to build upon one another and thus in some measure avoid being swept into the maelstrom of nonbeing" (*Music of Thought*, 84). Oppen, then, always retains, in tension with his romantic bearing, a populist bearing (to adopt the term he uses in "The Mind's Own Place"), a concern with our common world of the *polis*, as John Peck says, a concern with the common social world built by human work, as Burton Hatlen says. Hatlen, in "'Not Altogether Lone in a Lone Universe,'" a detailed and illuminating reading of *The Materials*, emphasizes the persistence of Oppen's marxist perspective into his later work. Oppen, he shows, is concerned with the way human labor builds a common world against the natural world, the bare ground, emblematized by stone and sea (338, 340, 344):

> Here [in 'Product'] as throughout *The Materials* Oppen's basic poetic strategy is to illuminate for us the significance of human labor by focussing on the materials which are transformed by that labor, the tools through which human beings exercise their energy upon these materials, and the end products of this exercise of human labor upon the world. [. . .] The task at hand here is the same task that Oppen confronts in all his various 'sea,' 'rock,' and 'city' poems: how to build a human habitation in a world in which even the creations of humankind confront us as alien, inhuman. Alienation is not, this poem ['Sara in Her Father's Arms'] promises us, our 'natural,' eternal condition. As we live, the world makes us and we in turn make it, not out of our minds, but out of the milk we drink and words we speak. That is, speaking here becomes, not a 'spiritual' or 'mental' process of creating meaning in an otherwise meaningless world, but an act of 'material' production—one of the many acts of production through which we constantly make and remake our world. (337, 344)

Even if he overstates his position, Hatlen argues persuasively here; he clarifies an important dimension of Oppen's work. Yet it is also true,

I think, that Oppen finds great value in the life of seeing, the life of the mind, the life of open wonder in relation to the whole. A measure of estrangement and fear amid the miracle is inevitable. Oppen is at one and the same time a populist and a romantic. He expresses at one and the same time a marxist or pragmatic sense of the world, as Hatlen says, and an existential-phenomenological sense of the world, as Nicholls says. Or, in John Peck's terms, he explores at one and the same time a common world in a "political" sense and a common world in an "archetypal" sense. Many readers have underlined the unresolved tensions at work in Oppen's poetry. The tension between a populist concern with the value of active building and a romantic concern with the value of meditative wonder, I think, is one of the most important of these tensions. It pervades all of Oppen's writing—poems, essays, daybooks, and letters. The maps I've sketched above (pp. 76–77) are meant to show this.

In this light, I think, the epiphanic turn at the end of section 26 takes on particular resonance:

> The power of the mind, the
> Power and weight
> Of the mind which
> Is not enough, it is nothing
> And does nothing
>
> Against the natural world,
> Behemoth, white whale, beast
> They will say and less than beast,
> The fatal rock
>
> Which is the world—
>
> O if the streets
> Seem bright enough,
> Fold within fold
> Of residence ...
>
> Or see thru water
> Clearly the pebbles

Of the beach
Thru the water, flowing
From the ripple, clear
As ever they have been

The "bright streets" here recall the "spot of light on the curb" glimpsed in section 11: glimpsed by the poet of the sequence, it seems, though perhaps also seen, also felt, by the "girl" named Phyllis who is said to have stepped out of a bus onto the curb, "her heart, she told me, suddenly tight with happiness—" (CP, 169). "So small a picture," Oppen says, "A spot of light on the curb, it cannot demean us // I too am in love down there with the streets / And the square slabs of pavement— // To talk of the house and the neighborhood and the docks // And it is not 'art'" (here, as often in this sequence, there is no end stop). These are the streets and slabs of pavement that return in section 26, first as "pavement" seen as "filthy," then as "bright streets" seen as folds of residence. The pavement is not only filthy: it is also bright. In section 26, as in section 11, there is a momentary reconciliation of the life of the mind and the life of the city. David McAleavey suggestively speaks of the "cerebral folds" here, hinting that the image is meant to evoke the brain itself ("Clarity and Process," 396), and surely there is a sort of rhyme between the folds of the street, holding residences or places of human dwelling, and the folds of perception and thought, finding another sort of dwelling. Both sorts of folds, both spaces, it would seem, provide protection from the vast sea or the fatal rock of the outer world: practical protection in the face of death, psychic consolation in the face of death. Hugh Kenner writes: "That glimpse of pebbles *liberates* 'The fatal rock which is the world': liberates it from portentousness" ("Disconnected Numerousness," 207). Yet it might be better to say that it liberates the mind from a portentous fear of the fatal rock. This, too, as both Hatlen and Weinfield underline, is part of our relationship to death: we fear it, search for stays against it, and, in this sense, deny it even as we acknowledge it. Weinfield recalls in this context Ernest Becker's existentialist *The Denial of Death* (*The Music of Thought*, 83). Oppen says in a long letter to Julian Zimet written in 1959: "yes, Nature, stone nature and the empty space must be the mother from which we were born since the others are deserted too outside a closed door of nothingness and therefore presumably our brothers [cf. the end of "Blood from a Stone"] [...] What are any of us worked up about --- if not metaphysics? My whole life is a fight against death. Yours hasn't? And death's around us in the dead matter we came out of" (SL, 31, 33). This whole letter lends considerable support to Hatlen's reading of Oppen. But, again, this is one dimension of an unresolved tension in Oppen's thought.

It is of interest that Hatlen is one of the few critics who has noted certain philosophical affinities between Oppen and Stevens; Hatlen raises this question in an interview ("Poetry and Politics," 42), but unfortunately the question is not pursued. This is of interest because Stevens's romantic conception of imaginative force—a pressing back against the pressure of reality—is clearly parallel to the marxist sense of labor that Hatlen finds in Oppen: a transformative pressing back against the pressure of reality. Elizabeth Bishop's great "At the Fishhouses," a deeply Stevensian poem, reads from this perspective like a poem in conversation with Oppen's work. It is romantic in its exploration of the human encounter with the sea as an emblem of our search for meaning in the vast of the flowing, astonishing, inhuman natural world (as in Whitman, Melville, Stevens, Moore, Crane, and Oppen). It is populist in its concern with the relationship between human work against the natural world and human thought in response to the natural world (as in Thoreau, Whitman, Sandburg, Williams, Snyder, and Oppen). And its powerful conclusion, as curiously given to repetitions of words as are many of Oppen's poems, enters a space akin in some ways to the space of the last poem of Oppen's "A Narrative" or a number of his later poems of the sea:

> I have seen it over and over, the same sea, the same,
> slightly, indifferently swinging above the stones,
> icily free above the stones,
> above the stones and then the world.
> If you should dip your hand in,
> your wrist would ache immediately,
> your bones would begin to ache and your hand would burn
> as if the water were a transmutation of fire
> that feeds on stones and burns with a dark gray flame.

If you tasted it, it would first taste bitter,
then briny, then surely burn your tongue.
It is like what we imagine knowledge to be:
dark, salt, clear, moving, utterly free,
drawn from the cold hard mouth
of the world, derived from the rocky breasts
forever, flowing and drawn, and since
our knowledge is historical, flowing and flown.

A Note on Belief and Language in Oppen

Truthfulness is essential to Oppen's poetry. In "The Mind's Own Place" he writes: "It is part of the function of poetry to serve as a test of truth. It is possible to say anything in abstract prose, but a great many things one believes or would like to believe or thinks he believes will not substantiate themselves in the concrete materials of the poem" (133). Peter Nicholls, as I mentioned above (in note 26), raises questions about this statement. Oppen's "account of belief," he says, "is curiously vague ('things one believes or would like to believe or thinks he believes'), vague to the point of trivializing the very notion of belief" (*George Oppen*, 54). Nicholls is particularly concerned with Oppen's suggestion that there is in this claim a basis for distinguishing between politics and poetry. The point is well taken. I think I see, more generally, what troubles Nicholls. A belief, as we use the concept, is something I can hold and state in plain terms without placing on it all the demands I place on genuine poems. Yet Oppen, it seems clear, wants to challenge this familiar concept of belief. He is concerned to write genuine poems. Here the statement makes sense in a way that is significantly analogous to a substantial issue in our lives. The issue at stake, in existentialist terms, is authenticity. Kierkegaard says that our task is to "reduplicate ideality" in our "concrete existence," that is to say, in the practice of our lives we are to strive to realize those ideals we profess (or think we believe). To become a coherent self, as Robert Pippin puts this, drawing on similar themes in Nietzsche and Sartre, has less to do with the general statements of belief I make, or with the retrospective narratives I tell about myself, which may be fantasies and self-deceptions, than with the extent to which I keep the pledges or promises I make to myself and to others ("On 'Becoming Who One Is' [and Failing]: Proust's Problematic Selves"). As Pippin shows, my ideals themselves are pledges or promises, if they are "mine," a part of "my" life, a life for which "I" take responsibility, and not just empty abstractions, not just rehearsed pieties.

If I keep these pledges, I am realizing an authentic and free life. If I fail these pledges from time to time, I am human and guilty; Kierkegaard at this point would say that this is inevitable, as indeed it is, and that therefore I need to acknowledge the source and end of my fractured being in a transcendent God who is my ultimate help, though those of us without this faith will have to rely on the saving human circle of apology and forgiveness. If I fail these pledges habitually, I am inauthentic and spiritually unfree, however free I may appear to be, at worst cynical and hypocritical, at best weak and without character. It may be, too, that what I say I believe is not finally what my actions show I believe but instead, as Oppen says, only what I would like to believe or think I believe or tell myself and others I believe. Then I can live in self-deception, or I can change my professed beliefs, or I can change my conduct. The question is the relationship between professed belief and concrete action. *Its analogue in a poem is the relationship between professed belief and concrete enactment in language.* This, I think, is what Oppen is getting at in the statement in "The Mind's Own Place." "I believe in technique as the test of a man's sincerity," as Pound says. Oppen's is a striking statement of a not unfamiliar thought, for writers and readers are in this sort of space whenever we judge that a novel has not "earned" its ending, that a drama has not "earned" its catastrophe, that a poem has not "earned" its epiphany or its consolation. If we say this, are we saying that a poet does not genuinely believe his or her insight, his or her consolation? Perhaps we are at times. But it may be, alas, that the poet simply has little talent, that the poet merely repeats our own unreflective repetitions, that the poet *sounds* worse than the poet *is*. Here Nicholls is right to voice unease with Oppen's extreme statement, for surely we cannot judge the integrity of people on the basis of their relative lack of artistic talent, and we would be equally unwise to move in the other direction, to infer lived integrity from artistic talent. Life and art are not the same (neither, of course, are life and scholarship). Yet, once we are in the presence of a serious writer, Oppen's statement bears all its cogency. For when a poem does work, or when a certain sort of poem does work, when there is a concordance of intention and linguistic enactment, of belief and articulate realization, we are moved, I think, less by verbal élan than by the encounter with the sort of concordance that we know we are meant to strive for in our actual lives. This is the analogy. Oppen places more weight on it than most writers. The contemporary poet who has most persistently made similarly severe demands on his own poetry and the writing of others is Geoffrey Hill. He addresses these issues in depth throughout the third and fourth sections, "Style and Faith" and "Inventions of Value," of his recent *Collected Critical Writings*.

At this point it may be worth noting that there is a statement in Emerson's "Spiritual Laws" that is similar to Oppen's statement. Emerson is discussing a theme to which he frequently returns in his work: the way a person's character, the latent presence or power of spirit, inevitably reveals itself in every glance, gesture, act, and word of a person. He writes: "I have heard an experienced counsellor say, that he never feared the effect upon a jury of a lawyer who does not believe in his heart that his client ought to have a verdict. If he does not believe it, his unbelief will appear to the jury, despite all his protestations, and will become their unbelief. This is that law whereby a work of art, of whatever kind, sets us in the same state of mind wherein the artist was when he made it. *That which we do not believe, we cannot adequately say, though we may repeat the words never so often*" (*Essays and Lectures*, 318, my italics). The echo here is less surprising than it may initially appear to be. For one dimension of Emerson's individualism that Oppen does share is a belief that "if we live truly, we shall see truly" (*Essays and Lectures*, 271). As we live, so we shall see, Emerson teaches, and as we live and see, so we shall speak and hear. We spend much of our lives hiding this from ourselves, and from one another, and thus our lives and relationships are often opaque, and thus our social life tends to drift in a haze of deception. In the real world, as we say, in the world of "natural" rather than "spiritual" seeing and judging, as St. Paul would say, deception and self-deception are pervasive and work all too well. Yet Emerson and Oppen, despite all, hold to a faith in this ideal of authenticity. This *faith* is akin to, if not exactly identical to, what I have called the *clairvoyance* manifest in Char's work.

Conclusion

Revisions of Axial Age Metaphysics in the Age of Modernity

Char and Oppen are poets as concerned with the question of freedom as with the question of the whole in which they find themselves. It is in this sense that I have characterized them as poets who, like the major existentialist philosophers, undertake not only a sounding of inwardness and concretely lived freedom but also a metaphysical search in a postmetaphysical age. They are philosophical poets, each with a distinctive meditative style, each concerned to articulate a horizon of the good life. Both, further, experience a collision in their lives between this basic existential orientation and the historical crises of the thirties and forties. Their poems explore the intersection—at times the severe tension—between a social horizon of concern and an existential and metaphysical horizon of concern.

At the end of my discussion of Oppen, I suggested that Seamus Heaney's account of the human range of Yeats's "The Stare's Nest By My Window" could be placed beside Oppen's work as well, in particular his sequence "Route." This sequence gathers all of Oppen's concerns in a widening existential, historical, and metaphysical meditation, measuring a vast weather of despair and hope, fear and gratitude, outrage and love.

Yet there is also some truth in the claim that Oppen, from the sixties through the seventies, gradually turns to a more inward lyric in which the social and historical concerns of a sequence like "Route" recede. Rachel Blau DuPlessis, near the end of the essay from which I've already cited several times, writes: "The most memorable fictive landscapes and actions of Oppen's recent poetry [the poetry collected in *Seascape: Needle's Eye*] are born from a desire to move beyond the struggle with alternatives. Having argued, posited, and negated, he will simply turn his back and move away from the necessity of this struggle into a beautiful, stark landscape of awe, almost devoid of man-made objects and certainly empty of a mass of people. In his most recent sequence, 'Some San Francisco Poems,' he turns away from the city, along with a few singular people who share this fictive landscape." I suggested earlier that this turn of Oppen's involves a change of emphasis rather than a stark reorientation. Yet DuPlessis's characterization nonetheless does justice to a general trajectory in Oppen's work. One might describe this as an expression of the common human passage of aging, or, in Blakean terms, the passage from the youth of a rebellious Orc to the maturity of an imaginative Los, which, as Blake and Oppen make clear in their different ways, needn't end in the hardened stance of a defensive Urizen. One might also say that we are familiar with this curve, not just in life, but in English-language poetry, for Oppen in his later years voices a movement that the young Wordsworth made nearly archetypal in the English-language romantic tradition. Wordsworth, it is true, later fell into a Urizenic decline, in both poetic and political terms, a fall he seems to have anxiously feared in himself even at the height of his powers. Yet it is worth pausing on this early turn and, more broadly, on the parallels and differences in the ways Wordsworth, Char, and Oppen wrestle with this sort of drama.[1]

Wordsworth felt as a child "elected" to become a poet: the faith in a calling received "in the dawn almost of life" is of course essential to his gift. He suffered the loss of both his parents at an early age, the first two of many losses that perhaps shaped his sense of vanishing as the substance of experience, but he was raised in a household that gave him love and time to roam the countryside. In his years in college he discovered radical politics, for the French Revolution began during his third year at Cambridge. In the summer of 1790 he took a walking tour in the Alps, evoked in the famous Book VI of *The Prelude*. A year later he returned to France, living there from November of 1791 through December of 1792, during which time he was involved in a love affair, fathered a child, formed a friendship with a liberal French aristocrat, took up a radical stance himself, witnessed the September Massacres in Paris a few weeks before the Republic was declared, and then made his way back to England, pressed for money and burdened with guilt. His inner uncertainty was taken further when war between France and England broke out in the spring of 1793. It was at this time that he took a long lonely walk across Salisbury Plain and saw Tintern Abbey for the first time, five years before the famous poem that would begin, "Five years have passed." He was disoriented, torn between his allegiance to the French Revolution and his allegiance to his native land, an England now at war with a France fighting for his own political ideals. He remained seriously involved with radical politics for the next three years, as repression and censorship extended their grip on England. Then, racked by doubt, in a condition of crisis, he reoriented his life, relying on the renewal of his companionship with Dorothy and the formation of a vital friendship with Coleridge. In 1797 he and Dorothy moved to Alfoxden, becoming neighbors of Coleridge, and an extraordinary literary friendship began, grounded in long walks, conversations, reciprocal challenges. A year later *Lyrical Ballads* was published, a book that opened with Coleridge's "The Rime of the Ancient Mariner" and closed with Wordsworth's "Tintern Abbey." The latter, a sort of compressed anticipation of *The Prelude*, has understandably been read as Wordsworth's testament to his rediscovery of his calling as a poet of time, memory, and the formation of the soul through an unfolding dialogue with natural presence. Yet the *Lyrical Ballads* as a whole shows that Wordsworth in the late 1790s was at least as deeply committed to a realist poetry of human suffering, or to a realist reshaping of traditional pastoral, as to a lyrical poetry of solitary encounter with the natural world. These would be the primary orientations of his poetry in the decade and a half of his greatest work, from 1797 through 1812.[2]

This story is well known. It is a story of a passage from a sustaining childhood, through a youth of radical political engagement, through an early adulthood of relative political disengagement and revived commitment to a more solitary calling. The interpretation of this arc that M.H.

Abrams presented years ago remains among the clearest we have. The poet who develops a lyrical dialogue with nature, Abrams argues, is a poet who celebrates an inward imaginative transformation as a compensation for the failure of the outward social transformation that he—like the young Coleridge, the young Blake, and, of course, countless others—saw promised in the French Revolution. Extreme political disappointment is absorbed and transformed through a meditative poetry of inward quest: a poetry that rearticulates in secular terms an older Christian tradition of inner light renewal. A century and a half earlier, the Quakers had emerged out of a similar trajectory of revolution, war, political disillusion, and spiritual recovery. Yet, Abram notes, there is a second and no less important voice in Wordsworth, a voice nearly antithetical to the Wordsworth of the great crisis poems and *The Prelude*, namely, the voice of the ballads of human disaster, or the related if deeper meditative voice of the great blank-verse poems like "Michael" that bear witness to suffering. This voice, Abrams suggests, is Wordsworth's translation into English poetry of the paradoxical low-sublime mode of the gospels. This bearing of Wordsworth's, further, allows him to sustain an allegiance to the "spirit of the age," to the democratic spirit of the French Revolution, even as his concrete political hopes wane. There is indeed a quietist and elegiac reorientation in Wordsworth, then, but it is qualified by this testimonial poetry of concern.[3]

Because I have already provided a sketch of the activities and works of Char, I need only recall these briefly here. Char, having abandoned school late in his teens, found his way to Paris and the surrealist movement by 1930, at the age of twenty-three. This initiated him into poetry in the line of Rimbaud and Lautréamont and a politics of provocation and revolt consonant with his anarchist temperament. By 1935, however, he had withdrawn from the surrealist movement, apparently for several reasons: a distrust of what he saw as an aestheticizing bent in Breton, a skepticism toward the movement's continually vexed approach to communist politics, and a concern to rethink the direction of his own poetic practice. He also went through a period of bad health at the time. After the rapid defeat of the French army in the summer of 1940, Char returned to L'Isle-sur-la-Sorgue and then, to escape police surveillance, went to live in the small mountain village of Céreste, where he began to form a resistance network of which he would serve as the commander from

1942 to 1944. In the late thirties he began to write most of the poems later collected in the section titled *They Alone Remain* in his major postwar volume *Fury and Mystery*. In 1942, at the very moment he was entering fully into clandestine activity, he wrote the aphoristic sequence *Formal Share*, a desperately lyrical affirmation of the metaphysical scope of poetry. This was followed by his war notebook, *Leaves of Hypnos,* an aphoristic sequence in which a similar romantic faith in the reach of poetry is embedded in the concrete tasks, preoccupations, and human relationships of the Resistance. His major work of the immediate postwar period, the sequence of prose poems gathered under the title *Le Poème pulvérisé*, includes elegies for fallen companions of the Resistance, hymns to the apparitional presence of beauty in the natural world, meditations on the art of poetry, and several major poems of creative recollection. Even in these expansive, luminous, and in some way softer poems of the immediate postwar period, however, one clearly feels the defiant energy of the poet's passage through the Resistance. The energy of Char's work of the early forties animates a journey lasting well into the fifties. The trajectory of Char's work in these years, then, is very different from the trajectory of the young Wordsworth or, to some extent, of English romantic poetry in general. The passage is from a phase of a youthful or natural rebellion, to a temporary disengagement and reflective reorientation, to a deepened meditative poetry of a sweeping metaphysical bent, which turns out to accompany a full and furious political engagement in the Resistance. A certain inner light romantic stance does not express a compensatory recovery from political disillusion but rather accompanies a bold political engagement. Orc remains wholly active alongside Los. A predicament often lived as either-or becomes a fury and a mystery lived as both-and. This is Char's version, as it were, of the surrealist alliance of Marx's "change the world" and Rimbaud's "change life." It is true that, after the war, Char tended to withdraw from politics (though he did in the sixties participate in an unsuccessful movement to keep nuclear missiles out of Provence). He became a meditative poet at a distance from the social world. In some basic sense, I think, Char was not a political animal; he did not think about politics, or society, in the ways in which politically engaged people typically do; his thinking about human life was existential, metaphysical, and, one might say, ultimately ethical rather than political; he was, in this respect, much like Camus, with whom he formed a close friendship in the fifties. The extreme situation of the war, which tended to reduce ordinary human predicaments to nearly mythical polarities, no doubt had much to do with the coming together in his life of an existential, meditative, visionary poetry and a defiant politics of freedom. But it is well to bear in mind that, in some situations at least, a politics of revolt and a poetics of vision are allies in a quest, not phases in a movement of aging, not turns in a familiar story of the experience of disillusion and the search for consolation.

Of Oppen's trajectory, too, I have already provided a sketch. He was born in 1908, a year after Char. Like Wordsworth and Char, he seems to have had an interest in writing at an early age. In the thirties, at a young age, like Char, he found a place in an inventive modernist movement, from which he then withdrew, not for poetic reasons, however, but for political reasons. In the winter of 1935, the year after his first book of poems was published, he joined the Communist Party and began to work as an organizer and a speaker. He would not publish another book for over twenty-five years. He responded to the crisis of the Great Depression by choosing to engage in political activity rather than to write poetry. He had no interest in writing populist or didactic political poetry, that is to say, he saw a tension, even an irreconcilable conflict, between the demands of politics and the demands of poetry. In later years he expressed himself in forceful terms on this matter. "If you decide to do something political," he said in his interview with Dembo, "you do something that has political efficacy. And if you decide to write poetry, then you write poetry, not something that you hope, or deceive yourself into believing, can save people who are suffering. That was the dilemma of the thirties" (IN, 187). He served in the American army from 1942 to 1945, fighting in France, "Burying my dogtag with H / For Hebrew in the rubble of Alsace," as he says in a powerful later poem that addresses Pound with severe clarity (CP, 218). In 1950 he went into exile with his family in Mexico rather than testify before the House Un-American Activities Committee. It is intriguing that at this point, for nearly ten years, he still did not return to the writing of poetry. It appears that he was concerned with being a good father; he may be the only serious writer in the world who felt reluctant to write certain despairing things because his daughter might read them (SL, 30, 55). Yet there is still a mystery here. He and Mary never spoke in detail about their experience as members of a Stalinist party, a party of the sort that, elsewhere in the world, had led to a totalitarian travesty of political hope. It seems clear that they were not particularly theoretical in their political engagement: they responded to a crisis of sheer misery by joining the organization that was doing the most to help. But perhaps—this is only conjecture—perhaps the fifties were for Oppen years of difficult reflection and self-reflection on the long path that he and his wife had taken. One easily imagines these as years demanding a gathering of forces in an aftermath. In any case he did return to poetry, in 1958, and as he said at the time, he felt he was "starting now from scratch" (SL, 26), beginning again. His poetry of the sixties and seventies, as I have said, is a distinctive sort of meditative poetry, deeply shadowed by disillusion. He engages political and social questions throughout his major sequences of the sixties, holding them in tension with his existential and metaphysical concerns, and then, as DuPlessis notes, comes in the seventies to step back from the social to a considerable extent. This is the turn that I have characterized as Wordsworthian: a turn from an involvement in radical politics to a meditation on the life of the mind and the wonder of presence. Oppen's wrestling with social issues in his later work, especially in the major sequences of the sixties, could be seen as analogous to Wordsworth's attention, in his "other voice," to the condition of the poor and the unemployed in the rural England of his time. There are of course enormous differences as well. Wordsworth had a passion for radical politics but was not a committed activist; Oppen took the risk of sustained engagement in the thirties and forties. Wordsworth turned from radical politics to meditative poetry in his late twenties; Oppen made a similar turn in his fifties and sixties, after two decades of an adult life in which his poetic vocation was set aside for the sake of a political commitment. Wordsworth, as he grew older, became politically conservative and lost his poetic power; Oppen, in his later years, continued to wrestle with his earlier political ideals and discovered a distinctive poetic voice that was anything but static or in decline. There is nevertheless a larger pattern visible in the trajectory. Oppen's life and work express, in a particularly dramatic way, the tension between political engagement and poetic vision that seems to have haunted modern culture from the romantic period on. It becomes a serious tension under the circumstances of modernity, when social hierarchy is no longer taken to be natural, when writers become aware of the complicity of culture with social injustice.[4]

There are of course many ways of characterizing this basic tension. Seamus Heaney, in the passage from his Nobel Lecture that I cited at the end of chapter 2, describes an intersection of different *qualities of the spirit*, a lucidity bearing witness to the truth of disaster and a tenderness sustaining the longing for a fully human life. Heaney himself, throughout his own work, notably in his "Station Island" sequence, has sought to hold these qualities together in a demanding and clearing oscillation. Oppen tends to think of this tension or intersection in terms of different *orientations of the spirit* or different *horizons of concern*. To put the matter in simple terms, when he speaks of the vertical concern, he speaks of a relationship to the depth of being or the miracle of place, and when he speaks of a horizontal concern, he speaks of a relationship to other persons, but the whole question is far from simple, not least because the horizontal can have to do with the social world as a whole, or with the world of friendship, love, and family, and in the latter case, as we have seen, it becomes profoundly embedded in the vertical concern with being, the life of the mind, and the questions of the whole and the meaning of one's mortal life in the whole. But if there are finally no simple terms in which to put the matter, there are nonetheless basic spiritual bearings and horizons of concern that do take on a certain clarity in Oppen's work. And these bearings and horizons in Oppen, as in Char, as in earlier writers as different as Blake and Wordsworth and Whitman and Rimbaud, are versions of a basic tension in our culture between the existential and the social, as this appears in one light, or between the metaphysical and the historical, as it appears in another light. This tension comes out with particular clarity, I think, in the entire existentialist tradition in philosophy. The debate between Hegel and Kierkegaard is emblematic in this respect. It has been continually revived, played out in different languages, for two centuries now.

*

The debate between Hegel and Kierkegaard is primarily a debate about the nature of human freedom. Their differences on this question are inseparable from their different accounts of transcendence, Christianity, the nature of society, and the relationship between social life and what Kierkegaard calls the concretely existing individual.[5]

Hegel's interpretation of the relationship between traditional Christianity and secular modernity would have a vast influence on all of modern sociology. According to this reading, Christianity was a phase in the discovery of subjectivity for itself, or in the discovery of spiritual transcendence. It promised freedom for all who turned to faith in the promise of the risen Christ, but freedom in a realm of spiritual equals before God, not in an actual social world, whose concrete hierarchies and inequalities it left untouched. In this respect Christianity was akin to Hellenistic philosophy. It was a religion of the unhappy consciousness in a phase of history where only thus could spirit begin to find its freedom. Modernity, however, marked by changes in the social whole and in particular by the American and French revolutions, transforms the older Christian promise of spiritual freedom into the promise of practical freedom in a concrete social world. The transcendent is to be made immanent. Christian theology, in turn, is to be comprehended as a mythopoetic anticipation of the truth at last conceptually articulated in Hegel's philosophy of the development of the World Spirit in historical time. While it is not difficult to follow Hegel's thought to this point—this sort of thinking would become familiar through its materialist reworkings in Feuerbach, Marx, Weber, and many others—there is still the problem of Hegel's social philosophy, which seems statist, even feudal, not consonant with the liberal individualism that has been the dominant trend of modern life and thought. Hegel, indeed, in the aftermath of the French Revolution, provides a critical comprehension of the individualist ideology of modernity. The freedom of the subject, for Hegel, is always social freedom, grounded in a network of institutions and practices within which subjects engage in work and contend for recognition, without which activities no inward or subjective freedom is possible, despite illusions that the subject may hold concerning its nonconformist freedom, its presocial or asocial independence. A social field of mutual dependence is the ground of independence. This remains a vital current in modern social theory, powerfully developed in recent years by Axel Honneth, who translates Hegel's account of the struggle for recognition into the *marxisant* terms of the

Frankfurt School and the naturalist terms of George Herbert Mead's anthropology.

Kierkegaard, ultimately, objects to this whole Hegelian philosophy. But initially, or on a certain level, he embraces important Hegelian insights. This can be seen most clearly in his account of the stages of existence of a genuinely existing individual. The aesthetic individual, living for pleasure, more or less reflectively moving from one set of circumstances to another, perhaps even becoming a romantic ironist delighted by its mobile negativity, is dwelling in despair, though a despair that can be concealed or repressed for an entire life. It is the despair of an individual who is merely a natural individual, that is, an individual with no coherent character and no coherent horizon of concern toward which it strives. The passage to the ethical stage of existence is a concrete spiritual decision, Kierkegaard says, and involves above all the decision to bind one's self to universal norms and, since such norms are embedded in the institutions and practices of a given social world, to commit oneself to a particular place in the social world. This transformation involves, then, the individual's decision to lend constancy and character to what is otherwise mere dispersive individuality (this is what it means to shape a self in relation to principles) and, further, to find meaningful work and to marry (these are the traditional markers, for Kierkegaard, of what it means to commit a self to a disclosed life in a social world of mutual acknowledgment). This is all Hegelian enough, so far, however audible the accents of Protestant individualism. At this point, however, the debate begins. The ethical stage of existence, for Kierkegaard, is not the end of the journey but a relative stage. Neither the transcendence of God, nor the inwardness of the concretely existing individual, can be wholly socialized, wholly immanentized. To believe so, Kierkegaard says, is disastrously to misunderstand human existence. If the despair of the aesthetic individual involves an encounter with emptiness, the despair of the ethical individual involves an encounter with failure, or guilt, and with the anguish of mortality. We are far from sufficient to the tasks to which our ethical ideals call us; and we are shaken by the shipwreck of our very existence that we see in death. The religious individual, haunted by guilt and death, turns in a movement of faith to the "objective uncertainty" of a transcendent source and end of its being. In this faith it discovers the full scope of its spiritual freedom, its genuine independence from the false consolations and invitations to self-deception of the social world, and a paradoxical flourishing that is at once an anguish of doubt and a joy of faith. The restlessness of the aesthetic individual turns out to have been a thin anticipation, as it were, of the genuine spiritual restlessness that is our true vocation: the restlessness of the religious individual who, holding firm to the demands of the ethical stage of existence, at the same time "makes the infinite movement" beyond this stage. It is a movement that transcends the social. It is incommunicable except through indirect discourse, and invisible except through indirect manifestation in a life of spiritual striving. The religious individual is indistinguishable from the philistine, in fact, except for the barely discernable lightness in his or her step, the sole outward sign of a genuine inward transcendence. Yet this lightness of step, in its hidden depth, is a poised readiness for love and self-sacrifice, and it thus quietly but powerfully shapes everyday conduct. Indeed, without this hidden inwardness in relation to a hidden transcendence, Kierkegaard says, we are not even capable of holding to the demands of the ethical stage of existence: we become depersonalized actors of social roles, lost in a spiritless rehearsal of conventions, not concrete individuals striving to realize our spiritual ideals in our actual lives.

Hegel, as is well known, sees where all this is coming from and, before Kierkegaard had ever written a word, forcefully criticizes it. Kierkegaard, he would say, is a romantic, a romantic Christian rather than a romantic ironist, to be sure, but a romantic nonetheless. The romantic is a typical modern figure of the unhappy consciousness, whose earlier figures in history include the Epicurean, the Stoic, the Christian, and the detached critical intellectual of the Enlightenment. The unhappy consciousness is the consciousness that, unable to find freedom, value, or significance in a particular social world, posits an absent world to which it turns in the depth of its inwardness. For Hegel, again, this was a necessary historical drama in the discovery of subjectivity for itself, in the liberation of spirit from the burden of mere being. Yet it is a drama that has been at once negated, retained, and superseded in a modern world that has made concrete social freedom a practical reality for all. The romantic—or, later, the existentialist, the modernist, the bohemian, the perpetual dissident—is a subject claiming a spiritual independence of the field of social interdependence that, in fact, is the unacknowledged ground of its independence. The refusal to acknowledge this ground is self-deception. The refusal to acknowledge the transcendent source and end of my existence, Kierkegaard responds, is self-deception. The divine cannot be comprehended in a concept or a system. Neither can the spirit of the self, the passion of the concretely existing individual. The claim that the inwardness of the concrete individual, grounded in an openness to transcendence, can be fully socialized is a claim that, were it carried out, would destroy the concrete individual's freedom and destroy the possibility of ethical life itself—if ethical life means a living forward, not a looking backward, an effort to realize our ideals in lives for which we are responsible, not merely a mechanical or prudent adoption of social roles and norms. Prudent, Hegel says, who said anything about prudent or mechanical? The debate goes on and on.

My basic response to this debate, as the way I've sketched it perhaps already suggests, is to say that Hegel and Kierkegaard are both right. The freedom I find in my life is based in a social world of interdependence and, ideally at least, this social world would be experienced not as an obstacle to the genuine conduct of my life but as its sustaining ground and resource. At the same time, the freedom I find in my life is an individual project, demanding that I inwardly and concretely realize those roles and norms I adopt, and the possibility of my losing myself in empty imitations and deceptive rationalizations is all too real. As Robert Pippin says, if the self is a project, as modern culture pervasively teaches us that it is, then it can certainly fail as well as succeed. Kierkegaard, a severe Christian Socrates, means not to let us forget this. Hegel needs to be supplemented by Kierkegaard, then, just as Kierkegaard needs to be supplemented by Hegel. Each lends an essential perspective to the other.[6]

Hegel's claim that the ancient promise of spiritual freedom had been practically realized in early nineteenth-century Europe was of course implausible in the extreme. It was therefore quickly subjected to critical revision. If the concrete individual is shaped by the social world in which it finds itself, the social world may not enable or sustain this individual so much as crush and alienate it. Then some version of an unhappy consciousness would be the only form of a still free, clear, dignified consciousness. Perhaps, further, this form of unhappy consciousness could turn its spiritual freedom toward an absent world located, not in a transcendent realm, but in an immanent realm of the future. Perhaps, too, one could clarify the road from the present of unfreedom to the future of freedom through a study that paid less attention to the unfolding of World Spirit and more attention to the development of material institutions and everyday social practices. With these steps, one arrives in the realm of a critical historicist sociology, whether in a radical version, a liberal version, or a conservative version. The Hegelian emphases on stages of historical development, a holistic social hermeneutic, and an understanding of the basis of individual freedom in social interdependence are all retained. But the whole approach is placed on a materialist footing (in a broad sense), gradually detached from a teleological narrative, and usually taken up less in a recollective or contemplative spirit than in a critical or activist spirit. This is the way Hegel has been transformed in modern sociology and social philosophy. The Hegelian perspective, in this broad sense, remains an important part of our culture.

What happens, then, to the Kierkegaadian perspective? Kierkegaard, in the middle of the materialist nineteenth century, defends a distinctive version of a Christian metaphysic and a Christian conception of the person. The spiritual dimension of the existing individual is ultimately grounded in and capable of turning toward the transcendent dimension of the whole. Neither this inwardness of the individual, nor the transcendence of the divine, can be comprehended in a discursive system; they can only be lived in faith, and they can only be indirectly communicated through exemplary lives or through indirect words that provoke, call, awaken. What happens if this faith in the divine wanes? What happens to this perspective in the age of what Nietzsche calls the death of God? Where is the inwardness of the individual—for Kierkegaard inseparable from its relationship to a divine transcendence—to be found if this transcendence is taken to be an illusion? In the wake of Kierkegaard, the major existentialist thinkers of an atheistic bent do tend to naturalize this spiritual dimension of the self, though not quite along the lines of a naturalist empiricism. The concern with freedom is still fundamental: the existing individual that would be authentically free must first of all detach itself from the shadows of the cave, that is to say, from the herd and its conventions (Nietzsche), from the they-self and its insistent demands to conform (Heidegger), from the many invitations to bad faith circulating in the social world (Sartre). The existentialist tradition tends to be as emphatically individualist as Kierkegaard. But where, in the absence of a transcendent horizon of concern, is the genuinely free individual to find its bearings? Where is the transcendent horizon to which this individual can turn in discovering the dimension of its freedom irreducible to the social? Karl Löwith, in a reading of the early Heidegger, has said that the answer here is no secret: the absolute horizon of a mortal existence is now not God but death. It is in relation to my death that I discover my spiritual freedom, my longing for transcendence, a concern to make my life authentically my own. Is this not after all what Socrates teaches his friends in the *Phaedo*? The Christian God and the Platonic Good or space of Forms are only two possible responses to this more fundamental and abyssal ground of spiritual freedom, of the spiritual gathering of the self that is concerned for itself. The care for the soul, the search for the good life, begins in the shadow of death. One could claim that Nietzsche explores this same issue in *Zarathustra*. It is, I have suggested, at least one important line of thought in both Char and Oppen.[7]

Yet it would seem that this perspective, finally, is not fully sufficient even for these tragic or pessimistic thinkers. In the end they all turn toward a horizon of our freedom that is not exactly the horizon of our death or shipwreck, though it is not exactly separate from this horizon, either. Nietzsche speaks of *amor fati*, love of fate, love of the whole, as though he were a sort of Dionysian Stoic. Heidegger speaks of Being as the clearing or opening into which we are called. Merleau-Ponty speaks of the intertwining of my embodied self and the Being that I have always already been drawn into as into a field of depths, contours, and openings. Camus speaks of the whole of nature that is intimately connected to our experiences of joy, love, and unity. Char speaks of the beauty that calls us to the slope of poetry in the unending ruin and renewal of the whole. Oppen speaks of the miracle of place and the marvel of what is there in the unending erosion of things. These are not all the same, of course, but they do all bear affinities with one another. The existentialist current in modern philosophy and poetry, when it is not religious, tends to follow romanticism in discovering in Nature or Being an unfathomable horizon of transcendence in relation to which the inwardness of the concretely existing self can take its bearings at some distance from the compass of the social self and the familiar social world. Nature or Being, in this sense, is approached as a sort of open question or open horizon in the space of the traditional metaphysical question of the whole. It is turned to in this way because these thinkers have not wished to abandon the Kierkegaardian perspective in a modern secular world whose dominant trends have left this perspective no less relevant to our lives than the post-Hegelian sociological perspective. The romantic, modernist, and existentialist currents in modern thought reinflect the Kierkegaardian voice, just as the marxist, historicist, and sociological currents in modern thought reinflect the Hegelian voice. I said above that, to my mind, Hegel and Kierkegaard are both right. I would say, similarly, that materialist sociology and existentialist philosophy and literature are both right.

How did Nature or Being come to be thought in this way in romantic, modernist, and existentialist literature and philosophy? What does it mean to think of Nature or Being in this way? It seems clear that Nature, in these traditions, is not exactly the Nature of modern Newtonian and post-Newtonian science—though the latter, an infinite space of matter and motion with no intrinsic significance for human life, seems to me always still there, in the background, in romantic, existentialist, phenomenological, or ecological efforts to think of our relational embeddedness in Nature in other ways. It is what the river of erosion and the fatal rock evoke in Oppen's poetry. Yet I have suggested that Nature in these traditions takes the place, in some sense, of the whole in traditional metaphysical thought. This would mean that the thinking of Nature in these traditions is intimately connected to the fate of metaphysics under the circumstances of modernity, that is, under the circumstances of a civilization that defines itself as primarily historical: historically conditioned, historically self-shaping, and, to this extent, anti-metaphysical. This is obviously a question that goes far beyond what I can address here. Yet I would like at least to work through a few hints and to suggest a few larger stories that might help us to see the stakes of this question a little more clearly.

This will require a roaming detour. The debate between Hegel and Kierkegaard, in an important sense, is a debate about what to do in the modern world with the religious transformations of the epoch that Karl

Jaspers calls the Axial Age. Jaspers refers in this way to the range of religious and metaphysical transformations that took place around the world in the first millennium before the Common Era: the emergence of Taoism and Confucianism in China (historians, it is true, sometimes describe Confucianism as less a religion than a social philosophy), Hinduism and Buddhism in India, Zoroastrianism in Persia, prophetic monotheism in Judah (the root of all three religions of the book), and Platonic metaphysics in Greece (the root of later Hellenistic philosophies that had an ample influence on Christianity). Some historians emphasize the importance of a somewhat later peroid—a second phase of the Axial Age, as it were, situated around the turn of the millennium—marked by the emergence of a series of "salvation" religions: a further altered Hinduism, Mahayana Buddhism, Christianity, and, centuries later, Islam. These salvation religions bring out fully the metaphysical dualism at times only implicit or emergent in earlier Axial Age religions. The transformations of this long period, in any case, include what historians often call the world religions. With some exceptions, they appear to have emerged in relative independence of one another. They of course did not emerge out of thin air. They were transformations of older religious traditions, even if some of them, notably Buddhism and Platonic philosophy, were more radical in their innovations than others. It is not easy to see what they have in common, nor to clarify why they took shape in this period of urban civilization, and yet there is clearly some sort of "great transformation" at stake here, to recall the title of Karen Armstrong's recent popular book on this dramatic period in cultural history. Nietzsche, notoriously, developed a polemical and complex psychological interpretation of this age of metaphysical longing and invention. Attempts at a general interpretation have been made not only by Nietzsche and Jaspers but also by Max Weber and, more recently, Louis Dumont, Marcel Gauchet, and Charles Taylor, among others. Samir Amin, from the point of view of contemporary world-systems theory, has sketched an unfamiliar interpretation, one that places the transformation at a later date, in what I have called the second phase of the Axial Age, finding in Neoplatonic metaphysics the synthesis at work in a range of religious constructs lasting from the Hellenistic period all the way through the Renaissance. Amin, in line with these other thinkers, underlines that all of these religions provide, in one way or another, a developed cosmogony, a quasi-rationalized cosmology, a conception of an absolute, a universalist morality, and some notion of either an immortal soul or a liberation from death. All tend to provide a dualist picture of both the world as a whole and the self. All tend to teach, at least for those who seek a full transformation, an ascetic path. An ascetic care for the self is the way to insight (wisdom, enlightenment, or faith) and virtue. One might argue that what all of these religions provide is a path to what we call spiritual freedom. It is a freedom discovered and lived by a self that takes a distance from a social world in which any freedom is far from generally sustained in practical, economic, or political terms (Dumont thus speaks of the "other-worldly individual" of these religious traditions as distinct from the "this-worldly individual" of modern political traditions). Gauchet, in his interpretation of Christianity as the religion that ultimately leads to an "exit from religion," clarifies the fundamental frame of this sort of spiritual freedom. What Christianity teaches—what, I would say, Axial Age religion in general teaches, in diverse terms and frameworks—is the presence of a transcendent world beyond the familiar outer world, the presence of an inward self beyond the familiar social self, and a way of unfolding the dormant freedom of this inward self by turning it toward the transcendent world (this transcendent horizon is no doubt quite different in Buddhism than in any other Axial Age frame). The self that is inevitably of this world is free insofar as it is not entirely of this world. Spiritual freedom is found through an inward discovery of a transformative relationship to a transcendent dimension of being. This frame not only provides the transformed self with a point of orientation beyond the familiar roles and norms of life in the cave, to recall Plato's figure, or in the world of the flesh, to recall the Christian figure. It also, as Charles Taylor underlines, provides the transformed self with a conception of the good life that may be antithetical to ordinary conceptions of the good or the flourishing: the Buddhist sage, the suffering servant, and the ascetic monk would be exemplary "types" or "figures" of this transvaluation of values. Yet these Axial Age transformations, as Taylor also notes, do not simply carry the day. They come to be re-embedded, as he puts it, in the social worlds they challenge with a vision of spiritual dis-embedding. Inevitably, they become ideologies of worldly practice and power—in this way they enter the course of history—but they remain present as counterframes of spiritual values within the social world of pragmatic values. An interpenetration takes place. They are the basis of a spiritual freedom always available to those who wish to undertake, to a greater or lesser extent, the quests they encourage. Stoicism—invented by a former slave, practiced by a famous emperor—provides a suggestive example of this ambiguity.[8]

It is no accident that the most ambitious interpretations of this age of metaphysics have been proposed by historians, sociologists, and philosophers primarily preoccupied with modernity. For modernity has defined itself as a negation of the sort of metaphysical frame that emerges, in different forms, in the Axial Age. The character of this negation is a complex and controversial question. Hobbes and Locke, preparing the way for the modern liberal economic order, seem almost to demolish the whole picture in a mere fifty years: the reflective or inward dimension of the self is reduced to a power of calculation serving the natural instincts of self-preservation, the avoidance of pain, the improvement of one's lot, or, as we say today, the finding of an effective way to get ahead: everything in the world is turned into an "obstacle" or a "means" for an instrumental self. This economic stance fully comes into its own, so to speak, in our own time. Nietzsche appears to denounce the whole picture for the sake of a revived paganism. Yet this is a misleading appearance: Nietzsche, for all his naturalism, is a spirit of metaphysical longing, calling for a demanding transformation of our lives, opposing any Hobbesian or Lockean version of naturalism. Hegel and those he influenced see this negation as a dialectical negation: the transcendent horizon and the transcendent dimension of the self are to be negated as dimensions of otherworldly transcendence and at the same time realized as dimensions of immanent social life. The ancient Christian promise of spiritual freedom for all, in the wake of the American and French revolutions, is turned into the modern promise of practical social freedom for all. So it is, liberals and marxists and other activists say, but this will have to be fought for, either through reform or through revolution. The reality has always been far from the promise, to say the least, and modern history has been a continual struggle in the space of this vast disjunction.[9]

Yet the old question of spiritual freedom does not simply vanish. There are two obvious features of our lives that make this clear. First, we all know that individuals with little social freedom—political, economic, cultural—can still be unmistakably free, in a way that is existentially lived, in a way that is felt by others as a presence and a dignity, in a way that can be ignored only in blindness. "The definition of the spiritual," as Emerson says, "should be, *that which is its own evidence.*" Second, conversely, we all know that individuals with a large measure of social freedom—political, economic, cultural—can still be basically unfree. We may be driven by compulsions, blocked by neuroses, dispersed or disintegrated in our habits and passions, lacking character or spirit, damaged by conformist pressures, obsessed with the wrong things, abandoned to callousness and cynicism, or what have you. I may, as Robert Pippin puts it, fail at the project of becoming a coherent self shaping my life. To speak of spiritual freedom in this context is to draw on an older language. An important current in modern culture speaks in this context of independence or moral autonomy. The existentialist current in modern culture speaks of the measure of authenticity of the existentially free self ever at risk of losing itself in an unreflective, uncommitted, unmeant adoption of conventions. Hegel and the sociological tradition draw our attention to the social ground of the self. Kierkegaard and the existentialist tradition draw our attention to the inward life—essential to the practice of life—of the self. Axial Age metaphysics, then, is not only translated into the frame of social ideals in modern society. It is also translated into distinctly modern versions of spiritual freedom in a world with altogether uncertain metaphysical moorings. Kierkegaard develops a paradoxical negative theology in defense of the Axial Age frame of traditional Christianity. Yet many existentialist thinkers in his wake have sought to articulate agnostic or atheistic versions of this perspective.[10]

There is one more station on the road of this detour. The debate between Kierkegaard and Hegel, as I have sketched it, is more frequently encountered as a debate between Kant and Hegel. Kant, writing at the end of the Enlightenment, develops a secular version of spiritual freedom that has been immensely influential. This is his picture of moral autonomy grounded in a universal power of reason whereby I "give" myself the ends to which I freely "bind" myself. The moral ends that I set for myself, out of my rational power, are imperatives that I freely obey under all circumstances (for Kant there are no excuses at the level of willing). Therein lies my dignity and my freedom as a spiritual being. This is not the place to address the whole history of this picture of spiritual freedom in modern culture. I will simply make two points. The first is that this Kantian picture of moral freedom is severely shaken when a faith in a universal rational power in every self is severely shaken. This happens, historically speaking, rather quickly. Historicism arrives in the generation after Hegel. Materialist and naturalist accounts of the self are everywhere by the late nineteenth century. In the wake of the fracturing of a faith in a universal reason, Kant's translation of traditional spiritual freedom into the terms of rational moral autonomy does persist in our culture, but only in forms that would have dismayed Kant. One of these is existentialist philosophy. The emphasis on my capacity to set the ends to which I freely bind myself becomes the emphasis on my capacity to adopt or choose the ends to which I freely commit myself. The faith in an "ultimate" rational ground for these ends is lost, but not the concern with my freedom, with my responsibility to make these ends authentically mine, to strive to realize them in the practice of my life. The language of resolution and commitment and striving, hallmarks of existentialist philosophies, in fact have their origins in Kant and, behind him, in Axial Age disciplines of spiritual freedom.

The second point I want to make has to do with the picture of the whole that Kant connects to his account of moral freedom. Freedom, he notoriously says, is an enigmatic "fact of reason" beyond which thought can go no further: it is there, felt in the force of the moral imperative, and it can only be denied through self-deception. Yet he finds this fact of freedom and the universal moral law of reason not quite sufficient, finally, for his larger philosophic picture of the free self. This self, it turns out, needs two other practical postulates, namely, a practical belief in the immortality of the soul and a practical belief in the existence of God. These postulates or practical beliefs are of a peculiar and ambiguous sort. They are not theoretical claims—we can have no knowledge of such things that are beyond the boundaries of empirical experience—yet they are, Kant says, necessary orientations if we are to live a morally free life. Otherwise despair, born of a clear recognition that the world as we know it hardly seems made for the realization of moral ends, will overwhelm us. A Kantian skeptical of these particular Kantian postulates, to be sure, can simply jettison them and call us to hold to a reason that operates as a firm transcendent horizon within our immanent lives. Yet it is of interest that Kant, for all his own skepticism, wants to hold on to this transcendent horizon of concern. The analogy at work is clearly an analogy with a traditional Axial Age metaphysical frame. The Christian is spiritually free, in an inward depth that shapes his or her practical life, in relation to a transcendent reality (God, the risen Christ, the Spirit). The Kantian autonomous self is spiritually free, in an inward depth that shapes his or her practical life, in relation to a transcendent horizon of concern that can be reached toward not through revelation or knowledge, and not through the passionate faith taught by Kierkegaard, but through a sort of sober practical faith. Modern atheists are likely to say that we will have to do without these postulates as they are simply illusions. Reflection and commitment will have to be enough. Hegelians and post-Hegelian sociologists will say that the horizon of concern transcendent to the self, in relation to which the reflective self can take its bearings, is the expansive horizon embodied in all the institutions, practices, languages, and ideals of the social whole, in which we participate with others. It is this claim, again, that vexes Kierkegaard. He finds it true on one level: the level of the initial education of the dispersive individual for life as an ethical individual. Otherwise he finds it false, dangerous, destructive of the self, and of a piece with the depersonalizing trends of modern social life in general. But Kierkegaard has a hidden God in relation to which the inward self comes to be transformed and reoriented. Atheistic existentialists, while sharing Kierkegaard's fear of a loss of the self in social routine, have only the shadow of death in which the lonely self is able to discover its groundless care for itself, its unmoored freedom. They no longer even have Kant's universal power of reason. But atheistic existentialists, I have also said, finally seem drawn to a picture of the whole that is not simply or solely a horizon of shipwreck. There is a wider horizon in relation to which the self takes at least a measure of orientation as it steps back from the shadows of the cave, the conventions of the social whole, although this wider horizon cannot provide the "final ends" that the Greeks found in the nature of things and Kant in autonomous reason. It is at this point that Nature or Being comes to take a place in romantic and existentialist thought precariously analogous to the place that the practical postulates take in Kantian thought. In both cases, despite all the differences, what we encounter are ambiguous versions of Axial Age metaphysical accounts of the whole in relation to which the self discovers spiritual freedom. Kant works out his vision of rational autonomy at the same moment that romantic writers begin this long meditation in modern culture on the whole of Nature or Being: a meditation that turns out to be intimately linked to a long meditation on some dimension of the self variously called imagination, creative power, the play-impulse, an intuitive openness, a mimetically responsive form of reason.

*

One way romantics of this period approach the natural world could be called dynamic or dialectical. There is felt to be a restorative or renovative promise in nature, and this is above all because nature is taken to be a resonant counter-presence to a fragmented social life. It is in an encounter with the natural world that all the poet's capacities of perception, response, passion, and thought are brought together in a movement of healing. "The poet, described in ideal perfection," Coleridge says, "brings the whole soul of man into activity." This vision of renewal discovered in the natural world is inseparable from a diagnosis of ills taken to be distinctive to modernity. Wordsworth is the preeminent expression of this perspective in English romantic poetry, though Blake, while opposed to any naturalism, develops this sort of critical diagnosis more capaciously than any other writer of his time except for Hegel. In these and other high romantic writers, we find not only a cross-mapping of social divisions and psychic divisions but also a vision of the utopian surpassing of these divisions. The project is spelled out in clear conceptual terms in Schiller's *Letters on the Aesthetic Education of Man*, a work that exerts a substantial influence on Hegel and, later, on a whole line of Hegelian Marxist thought. The romantic diagnosis of our fragmented social and psychic life is recast by the young Marx, and then unfolded further by Lukács in *History and Class Consciousness*, a work in which the concept of "reification," an impressively roomy concept, manages to embrace at one and the same time what Marx means by "commodification," what Weber means by "rationalization," and what the whole romantic tradition means by "division" and "fragmentation." Lukács's approach is in turn extended by the Frankfurt School, most brilliantly by Adorno, who supplements it with both a messianic vector and an agile interpretation of artistic modernism as an embodiment of reification that resists reification. The utopian horizon, throughout this tradition, is a renewed psychic and social wholeness that neither evades nor reduces differentiations but gathers them anew on a higher level.[11]

For all the nuances and transformations in this long tradition, the basic story is a triadic story of mythopoetic scope and resonance: a story of an initial but insufficient unity, followed by a division and fragmentation, or a development of human powers that is at the same time a wounding of human life, and then a promise of the recovery of complex wholeness on a higher level. This is a developmental story that can be told in existential terms, or social terms, or, as in Schiller and Blake, both at once—this ambiguity probably has much to do with the staying power of this story in modern culture. First there is an always already lost Eden, where work was play and play was work, a non-alienating tilling of a garden, and then there is the long history of work and alienation and repression and suffering, where we have always lived, wondering how we have so badly missed what we are meant to be, and then, always, there is the promise of the messianic age that will heal all these wounds, permitting us to live the fully human life that we have glimpsed only in the depths of memory or in the far places of hope.

This sort of philosophy of history is developed as nowhere else in Horkheimer and Adorno's *Dialectic of Enlightenment*. To recognize the mythopoetic matrix of this work is not to ignore its provocative synthesis of interpretative approaches to modernity. Horkheimer and Adorno draw into their bleak narrative at least the following perspectives: Nietzsche's theory of the will to power as the ground of a reason that has become irrational and nihilist in its bent toward technical and social control; Weber's account of a world-historical process that culminates in the reduction of all reflection to instrumental rationality, or the rationality of efficiency, in the iron cage of the modern world; Marx's emphasis on the organization of work against nature as the ground of social life that, under the conditions of capitalist modernity, leaves individuals of all classes subjugated to a reifying machine of production so vast it extends even into the cultural sphere and the domain of psychic life; and Freud's account of the instinctual renunciation that, constitutive of subjectivity, comes to be intensified in the modern order of productivism, leaving the subjects of this order prey to explosive discontent, the return of the repressed in the form of paranoid rage, or projective rage in search of a scapegoat. All these interpretative approaches are brought together in an apocalyptic story written by two German Jewish exiles living in America in the early 1940s, responding to the realities of Stalinism in eastern Europe, fascism in western Europe, and devastating war on a global scale. The ruined promises of modernity are seen entirely under the aspect of fear, power, and division. Yet the deep mythopoetic narrative of this book is the romantic narrative earlier elaborated by Schiller and Hegel. In this version of the narrative, the basic historical periods are the pre-modern, the modern, and the utopian, periods or narrative chapters that those suspicious of the story are likely to find a touch too general. The pre-modern period embraces the millennia of deep history in which all societies were in a profound sense at the mercy of nature, in which the power of nature was felt to be overwhelmingly superior to human power; this is the realist rethinking of Eden, as it were, according to which the only true paradise is the paradise to come. This pre-modern period, in Horkheimer and Adorno's narrative, in fact includes two phases. The first is the vast history prior to the rise of urban civilizations and, later, Axial Age religions. This was the age of simple hunter-gatherer societies or, after the neolithic revolution about ten thousand years ago, elementary forms of agriculture. Animistic religion (in the broadest sense) was the cultural frame through which these societies attempted to engage with natural power, understand their precarious place in the world, and sustain their cohesion in the face of internal and external violence. If the first religions that emerged with the new urban civilizations were fairly transparent cosmological projections of social power, the Axial Age transformations of the first millennium were far more ambiguous. They were indeed, on the one hand, rationalizations of a vast increase in social domination: the domination of nature by the organization of work, the domination of the many by the few, and the domination of inner nature by the repressive demands of highly organized work and new forms of social life. Yet the major Axial Age religions, at the same time, were contestations of this whole world of domination in the name of spiritual freedom and a life shaped by horizons of the good at odds with the defining realities and severe limitations of this world. They thus brought with them a vast promise even as they remained bound to the civilizations they challenged. The modern period, in Horkheimer and Adorno's dystopian narrative, is not only the period of the secularization of Axial Age promises of freedom under the sign of progress: now promises of increased material prosperity, a liberation from the damages of scarcity, the reshaping of society in the light of scientific and critical reason, and the expansion of individual freedom and democratic politics. It is also the period of the technological conquest of nature (with Bacon and Descartes as heralds and Nietzsche as wild diagnostician), the growth of the bureaucratic state (with Hobbes as herald and Weber as sober diagnostician), and the rise and spread of a capitalist economy of production for profit (with Locke and Smith as heralds and Marx as dialectical diagnostician). These processes complete the disenchantment of outer nature begun by Axial Age religions; in fact they carry this disenchantment further, into the substance of human life, gradually disenchanting the social world and the human person as well. At the same time they extend and intensify, to an unprecedented degree, the divisions that had always been a feature of complex civilizations. The vast expansion of human powers and promises that marks modernity—including, notably, the possibility of a substantive social realization of the freedom promised solely to the spirit in Axial Age religion—thus turns out to be inseparable from a deepening of social and psychic fragmentation. The romantic turn to an elusive natural presence, either to wild nature or to the rural life-worlds being dominated and destroyed in this very unfolding of modernity, is an elegiac and utopian search for the promises of spiritual freedom and wholeness once held out in Axial Age religions and now, it is feared, difficult to locate anywhere. Adorno's idiosyncratic version of this romantic turn is already at work in this book that he co-authored with Horkheimer. If paranoid rage is the unreflective, nihilist form of the return of repressed nature in a society scarred by domination and fragmentation, then the question is where a reflective, healing form of the recovery of repressed nature is to be found. Part of the answer on a practical level, it is clear, would be a radical transformation of society, though Horkheimer and Adorno, here as elsewhere, do not shed much light on this question. Part of the answer on a cultural level, for Adorno, is the unfolding of a "mimetic" moment in reflection itself: a moment fully responsive to all that remains outside the identifications and schematizations of instrumental thought. This promise is found, first of all, in art, characterized as it is by an attention to the material texture of things and a responsiveness to the experience of suffering. It is the task of philosophy in an age that has betrayed the promises of the enlightenment to develop this mimetic capacity in a movement of thought that is at once narrative, holistic, and hermeneutic, that is to say, concerned not simply with a conceptual mapping of the world but with an articulation of the meaning of what has happened in the world. For Horkheimer and Adorno, it is true, the only promise left appears to be that which can be paradoxically sustained through a totalizing critique of modernity, an exposure of the failure of the historical promise of freedom, reconciliation, and redeemed nature. This is the romantic appeal to nature in the mode of a negative dialectic. There does, then, remain a certain division of labor within this romantic diagnosis of social and psychic division: if romantic poetry and romantic social philosophy alike seek to clarify the correlation between the social and the psychic, the task of social philosophy has largely been to comprehend the larger historical process at the level of social life, while the task of poetry has usually been to illuminate the way this is all played out at the level of concrete individual life. In Wordsworth's "Tintern Abbey," for instance, the sequence of pre-modern, modern, and utopian appears as the sequence of exuberant child, troubled and disoriented youth, and elegiacally poised adult for whom the life of the mind and the life of friendship, vision and companionship, are the things to be found and held to in the falling away of everything else in loss and absence.

 Rousseau, I think, ultimately belongs to a different tradition of the romantic turn to Nature or Being, one that I will address below, but his thinking does cross through this dialectical tradition in important respects. Rousseau, too, discerns in modernity an increase in social complexity or social differentiation. He, too, discerns in these new forms of differentiation a whole range of social and psychic illnesses. But he does not, as in the tradition running from Schiller through Adorno, emphasize the spread of instrumental reason and its disintegrative consequences. He concentrates, rather, on the disintegrative consequences of new forms of social dependence in collision with new forms of individualism. Rousseau, as Pierre Manent has shown in a brilliant essay, is the first Proust of our literature. He has studied our vanities and pretentions, our deceptions and self-deceptions, and above all our corrosive habit of comparing ourselves with others all the time: "the man who is always comparing," as Manent says, "is the man who, in his relations with others, thinks only of himself, and in his relations with himself, thinks only of others." This is the divided modern self. This is the self of envy and *ressentiment* studied by Blake, Tocqueville, Kierkegaard, Dostoevsky, Nietzsche, and, again, Proust. This is the self of latent paranoid rage studied by Horkheimer and Adorno. In his major constructive political work, *The Social Contract*, Rousseau sketches a surpassing of this divided self through the construction of a civic order in which a moral equality is to replace a vanished natural equality: a civic order that is to turn damaged natural individuals into integrated citizens of the social whole. Yet Rousseau, in his influential diagnostic writings, nonetheless appeals to a sort of natural standard for any political project. He, too, looks to Nature, to a natural independence, for a standard of spontaneity and poised freedom, the ground of a self not torn apart by the distorted relationships of an individualist, ideologically egalitarian, actually inegalitarian society. He, too, looks for the lost inner nature that, free and sane, has been damaged in modern society: a nature to be found anew on a further horizon, in a transformed society. But at this point it becomes clear that the lost nature to which Rousseau appeals, like that to which the tradition from Schiller to Adorno appeals, is largely indeterminate, less a reality that could be clearly found than the sign of a life we are missing, an invocation to a life we are longing for. It is a figure of a healing of the damages of our social life, part of a vision of social and spiritual renewal. The ultimate horizon of promise in this sort of romantic approach to Nature, indeed, is a reconciliation of free humankind and the whole of nature: inner nature, the nature of other persons, and outer nature. These ideals, including a reconciliation of the built world of human work and the natural world itself, are as old as Isaiah, and to recall this is to recognize the biblical horizon of redemption that has been translated in this critical-utopian interpretation of the ambiguities of modernity. Perhaps the utopian indeterminacy of the translation, a sort of palimpsest of immemorial longing, has been at once the strength and the weakness of this dynamic or dialectical approach to Nature in modern romantic thought.[12]

Yet there is in modern thought another sort of romantic approach to Nature or Being that is less dynamic, less shaped by the biblical pattern of historical journey and ultimate reconciliation. If Rousseau belongs to the post-biblical tradition in his diagnostic works of social philosophy, including both the *First Discourse* and the *Second Discourse*, he belongs to this other tradition in his works of educational philosophy and of solitary meditation, including *Emile* and *The Reveries of a Solitary Walker*. The latter evoke a care for the self that takes place at a distance from the familiar social world, either in a small community of family and friends and teachers, or in solitude. What is affirmed is the possibility of an organic development of the powers of the self and, above all, of the poised independence of the self in relation to its own being and to natural being as a whole. The Axial Age frame of spiritual freedom that is retrieved and translated here, I think, is at least in part that of Hellenistic philosophy. It is the figure of the Stoic or the Epicurean sage, perhaps as mediated by Montaigne, that shapes this picture of a genuine independence discovered once the lures, obsessions, and perilous forms of dependence of the social world have been set at a distance. Stoicism and Epicureanism, it is true, provide very different pictures of the whole: the former teaches a picture of a divine providence at work in the manifold of being, in which the sage can participate by inwardly unfolding the life of wisdom and virtue, while the latter teaches a picture of atoms falling into patterns in a void, the contemplation of which, however, permits a serenity of wisdom and virtue akin to that of the Stoic. In both approaches, as Pierre Hadot has emphasized, the ascetic care for the self that leads to independence is inseparable from a practice of philosophy as a way of life, as a daily discipline of conduct, reflection, spiritual freedom. Rousseau owes more to Stoicism than to Epicureanism in his own naturalist philosophy of independence—at least if the Savoyard vicar's meditation on religion in *Emile* is to be taken as a guide. What is sought, again, is an independence found through a life in nature that is simple, open, balanced, self-shaping. One can surely see affinities between Rousseau's vision and the turn to Nature of influential romantic writers like Wordsworth and Thoreau.

Even Emerson, for all his post-Christian inner light idealism, can be seen in this way. "Compensation" reads like a luminous translation of an ancient Stoic perspective. Nature in this current of romanticism is approached less as a dynamic promise of a total transformation of self and nature alike than as the outer bedrock, as it were, the abiding objective whole that lends perspective to the self that would be spiritually free.[13]

There are in the existentialist tradition after Kierkegaard, too, elements of this translation of a Hellenistic perspective. It would be an error to overemphasize these. Existentialist philosophy in general is decidedly post-biblical in its orientations. The concern with inward striving, the emphasis on wresting an inauthentic self away from its dispersion in idols for an authentic, free, self-gathered existence, the dramatic preoccupation with an affirmative stance in the face of death, the concern with a committed conduct of life in the absence of secure foundations: all this is surely the translation of a "strenuous" or "activist" biblical tradition that goes back to the prophets. Yet, too, there is in the existentialist tradition a recurrent turn toward Nature or Being as an abiding whole that is of compelling if elusive relevance to the self seeking an independent presence of mind and authentic presence to itself. Nietzsche's teaching of *amor fati* sounds like an attempt to rearticulate a Stoic perspective. One sees something of this in Camus, as well, and even in Merleau-Ponty. Perhaps, finally, these two versions of the romantic turn to Nature or Being, as I've characterized them, cannot be clearly separated: they seem to cross through one another in complex ways. What is essential is some horizon of the whole in relation to which the self that would be spiritually free takes its bearings.[14]

A long perspective like this one, further, casts light on the transformation of pastoral in romantic and post-romantic poetry and, surprising as it may sound to say so, in existentialist philosophy at times. This is not the space to address this vast question in any detail, but a helpful hint might emerge in this light. Pastoral in modern culture is inevitably sentimental, as Schiller puts it, rather than naïve—though pastoral is already sentimental, or reflective and ironic, in Virgil. Pastoral is developed in two directions from the romantic period on: the most traditional feature of pastoral, the representation of shepherds or ordinary workers of the rural world as emblematic of the human condition, is occasionally renewed, as in Wordsworth, but over time abandoned out of a distrust of the illusions and problematic class hierarchies involved in the whole strategy; the other feature of pastoral, the replacement of the shepherd by the solitary "pastoral speaker," as Paul Alpers puts it, unfolds into the romantic poetry of nature. The shepherd becomes the meditative poet that the shepherd always was in any case: but the literary trope is now adopted with earnestness and explored as a path to spiritual freedom. There is still at work in all this the traditional pastoral movement of a retreat to the renovative natural world—a hill in the country, a garden, a Walden Pond, a Sorgue River, a place to the side of the road—and a return to the complex and perilous social world, a back-and-forth movement whose promise of transformation is given an influential development (at least in English-language traditions) in Shakespeare's comedies and romances. The measure of irony at play in the pastoral tradition is therefore maintained, inevitably, even as the literary genre is transposed into a resonant philosophical mode. Virgil, one could say, already pointed in this direction. He had hoped to become an Epicurean philosopher. In Book II of *The Georgics* he affirms that a poetry of the rural world, or of nature as a whole, can serve as a sufficient path to poised independence in the absence of philosophy:

> For my own part my chiefest prayer would be:
> May the sweet Muses, whose acolyte I am,
> Smitten with boundless love, accept my service,
> Teach me to know the paths of the stars in heaven,
> The eclipses of the sun and the moon's travails,
> The cause of earthquakes, what it is that forces
> Deep seas to swell and burst their barriers
> And then sink back again, why winter suns
> Hasten so fast to plunge themselves in the ocean
> Or what it is that so slows the lingering nights.
> But if some chill in the blood about the heart
> Bars me from mastering these sides of nature,
> Then will I pray that I may find fulfillment
> In the country and the streams that water valleys,
> Love rivers and woods, unglamorous. O to be
> Wafted away to the Thessalian plains

Of the Spercheus, or Mount Taÿgetus
Traversed by bacchant feet of Spartan girls!
O who will set me down in some cool glen
Of Haemus under a canopy of branches?[15]

The Hellenistic philosopher and the pastoral poet or, more broadly, the poet of nature thus have similar concerns: in Lucretius these concerns come together in one and the same voice; in Virgil they are evoked as analogous paths. The life of the mind, in Oppen's sense, or the life of spiritual freedom, is found through wonder, openness, and attention to the whole wherein the existing self comes to awareness of itself, comes to care for itself. This requires a certain stepping back from life in the cave, as Plato puts it, or of life in the city of struggles for power and wealth and prestige, as the Hellenistic philosophers and the philosophical and pastoral poets of the age of Lucretius and Virgil put it, or of life amid the dispersive illusions and conformist pressures of the world of the public and the herd and a savage torpor, as modern romantics and existentialists put it. This, I think, is an important part of the deep Axial Age background to modern existentialist searches for a spiritual freedom demanding a measure of solitude that, at the same time, remains dialectically related to social life.

Axial Age paths of spiritual freedom, I noted above, involve not only an inward turn to a transcendent horizon but also an ascetic discipline. This can be severe, as in the Christian tradition, or mild, as in the Epicurean school, but it is always there in some measure. It is one of the meanings of the detaching of the self from the shadows of the cave, the corrosive struggles of the city, the idols of the world, the illusions of unreflective desire. It is one of the meanings, in the first millennium before the Common Era, of the liberation of spirit from the familiar world. Existentialist traditions in modern culture, in rearticulating Axial Age paths of spiritual freedom, rearticulate, too, Axial Age paths of ascesis.

In the context of ancient Greek philosophy, as Pierre Hadot reminds us, the term *askesis* referred to practices of spiritual *exercise*, of spiritual discipline. Hadot is concerned to clarify the place of such practices in an ancient world in which, he argues, philosophy was understood first of all as a way of life, based in an existential choice, and only then as a form of discourse as well. He provides a detailed account of the characteristic spiritual exercises of the Hellenistic schools in particular: the gathering or concentration of the self at risk of dispersal; the reflective examination of the conduct and disposition of the self; the meditation on death; the meditation on the whole; the bracing and exhilarating contemplation of things under the aspect of the whole. All of these practices were meant to serve a transformation of the self. The Christian tradition, Hadot points out, later borrowed such exercises for its own spiritual and metaphysical horizons. This is true, yet it is also true, even if we are unable to trace all the connections, that ancient Greek philosophers themselves borrowed such exercises from older religious traditions, notably, in the case of Plato, Orphic and Pythagorean traditions. This reminds us of the other meaning that ascesis has long had in our culture, namely, asceticism, a practice of renunciation, self-renunciation, and sublimation. "Spirit is the life that itself cuts into life," as Nietzsche has Zarathustra say, not only opening a door to Freud but also providing a suggestive hint for a theory of the origins and unfolding of culture in general. In our own culture, shaped by Jewish and Christian ethical and devotional traditions, the whole Greek philosophical tradition is likely to seem chilly in its quest for independence. We value an independence that is not simply virtuous, in the resonant ancient sense of the term, but at the same time responsive, concerned, compassionate. Yet all of these Axial Age currents, in time, come to cross through one another. What is the place of such paths of spiritual ascesis in the modern world?[16]

The question of the attitude of modern society as a whole toward the ascetic emphasis of Axial Age metaphysical frames is a vast question, to be sure, one that I can hardly hope to address in detail here. A few broad trends do have to be held in mind, however, in order to see clearly the significance of the orientations that existentialist traditions lend to modern culture.

It might seem, at first glance, that modernity in general has been a long repudiation of the Axial Age concern with ascesis as a way to freedom. We think of modernity, after all, as an epoch of naturalism, the body, a decisive worldliness, a turning away from transcendent horizons, a commitment to the technological transformation of the natural and the social world for the sake of prosperity and well-being, a generally materialist or even hedonistic stance, and so forth. Yet things are more ambiguous. Charles Taylor has coined the expression the "Great Reform" to refer to a movement in modern culture that runs from the late medieval period through the entire modern epoch. This movement, he argues, begins with the effort on the part of social elites to establish, among themselves as well as the lower classes, a greater measure of civility and a greater attention to religious practice and moral improvement. This concern with self-fashioning and civic organization includes a range of projects, from efforts to subdue the violence of the nobility to attempts to defuse the extravagance of popular religious celebrations and social rituals like carnival. In the sixteenth and seventeenth centuries, under the pressures of the wars of religion, the formation of large bureaucratic states, and the emergence of the modern capitalist economy, this older project of religious and civic reform becomes intertwined with a project of military, political, and economic organization. "The ideal of civility," Taylor writes, "with its core image of taming raw nature, already involves what we might call a stance of reconstruction towards ourselves. It takes form in programmes and methods of 'self-fashioning' [...]. We treat our own baser nature as raw matter to be controlled, reshaped, and in certain cases eliminated, in order to impose a higher form on our lives. Of course, there are affinities to traditional ethical outlooks, Christian and ancient. [...] But what is special about this new outlook is the emphasis on will, and on the imposition of form on an inert and refractory matter." A transformative will, then, is directed at the natural world, the social world, and the inner world of the emergent modern self: this connects the Cartesian project of the conquest of nature and the Protestant project of the shaping of the social body as a vehicle of the divine will (or, more generally, as a vehicle of a national will in struggle with other national wills). No doubt this distinctly modern preoccupation with the transformation of the given is intensified with the passage to the industrial phase of capitalism. The defining ascetic discipline of modernity, from this point of view, is not a spiritual discipline but a discipline of production imposed on everyone, the ascendant commercial classes as well as the new types of working classes, and enforced by the demands of an unprecedented economic system. This is the sort of discipline that Weber sought to illuminate in his study of the

Protestant ethic and the spirit of capitalism. This whole ascetic world of disciplinary production, in fact, has been theorized in different ways in a line extending from Marx and Weber through Adorno and Foucault. Taylor brings out what Foucault, too, if read beyond the striking images of nightmarish enclosure, clarifies: that this modern project is effective in part because it relies, not simply on external enforcement, but on a disciplinary education whereby subjects of the modern order are taught to internalize a range of techniques for improvement, efficiency, heightened performance, productive self-fashioning. The technocratic academy is a fine example of the process. A certain type of ascetic discipline becomes a requirement for making one's way in the modern world.[17]

Yet from the Renaissance on, of course, there have always been counter-currents in modern culture as well. The humanist movement of the Italian Renaissance, if in part a dimension of the project described by Taylor, is in part an orientation that widens this project in the name of creative life and breadth of spirit. The rescue of the life of "sentiment" and concrete perception is an important counter-current of the Enlightenment, one later taken further by the romantic movement, where a concern with full development of the individual, an old Renaissance ideal, is revived and attached to an affirmation of passion, spontaneity, imagination, expression, the natural individual, and the horizon of nature as a whole. The romantic movement in turn gives rise to the whole adventure of wayward, anti-puritanical desire explored in bohemian and avantgarde sub-cultures, an adventure later popularized in the counter-cultural movements of the sixties. Here, too, one would have to recall the vital history of countercultures like jazz that have always refused the productivist discipline gradually imposed on the entire world. From the point of view of contemporary life, it is true, all of these currents may seem to have been simply preparations for the circus of consumer culture. But this is an optical illusion. Voices in these traditions are hardly prophets of such a culture. They are prophets, or exemplary voices, of another path that our culture as a whole has not taken, one still available, barely, as Char says, on the footpaths to the side of the road (PA, 179).

It is nevertheless fair to say that consumer culture readily draws into its field of operation any impulse it finds that is not already productivist. Contemporary society, seen in this long perspective, is a thoroughly paradoxical reality. It involves, in particular for the privileged classes but to a considerable extent across class boundaries, a heightened individualism, a release of the individual from traditional social and cultural forms of embeddedness. This trend is accompanied by the widespread ideologies in our time of mobility, flexibility, plasticity, dispersive intensities of feeling, and so forth. It is accompanied, too, by what Nicole Aubert has called the "manic-depressive" rhythm of subjectivity in our "hyper-modern" social world. This is not, as was sometimes said twenty or thirty years ago, a surpassing of the bourgeois ego: it is the dominant form of the bourgeois ego in our time. And it would be an error to see in this reality some simple vanishing of the iron cage or normalizing grid that Weber and Foucault have described in their studies of an older phase of capitalist society. For the dislodging of the individual from traditional forms of embeddedness and frames of coherence, in fact, takes place amid a staggering acceleration of the same old productivist order. The postmodern phase of this order at once trains us to perform and scatters us in unreflection. The risk is that desire and discipline alike will be made stupid. The thing we are all encouraged to be, it would seem, is an unhappy synthesis of the disciplined individual of Foucault and the aesthetic individual of Kierkegaard: a highly efficient, strategically savvy, basically dispersed self, threatened by disintegration, adrift in a high-speed network of production and consumption, a network as unrelenting in its performative demands on the individual as it is indifferent to the coherence of the individual. This is life for the fortunate and the relatively fortunate. For the unfortunate, the dispossessed, there is life in the desolate spaces of what Mike Davis has called a planet of slums.[18]

These are not the issues I mean to address here. Yet some background of this sort needs to be borne in mind in order to understand the significance of modern rearticulations of Axial Age disciplines of spiritual freedom. I've tried above merely to sketch some of the shadows on the walls of the cave. I've meant to suggest that the dominant ascetic disciplines of the modern world are less paths to spiritual freedom than paths to efficient performance or instrumental success. The system, as we say, would like us to ignore the difference. Romantic and existentialist traditions have tried to remind us of the difference.

What happens in these traditions, I think, is that they unfold immanent analogues of ancient modes of spiritual exercise. One sees this, first of all, in a common romantic pastoral movement, a *turn* from the social world to the open of Nature, or Being, in the hope of discovering some fuller human life that has been narrowed, flattened, damaged, forgotten. "How have we forgotten / That which is clear, we / Dwindle, but that I have forgotten / Tortures me" (CP, 152), Oppen says in one of his poems. One finds this sort of analogue, too, in the common existentialist theme of *stepping back* or *wresting oneself away* from the practices and norms that are familiar in a given social world, in the hope of disclosing the movement of freedom that is the source of an authentic life. Solitude is shown to be a moment of genuine life with others. One sees this sort of analogue, in a particularly suggestive way, in one of the major practices of existential phenomenology: the attempt to *uncover* the character of human being in the world at a primordial level prior to the reified frameworks that condition our habits, feelings, thoughts, and responses. The task is to clear away the accumulated abstractions that hamper our capacity for genuine encounter with the world: or, as Char says, "to cast off life's ugly accretions and find again the gaze that loved it enough in the beginning to display its foundation" (PA, 135). In the phenomenological tradition, it is true, this involves first of all a critique of epistemology, an attempt to see who and how we are in the world at some level occluded by the dominant modern frameworks of science and philosophy (generally taken to be Cartesian, Lockean, or Kantian in nature, that is, taken to be bound to a subject-object paradigm that this phenomenological approach then shows to derive from some more basic participation of human being in Being). Yet to recognize the impulse animating this philosophic project is to see that it goes beyond a solely epistemological concern: it is part of a romantic protest against the fragmentation of the self in the whole instrumental world of modernity. It is part of the existentialist concern to get back to what, half a century ago, was called the human condition. Romantic and existentialist writers want to discover some vital space of eros, attention, openness to the whole, and reflection on where we are that, they fear, tends to be blocked in our everyday social world. How will we get near, how will we bring to speech, our own experience? Oppen, with the powerful simplicity that is one of his gifts, says in "Of Being Numerous": "He wants to say / His life is real / No one can say why // It is not easy to speak // A ferocious mumbling, in public / Of rootless speech" (CP, 173).

Axial Age paths of spiritual exercise, like modern rearticulations of these paths, have always been concerned with this disclosure of what is existentially basic, with "what matters," as Oppen says in a letter (SL, 161), with "the sense of where we are," as he says in "A Narrative" (CP, 155). Erich Fromm traces the long arc of this connection in a passage I will cite at length:

> One cannot fully appreciate the nature of alienation without considering one specific aspect of modern life: its *routinization*, and the *repression of the awareness of the basic problems of human existence*. We touch here upon a universal problem of life. Man has to earn his daily bread, and this is always a more or less absorbing task. He has to take care of the many time- and energy-consuming tasks of daily life, and he is enmeshed in a certain routine necessary for the fulfillment of these tasks. He builds a social order, conventions, habits and ideas, which help him to perform what is necessary, and to live with his fellow man with a minimum of friction. It is characteristic of all culture that it builds a man-made, artificial world, superimposed on the natural world in which man lives. But man can fulfill himself only if he remains in touch with the fundamental facts of his existence, if he can experience the exaltation of love and solidarity, as well as the tragic fact of his aloneness and of the fragmentary character of his existence. If he is completely enmeshed in the routine and in the artefacts of life, if he cannot see anything but the man-made, common-sense appearance of the world, he loses his touch with and the grasp of himself and the world. We find in every culture the conflict between routine and the attempt to get back to the fundamental realities of existence. To help in this attempt has been one of the functions of art and of religion, even though religion itself has eventually become a new form of routine.

Art, too, one might add, readily becomes a new form of routine. Fromm suggests that an important task of art in our world is to renew our awareness of what existential phenomenologists call our fundamental being-in-the-world. This is a dimension of the task that I have characterized as an immanent analogue in existential writing of an ancient spiritual discipline. It is clear that in this passage Fromm draws loosely on existentialist currents in modern culture, on the phenomenological tradition in twentieth-century philosophy, and on the Hegelian Marxist thought of his old Frankfurt School companions (they would speak of "reification" where he speaks of "routinization" and "repression of awareness"). The book in which the passage appears, *The Sane Society*, was published in 1955, the same year in which Marcuse's *Eros and Civilization* was published. It is representative of a way of thinking that was quite widespread in the counterculture of the fifties and sixties. Indeed, it is my sense that many readers in our time will find a passage like this one to be naïve or nostalgic. In part, I think, this is because the call to step back from routine in order to encounter the essential has itself become a routinized piece of rhetoric in our culture, notably in the whole realm of advertising that surrounds us. Thomas Frank, in *The Conquest of Cool*, has described this predicament in detail: the marketing executives of the fifties, it turns out, did not appropriate beat or existentialist languages; in fact they were walking in exact step with countercultural voices; there was no temporal lag; the whole culture was mobilizing older romantic and existentialist stances at the same time, for different purposes. Yet, too, this really should not surprise us. There is nothing good in human life that has not been travestied throughout history (one need only call to mind what has been done in the name of, say, freedom, democracy, salvation, or charity). What genuinely matters always has to be retrieved from its spurious and destructive imitations. A second reason why the passage I've cited may sound naïve or nostalgic in our time, I think, is that a radical historicism is something like the air we now breathe and, therefore, we are not as confident as Fromm that there are "fundamental realities of existence" to be discovered beyond or beneath the built world of historical life. The sheer historicist climate of our time is the cultural correlative of an unprecedented material social context. We are creatures of a totally built world. This condition, on the one hand, sustains the extraordinarily promising circulation of multiple cultures and perspectives in the contemporary world: it is, as it were, a material support for the sort of critical, defamiliarizing, cosmopolitan ethos that keeps alive the ideals of all the liberal and utopian social movements of the last sixty years. The openness of this condition is a great promise of our time. This condition, on the other hand, is potentially blinding: an artifice so vast, dynamic, pervasive, and continually changing that we are perhaps no longer sure we can see anything outside it. Its openness can come to seem closed. This is the condition that Jean Baudrillard has described in a language of hyperbole and Borgesian paradox, and that Fredric Jameson has redescribed in a more philosophically respectable language, so to speak, the language of a capacious Hegelian Marxist hermeneutic. Baudrillard and Jameson suggest that Nature is gone. They mean first of all that older agricultural rhythms of life are gone, or that a traditional rural world is in the process of being brought to an end, but they clearly want to suggest something else as well. What would it mean if Nature were gone? It would imply a vast change in the way we experience and imagine human nature. We are in the Matrix. Everywhere we look, on all sides, we see not Nature, or Being, or the Whole, or the Transcendent, or the Open: we see, extending in every direction, the life-world of contemporary high-tech capitalism. We do not even perceive the depth of time in this space. Mystics, it is said, experience eternity as a visionary deepening of the here and now. The perpetual present of our world is the dimensionless parody of such an experience. Eternity has been cancelled. It was not productive. The depth of time has been erased. It was not quick enough to keep up. The blue-gray of the sky at dawn and dusk has been replaced by the blue-gray of the computer screen, pulsing and glowing round the clock, every second of your life. You are not supposed to sleep, or rest, or pause for thought.[19]

Nevertheless. It has always been the task of religion, philosophy, and art, the three forms of what Hegel calls absolute spirit, to see what matters, to call us back to what matters, to call us outward to what matters. Religion, philosophy, and art, in their different ways, have addressed the question of the whole and our life in the whole. Axial Age metaphysics articulated pictures of the whole, horizons of the good, and paths of discipline required for spiritual freedom. But the question of the whole, in modern culture, has been fragmented: it is variously taken up by natural science (post-Newtonian cosmology), sociology and philosophy of history (interpretative narratives of the historical whole), and poetry and existentialist philosophy (untimely pictures or glimpses of the lost or hidden whole of metaphysics). This threefold picture is meant to recall, in different terms, Kant's threefold differentiation of modern culture. The scientific picture, the background picture, is divorced from questions of existential significance for us. I have argued that the Hegelian and the Kierkegaardian approaches to our search for meaningful freedom, or the approach of historicist sociology and the approach of existentialist philosophy, are perspectives equally necessary to our self-understanding. They complement one another. Each, in the absence of the other, risks dogmatism, one-sidedness, blindness. It has been the task of both, in modern culture, to take us out of our cave, out of our enclosure in a reified and routinized artifice of productive performance and instrumental thought. The great modern sociologists awaken us to the social ground we stand on as we seek lives in freedom. The great modern existentialists awaken us to the groundless burden and freedom of the concretely existing individual not only socially situated but also open to the mystery of the whole.

The shared task of historical sociology, on the one hand, and of existentialist literature and philosophy, on the other, then, has been, in Fromm's terms, to unsettle our routines and place us back in touch with the fundamental realities of our existence. It is worth setting beside one another two clear statements of this project from these different points of view. An impressive account of this task from a sociological perspective is provided by Fredric Jameson, in an early book, in terms of an Hegelian Marxist or a dialectical hermeneutic:

> In the long run, therefore, what we have called the idealizing tendency inherent in abstract thought reflects the establishment of the various specialized disciplines, or in other words the division of labor itself; it is because thought has become a specialized domain, and the property of specialists, that it tends thus to hypostasize itself. In this sense the anti-idealistic thrust of Marxism simply aims at breaking the spell of the 'inverted world' of conceptual thought. The dialectic is designed to eject us from this illusory order, to project us in spite of ourselves out of our concepts into the world of genuine realities to which those concepts were supposed to apply. We cannot, of course, ever really get outside our own subjectivities; to think so is the illusion of positivism; but, every time they begin to freeze over, to spring us outside our own hardened ideas into a new and more vivid apprehension of reality itself is the task of genuine dialectical thinking.

Such thought is therefore essentially process: it never attains some ultimate place of systematic truth in which it can henceforth rest, because it is as it were dialectically linked to untruth, to that mystification of which it is the determinate negation and against which it is perpetually forced to reclaim a fitful apprehension of reality, itself perpetually in danger of losing contact with the real in its turn. In the context of our present description, which limited itself to an account of the dialectic as a mental operation, dialectical thinking thus proves to be a moment in which thought rectifies itself, in which the mind, suddenly drawing back and including itself in its new and widened apprehension, doubly restores and *regrounds* its earlier notions in a new glimpse of reality: first, through a coming to consciousness of the way in which our conceptual instruments themselves determine the shape and limits of the results arrived at (the Hegelian dialectic); and thereafter, in that second and more concrete movement of reflection which is the specifically Marxist form, in a consciousness of ourselves as at once the product and the producer of history, and of the profoundly historical character of our socioeconomic situation as it informs both solutions and the problems which gave rise to them equally.

Existentialist thinkers, again, undertake a similar movement of defamiliarizing thought at the level of the concretely existing individual, always situated, always with others, always part of a social whole, and at the same time groundless, free, haunted by death, open to the mystery of "the whole thing," as Oppen puts it (CP, 113), and never simply reducible to a moment of a social whole. The inward freedom of this concretely existing individual, as Kierkegaard makes clear, is never simply given but is attained by the individual who chooses it, seeks it, strives to live it out in what Kierkegaard calls "a repetition forward," that is, a commitment to the practical accomplishment of an inward bearing. Gabriel Marcel, in a description of the recurrent movement of stepping back and returning again that this requires, draws on the ancient concept of "recollection," a concept that Kierkegaard himself distrusted owing to the use that Hegel had made of it. Yet Kierkegaard and Marcel are talking about the same thing, a gathering of the self out of its dispersions in things that blind it, in routines that flatten it, a reflective pause in which the self clarifies its relation to its own existence and to wider horizons of life:

> And this at last brings us to recollection, for it is in recollection and in this alone that this detachment is accomplished. I am convinced, for my part, that no ontology—that is to say, no apprehension of ontological mystery in whatever degree—is possible except to a being who is capable of recollecting himself, and of thus proving that he is not a living creature pure and simple, a creature, that is to say, which is at the mercy of its life and without a hold upon it. It should be noted that recollection, which has received little enough attention from pure philosophers, is very difficult to define—if only because it transcends the dualism of being and action or, more correctly, because it reconciles in itself these two aspects of the antinomy. The word means what it says—the act whereby I re-collect myself as a unity; but this hold, this grasp upon myself, is also relaxation and abandon. *Abandon to . . . relaxation in the presence of . . .* — yet there is no noun for these prepositions to govern. The way stops at the threshold.
> [. . .]
> It is within recollection that I take up my position—or, rather, I become capable of taking up my position—in regard to my life; I withdraw from it in a certain way, but not as the pure subject of cognition; *in this withdrawal I carry with me that which I am and which perhaps my life is not.* This brings out the gap between my being and my life.

The re-collecting of the self in reflection is a moment of its passage toward the world in abandon, in openness. Spiritual concentration is a dimension of widened encounter. One hears in this echoes of the sort of ancient spiritual exercise studied in detail by Hadot. One hears in it echoes of a range of Axial Age spiritual disciplines. An ancient concern with spiritual freedom returns, in altered ways, under radically altered circumstances, in the existentialist currents in modern culture. These currents are ultimately allies of, not antagonists of, modern critical sociologies. Char and Oppen develop distinctive versions of this sort of modern existential search. This means that they develop, too, distinctive analogues of an older sort of spiritual practice.[20]

* * *

In our time, amid the high-tech world of the postmodern, how exactly do we hear poets like Char and Oppen? Both are not so far from us in terms of simple chronology. Oppen died in 1982, Char in 1989. Yet their concerns with certain meditative practices and with the sort of solitude these involve might seem to place them at a great distance from our world and its rhythms. While the political questions they engage are still with us in our altered context, it is often said that the existential and metaphysical questions they explore are no longer our questions. Is this true? How do we hear these poets in a world given over to speed, to flows of information, to flickering planes of attention? How do we read them in a world in which technological or constructivist habits of action and thought are as familiar as the phones we use?

I've suggested that we think of both Char and Oppen as meditative poets in search of a space of genuine encounter. For all the differences between them, which are considerable, there are affinities as well. The rhythm of their lives is a measure of their longing to discover what is there, to find all that, as Fromm says, is so often lost to us, hidden to the side of our lives. Char and Oppen travel from the countryside to the city, from the city to the countryside, back and forth, in Oppen's case from country to country and continent to continent as well. They lean into things; they want to find out; they want to see. Figures of this simple and essential movement are everywhere in their work. "Beauty makes its sublime bed all alone," Char writes, "strangely builds its fame among men, beside them but off the path" (M, 149; cf. PA, 179). "Perched in the dawn wind / Of that coast like leaves / Of the most recent weed," Oppen writes, he and his beloved are able to see "the thing happening" (CP, 110). Where weeds lean in the wind, vision takes place, a transparence is found. It is the sort of transparence in which Char's free-spirited Transparents dwell. The *Matinaux* take their baths in a river at the break of day. "When one's vocation is to stir awakening, one begins by washing in the river. The first delight and the first astonishment are for oneself" (M, 75). We cannot be existentially free if we cannot see where we are, and we cannot see where we are if we do not from time to time take a step back, a step to the side: "what was there to be thought / comes by the road" (CP, 199). "Once again we had to leave [...] and this road, which looked like a long skeleton, led us to a country that had only its breath with which to climb the future" (OC, 803).

If it is important to find our way to what Fromm calls the fundamental realities of our existence, or to what Oppen in "The Mind's Own Place" calls the "common experience, the ground under our feet," it is no less important to find the words for this search. Our words or ways of talking, too, have often lost their way in the blinding enclosures of our lives. Among the consequences of social reification, Horkheimer and Adorno underline, are a withering of the imagination, a decay of the practice of judgment into a filing according to stereotype, and a reduction of language to blank pointing. "There are words that mean nothing / But there is something to mean," Oppen says (CP, 149). Char and Oppen are writers with very different styles. Char's poems are quick, carved, compressed, abrupt; Oppen's are patient, bare, quiet, circling. Char's poems, "words in archipelago," traces or fragments of a larger quest always beyond them, are almost invariably bold, decisive; Oppen's poems, though they include moments of conviction and epiphanic disclosure, are on the whole hesitant, measured, riddled with silences, questioning, self-questioning. Char speaks of an art of "premonition" and a "transhumance of the word": he seeks a word at once vividly felt and disclosive of distances. Oppen speaks of an exact or even exactly impoverished word: he seeks a truthful word bound to the contradictions of a patiently searching mind. Yet both of these poets are meditative writers. The poems of both seem to arrive out of an amplitude of pause. Both turn words, phrases, and images over and over in their minds, come at them again and again from different points of view, embrace contradiction as the substance of our lives and our efforts at understanding, seek an unfamiliar texture of articulation true to their concern to discover a genuine freedom of encounter, response, reflection, orientation.[21]

One feels that, for both of these poets, writing is a sort of spiritual exercise, the disclosive tracing of the life of the imagination, as Char sees this, the articulated path of the life of the mind, as Oppen understands it.

Such a meditative practice of writing, emerging out of the circumstances of a particular life, addresses what Oppen calls the "old questions" (CP, 109), including who we are, where we are in relation to others, where we are in relation to the whole, what horizons we are to turn our care toward, how we are to live. Both Char and Oppen, as I have underlined at various points in this book, respond fully to the world around them, in their poems as in their lives. At the same time both undertake a sounding of the traditional metaphysical question of the whole in which one lives: the whole, for both, as for a long tradition of romantic and existentialist writers, is approached as Nature or Being. I have tried in this chapter to cast some light on this dimension of modern literature and philosophy from the romantic period on. I have tried, in earlier chapters, to clarify the different ways in which Char and Oppen explore the question. Char comes out of a visionary tradition, one that includes Nietzsche as well as Rimbaud and Éluard, and he opposes at one and the same time traditional metaphysical dualisms and modern empiricisms or realisms. The immanent transcendence of poetry, figured as the apparitional light and erotic call of beauty, is imagined as a slope, a passage along a certain slant of light that arrives unexpectedly, a scaling of a hill or a mountain, an ascensional power in the open spaces of the whole. "Born of the call of becoming and the anguish of retention, the poem, rising from its well of mud and stars, will bear witness, almost silently, that there was nothing in it that did not truly exist elsewhere, in this rebellious and solitary world of contradictions" (FM, 169). "The urgent, jagged, bold writing of a blue lantern—of Ventoux in its childhood—always ran on the horizon of Montmirail that at every moment our love brought me, took away from me" (PA, 203). There is, for Char as for Oppen, no other transcendence than this immanent rising, returning, finding a slope again. The outer world is a night of ruin even wider and deeper than the night of transparence and the occasional daylight we find there. To see the elsewhere of the widened life, to partake of this life found only in the motion of the quest itself, demands the sort of analogue of faith (or what Char calls hope) and the practice of clairvoyance that I tried to describe at the end of my chapter on Char. Oppen, though he comes out of a realist tradition, also turns in wonder toward an immanent transcendence that he finds to be inseparable from spiritual freedom, from an openness of response that is a basic dimension of freedom. He, too, imagines this as a vertical space analogous to the height of a traditional frame of transcendence. It is a space where, he says, the mind "rises into happiness, rising into what is there," a space where this rising is at the same time a passion, an event of encounter in which one is swept up in something larger than oneself: "thought leaped on us in that sea" (CP, 155–56). All is ruin, car wreck, shipwreck, failure, erosion, fatal rock, Oppen says again and again, and at the same time all is clearing, openness, luminosity, disclosive miracle of place, clarity of pebbles in the water of a shore. Perhaps religion began in helplessness and fear, fear of the power of nature and fear of death, as a long enlightened tradition claims, or fear of our own violence, as Durkheim and Girard suggest in different ways. Perhaps, as Nietzsche says, it began in an attempt to give meaning to our suffering. As world religions unfolded, they tended to affirm the wonder that is a dimension of our opening to the whole, to the good, and to a deeper horizon of spiritual freedom. Axial Age philosophy borrowed this affirmation, linked it to curiosity, and called it one of the fundamental roots of the search for wisdom. "Though it's against the law to harbor wonder // In the prison of the post-Hellenic world," as Lucie Brock-Broido puts it, modern poetries and existentialist and phenomenological philosophies have kept this a part of our horizon. We cannot live without some measure of it. Wonder awakens energy, care, openness to life. Wonder stirs the advent of generosity. Wonder inspires praise amid the endless weather of elegy. If there is a poet who hovers beside the work of both Char and Oppen, and whom each of them only rarely mentions, it is Rilke, in particular the Rilke of the *Duino Elegies* and the *Sonnets to Orpheus*.[22]

Wonder awakens eros as eros awakens wonder. Both Char and Oppen are love poets. This is immediately palpable in Char's work. Like Shelley, like Éluard, Char is a love poet in almost all his poems, from beginning to end. Eros is the animating élan of his response to reality, including the natural world, which enters the space of his poems under the aspect of the near and far beloved. Love is a desire for a sheer apparition in the texture of things. "Emerge, appear," Char says, in a poem written in the dark of the early forties, addressing at once beauty and the beloved. "We have never finished with the sublime well-being of the slender swallows. Avid to approach the ample lightening. Uncertain in time love has widened.

Uncertain, they alone, at the summit of the heart. Such hunger I have" (FM, 45). The ruin of the whole is countered by the passion of the lover, for only in this light is the miraculous scope of things disclosed, only in this light is the *allègement*, the lightening, found (FM, 28). Oppen is a quieter sort of love poet. He does not belong to the extended company of Shelley. His love poetry is a song of gratitude for a deepening of fidelity, care, and conversation in time. This is not exactly a major tradition in our literature. For Oppen, in any case, as for Char, the luminous disclosure of Being, against the groundless abyss of ruin, is embedded in the life of love. For Char, call and response, the life of the hunt, are the way to presence, to spaciousness. For Oppen, care and response, the turn and return of conversation, are the way to presence, to the light of things.

Romantic and existentialist traditions in modern culture, I have said, rearticulate Axial Age paths of spiritual freedom. In Char and Oppen the rethinking of ascesis involves all the bearings I've just sketched: a stepping aside from the routines of our lives; a meditative immersion in words turned over and over in the mind, sounded over and over on the page; a turning to the whole of Nature or Being, the whole of ruin and wonder where we find ourselves at once frightened and astonished, where we are drawn to a strange, groundless, nearly incredible freedom. That they are both love poets tells a still deeper story. A spiritual discipline that both Char and Oppen could be understood to rework, in different ways, is one of the most memorable of the Axial Age disciplines: the path of visionary Eros that Plato has Socrates teach in *The Symposium*. This is an inexhaustible parable for the life of lyric poetry. Socrates, according to the dialogue, has learned this path from Diotima, perhaps a priestess of the Eleusinian mysteries. In Plato the mystery is transposed into the conceptual and dialectical terms of a journey to transcendence. Love of a beautiful body, Socrates says, reciting Diotima's visionary recital, leads to love of all beautiful bodies, which in turn leads to love of beautiful minds, love of beautiful cities and laws and constitutions, love of concepts and forms of wisdom, and, ultimately, love of the beautiful itself, an abundant light akin to what in *The Republic* is called the overflowing light of the good. At each step along the way, it turns out, love and insight are not quite enough: they require beautiful "discourses" to accompany them, words that recall the route taken and presage the route to come, words that awaken us, call us to the horizon of the good we desire. These are words of recollection and disclosure at once. Char and Oppen, as I suggested in the earlier chapters of this book, place all this back on an immanent footing. Eros walks abroad in the tragic world of time. Eros is the source of companionship, vision, and disclosure. It is a dimension of openness. It animates our turning to horizons of value. Child of poverty and resource, barefoot and indigent, spending nights on the side of the road, Eros is the source of the search for the slope of poetry, as Char says, or for the clarification of what matters, as Oppen says. To sustain the genuine search of illuminative Eros, in the face of the sophistries on all sides, is to practice a sort of ascesis. We become what we behold, as Blake says, and we become free in the light of what we turn toward with care. Plato teaches this, too, as do the prophets, as do finally all the sages. Thus, if we would be free, we are responsible for the directions in which we turn. There is an ascesis of care in this that is a path of disclosure. It is not a narrowing but an opening. "If I come out of this alive," Char says in a passage in *Leaves of Hypnos* that I cited in chapter 2, "I know I'll have to break with the aroma of these essential years, silently push away from myself (not repress) my treasure, take myself back to the beginning, to my most indigent bearing in those years when I was in search of myself, without claim to mastery, in naked unsatisfaction, with a barely glimpsed knowledge and a questioning humility" (#195). Oppen calls himself to this sort of path in a poem whose conclusion I cited in chapter 3 and recalled again above, "Guest Room," which ends with the poet and his wife "perched in the dawn wind" of a cliff on the coast, looking out at what is there, "the thing / Happening, filling our eyesight / Out to the horizon" (CP, 110). Earlier in the poem Oppen wrestles with two fears: a fear of homelessness, of a defeat from which recovery is impossible, and a fear of what in his interview with Dembo he calls a condition of "over-protectedness," the unreality of a life hiding from life, in this poem the unreality of the houses and habits of the wealthy. In the penultimate section of the poem, prior to the concluding passage of vision, Oppen recognizes that death is the leveller, "The unspeakable / Defeat," toward which "they," the rich, and he, the wayward son of the rich, and everyone else, after all, live. He speaks of acknowledging our fear and at the same time setting aside our armor: "Like theirs // My abilities / Are ridiculous: //

To go perhaps unarmed / And unarmored, to return // Now to the old questions" (CP, 109). The whole last part of "Route" is a meditative unfolding of this approach to experience, this open life of encounter, from an uncommonly widened perspective.[23]

Time is our "wealthy host," Char says in a late poem (NP, 97–98), a poem that reverses the images of Oppen's "Guest Room" while affirming its existential bearing. We readily invent defenses against time and so block ourselves from what Char in this poem imagines as the far calls and the hidden fountains of the hours. It is no surprise, of course, that we build walls against the erosions of time. We are afraid. There is something missing in the metaphysics of Plato that was not missing in the life of Socrates or the life of Plato: tragedy, anguish, failure, defeat. Plato sees all this, no doubt, but he would like to talk us beyond it. He would like to persuade us that no real harm can come to the just soul, the wise soul, the soul genuinely turned to the good. If we think of the soul as embodied, as having no life beyond its embodied life, then this teaching immediately runs into difficulties. It runs into serious difficulties anyway. Souls inflict harm upon one another, suffer harm from one another, all the time. And yet some version of Plato's teaching is found not only in all Axial Age religions but also in Rousseau, Kant, Emerson, and other modern philosophers. There is some longing at work in this that must be very powerful. In fact a revised version of this teaching returns, surprisingly, in the philosopher who more fiercely than any other attacks Plato's rational idealism, namely, Nietzsche. The young Nietzsche, in *The Birth of Tragedy*, begins his philosophic journey by denouncing Platonic metaphysics in the name of a tragic wisdom. It is against the pointless flux of things that our cities, the social ground we stand on, and our religions and philosophies, the cultural space we find consolation in, are built. Nietzsche would take us out of our enclosures. He would return us, unarmed and unarmored, to the old questions, to the fundamental realities of our existence. He would do so, he says, not out of callousness, not out of cynicism, but out of a concern to discover a fuller life, a deeper encounter with where we are. In *Zarathustra* the tragic artist of *The Birth of Tragedy* comes back as Zarathustra himself. Initially he proclaims a prophetic teaching of an unprecedented form of human life. This teaching is severely revised after an encounter with the nihilist teaching of the soothsayer and the thought of the eternal recurrence. The latter is an eccentric teaching that I set aside here. The issue I want to underline is that Zarathustra, at the end of his three-act drama, sings hymns to the whole and affirms an ecstatic *amor fati* or love of fate. Nietzsche, in this work, through Zarathustra, would like to affirm something analogous to what Plato, in the *Phaedo* and *The Republic*, through Socrates, would like to affirm: that genuine spiritual freedom can sustain a poised affirmation in the midst of suffering, in the face of death. In one important respect, that is, Nietzsche represents Zarathustra in the way Plato represents Socrates: as a free, noble, spirited person to whom all harm may well come but to whose soul no further harm can come. While the dream that something like this is possible has a deep hold on our imagination, as I said a moment ago, it is nevertheless always startling to encounter such a picture. It is so far from our lives. It has been said that Nietzsche's picture fails, in part, because Zarathustra, like Nietzsche, is too frantic or theatrical in his affirmation. His laughter, as Stanley Rosen has put it, is less the laughter of joy than the laughter of hysteria. He protests too much. There is truth in this. And yet those of us without Plato's faith, or without any Axial Age faith, are likely to think that Nietzsche has at least journeyed in the right direction: into the ruinous and wondrous mystery of time. Further, his vision, despite himself, is finally indebted less to the tragic vision of the Greek dramatists than to the redemptive vision of the ancient Jewish prophets. Nietzsche, for all his courage, lost his way in hopeless isolation. Yet his vision is a vision of suffering deepened, gathered, and redeemed in time. It is a vision that can thus be reconnected to the compassion that Nietzsche himself so scrutinized because, like Blake, he saw all the hatred that so often walks to and fro in what we call our love. This is the challenge he leaves for those of us not inclined to abandon the prophets on this point. Failure, defeat, and anguish are the given. The question is what we will do with them.[24]

It is a vision of this sort, with greater poise, that both Char and Oppen unfold in their poetries. The movement of Platonic Eros, the passionate search for what matters, is drawn into a tragic vision of our lives in history and in the boundless whole. The accent of failure may be deeper and clearer in Oppen than in Char. In part this has to do with the distinctive path of Oppen's life, with the weight of disillusion he works through, which I addressed at the end of chapter 2. In part, I think, it has to do with Char's tendency simply to assume his own deepest intuition, an intuition so basic that it literally goes without saying in many of his poems, namely, a pessimistic fear of pointlessness and fatigue that has to be overcome again and again (FH #80). It is this fatigue that his lyricism of hope is meant to counter. "Resistance is only hope. Like the moon of Hypnos, full in every quarter tonight, tomorrow a vision of the passage of poems" (FH #168). "These are the pessimists the future raises. In the course of their lives they see their apprehensions come to pass. Yet the grape cluster that has followed the harvest, above the stock, bends; and the children of the seasons, not ordinarily gathered together, quickly pack the sand at the edge of the wave. That, too, pessimists perceive" (PA, 152). This is the rhythm of pessimism and vision that characterizes the whole of *Leaves of Hypnos*. It is the rhythm that animates *To a Tense Serenity*, a sequence of the early fifties in which Char calls for *une santé du malheur*, a health of misfortune, an expression that could be gathered out of a long tradition of crisis poems. "Today we are closer to disaster than the alarm itself. So it's time to compose a health of misfortune. Even should it appear with the arrogance of a miracle" (RBS, 128). These words, if something like "the wonder" were to replace "the arrogance," could almost serve as an epigraph to Oppen's "Route." There is in Oppen's sequence, too, a rhythm of pessimism and vision, of sobriety and, if not exactly hope, at least presence of mind, persevering clarity. In this ranging poem there is gratitude, as well, salvaged against all odds in a space of disillusion and fear of catastrophe. The major sequence in Oppen's next book, "Some San Francisco Poems," shows a similar rhythm of grief and gratitude. One could perhaps draw a parable out of these sequences by Char and Oppen. There is first a movement of disclosive eros in time. This meets with shipwreck almost from the beginning. Then there is the discipline of the renewal of searching eros in the passage through suffering and disillusion. This is a task to be renewed for the rest of a life. What is found there?

It depends, of course, on the life, on the writer. An old vocation of the lyric has been to lend voice to the work of beginning again. It is my sense that, in the field of contemporary American poetry, the poets who most fully respond to this question, who most deeply explore a renewal of eros in the passage of despair, are women. Why this is so is a question I'll leave for another time. I think in this respect of Thylias Moss and C.D. Wright in particular, two poets who step into the whirlwind of their own lives and our troubled times with uncommon boldness, with passionate curiosity and care. Yet I will conclude here by citing Louise Glück. She is as spare a writer in her way as Oppen. She likes to cut to the bone and see the changes there. Invited to give a commencement address, she speaks of desolation, impoverishment, despair. There are, she says, two ways of responding to despair that are evasions: wild activity, a frantic flight from despair, and simple capitulation, a passive going under in despair. Then there is the response that she calls "the work done through suffering." She speaks of the way this sort of passage through the dark yields renewal, a deepened gratitude, an altered sense of scale:

> The alternative? A life made entirely of will and ultimately dominated by fear. Such a life expresses itself in too prompt, too superficial adjustments of what can, in the external environment, be manipulated, or in a cautious clinging to those habits and forms which, because they are not crucial, cannot, in being lost, do much damage. The deft skirting of despair is a life lived on the surface, intimidated by depth, a life that refuses to be used by time, which it tries instead to dominate or evade. It is all abrupt movement or anxious cleaving; it does not understand that random action is also a kind of stasis. In its horror of passivity, it forgets that passivity over time is, by definition, active. There exists, in other words, a form of action felt as helplessness, a form of will that exhibits, on the surface, none of the familiar dynamic properties of will. Fortitude is will. Can it be taken too far? Yes—but the same argument can be made against all action: when response becomes policy it has ceased to engage directly with circumstance. And I suppose patience, in its various forms, is particularly susceptible to this deterioration.
>
> It is very strange to stand here, wishing you desolation, like the bad fairy at the cradle. You have, all of you, a vocation for learning. And you have been well taught here. Realize, then, that impoverishment is also a teacher, unique in its capacity to renew, and that its yield, when it ends, is a passionate openness which in turn re-invests the world with meaning. What I remember of such moments is

gratitude: the fact of being born immerses us in the world without conveying the daily immensity of that gift. To live in the world in the absence of such knowledge may not be tragic: I don't know; I have no prolonged experience of such a life. But I think some intensity of awareness must be lost, since it depends on contrast. And that intensity is impoverishment's aftermath, and blessing: what succeeds temporary darkness, what succeeds the void or the desert, is not the primary gift of the world but the essential secondary gift of knowledge, a sense of the significance of the original gift, the scale of our privilege.[25]

NOTES

Introduction

1. Claudel, *Art Poétique*, 36; Merleau-Ponty, *The Visible and the Invisible*, 103–05; Rosen, *The Limits of Analysis*, 127–28 and 149–89, and *The Elusiveness of the Ordinary*, 204–50; and Pierre Hadot, *Qu'est-ce que la philosophie antique?* I've slightly modified Alphonso Lingis's translation of the passage from Claudel that Merleau-Ponty cites. Rosen and Hadot, from different perspectives, emphasize the metaphysical search for an articulate vision of the whole. This is not quite the same as the search for a transcendent source or an ultimate foundation. To try to see the whole is to try to see where we are. "Where have you come from, my dear Phaedrus, and where are you going," Socrates says in the first sentence of Plato's *Phaedrus*. "The most crucial question to be asked about any philosopher," Walter Kaufmann writes, "even more important than the question 'What did he mean?', is: What has he seen?" (*Critique of Religion and Philosophy*, 92; cf. 72–73). Julie Annas, in describing the basic shape of Plato's *Republic*, gives a suggestive account of the place of imaginative seeing in the quest of philosophy: "In Book I of the *Republic* we see the ineffectiveness of Socratic methods in dealing with the powerful claim of the moral sceptic, that there is really no reason to be just, and that one should, if one is rational and intelligent, look after one's own interest. Plato took the point, and realized that it was not only particular people like Thrasymachus who were not convinced. In the rest of the *Republic* we move to a different style of arguing. There are no more snappy little arguments with disputable premises. Instead of that, the discussion is expanded; Plato's defence of justice is built up against a large and rich background theory of the nature of the person and society. The claims which Socrates failed to make convincing are fleshed out and become part of a much larger discussion which makes appeal to the philosophical imagination as well as to the narrower kind of cleverness tested by Socrates' methods of arguing" (*Plato's "Republic,"* 57).

2. For detailed accounts of our modern experience of taking place in history and making history, see Pierre Manent, *La cité de l'homme*, and Marcel Gauchet, *La condition historique*, *La révolution moderne*, and *La crise du libéralisme*. It is of course plausible to think of Hegel as the first great thinker of this historicist perspective. Yet, as Manent and Gauchet show, it is a perspective that emerges in the Enlightenment. The "encompassing" or "comprehensive" were once more familiar terms than they are now: they are translations of Karl Jaspers's term, *das Umgreifende*, for the no longer clearly bound or clearly conceptualizable whole (see his *Reason and Existenz* and *Way to Wisdom*). Adorno concludes one of his lectures on metaphysics by evoking the sheer openness that thought reaches toward: "Philosophy has the curious characteristic that, although itself entrapped, locked inside the glasshouse of our constitution and our language, it is nevertheless able constantly to think beyond itself and its limits, to think itself through the walls of its glasshouse. And this thinking beyond itself, into *openness*—that, precisely, is metaphysics" (*Metaphysics*, 68).

3. The modern realist novel emerges at about the same time as the emblematic opposition between sociology and existentialism that I've just sketched. Erich Auerbach, in *Mimesis*, underlines the crucial decade of the 1830s in the emergence of the realist novel (454–92). Stendhal's *Le Rouge et le Noir* was published in 1830, Balzac's *Le Père Goriot* in 1834. Auerbach's book is of course a sweeping history of the representation of reality in western literature from Homer and the J Writer through Virginia Woolf. But in a sense this whole story is told in order to illuminate the way the realist novel takes shape in mid-nineteenth-century France (Auerbach gives less weight to the English novel of the time). The realist novel, Auerbach argues, has two defining characteristics. One is the representation of ordinary people as serious, problematical, or tragic, a stance whose distant origins Auerbach locates in the J Text of the Hebrew Bible and in the gospels of the New Testament. The other is a representation of people as intimately shaped by and responsive to historically "evolving" or "developing" social forces. This sense of reality, if it has distant origins in a Jewish and Christian experience of providential time, more specifically emerges in the French Revolution and its aftermath, coming to philosophical articulation in early nineteenth-century historicism. The realist novel, then, registers the tension between existential and sociological approaches to our lives *from within* a sociological or historicist perspective.

4. Stephen Fredman, in "'And All Now Is War': George Oppen, Charles Olson, and the Problem of Literary Generations," argues that Olson and Oppen, considered as "existentialist" writers, may have as much to do with writers as diverse as Sartre and Celan as with the poets with whom they are usually associated. Eric Mottram, in "The Political Responsibilities of the Poet," similarly characterizes Oppen as an "existentialist," in a broadly Sartrean sense, that is, in a sense that involves an emphasis on social awareness

and political engagement; Mottram also, in passing, likens Oppen to Char in this respect (152). "For Oppen, as for Sartre," Peter Nicholls writes, "the insights of Marxism and existentialism came to be regarded not as incompatible but as complementary" (*George Oppen and the Fate of Modernism*, 52). In "'Not Altogether Alone in a Lone Universe,'" Burton Hatlen emphasizes the weight in Oppen's later poetry of all that Oppen lived through in the thirties, forties, and fifties. Oppen criticizes Char's poetry as rhetorical and abstract in one of his daybooks (SP, 69). His distrust of "Pound's organization of the world around a character, a kind of masculine energy" (IN, 183), would probably inform his response to Char as well. My sketch of Char's life relies on Laurent Greilsamer, *L'éclair au front: la vie de René Char*, Jean-Claude Mathieu, *La poésie de René Char*, Jean Roudaut, "Introduction" to Char's *Oeuvres complètes*, and Dominique Fourcade, "Essai d'introduction," the introduction to a special edition of *L'Herne* devoted to Char's work. My sketch of Oppen's life relies on Mary Oppen, *Meaning a Life*, Rachel Blau DuPlessis, "Introduction" to Oppen's *Selected Letters*, Peter Nicholls, *George Oppen and the Fate of Modernism*, and Oppen, "George Oppen" (the interview with Louis Dembo, abbr. IN). Northrop Frye's characterization of "existential writing" is relevant to the questions I've raised here: "I am not fond of the word ['existential'], but I know of no other that conveys the sense of anchoring an interest in the transcendental in the seabed of human concern. The great systematic thinkers are all aware of the analogical nature of their language, but they throw the emphasis on the unifying of their thought. Unity, or rather unification, of language is for them the appropriate way of responding to a transcendental form of being. Luther, Pascal, and Kierkegaard differ from St. Thomas or Leibniz or Hegel in stressing the negative aspect of analogy, in showing how experience in time eludes final or definitive unification in thought. [. . .] Most 'existential' writing, at least in our day, carries on the transcendental perspective of religion and metaphysics in a language profoundly unsympathetic to any separated realm of immutable being. A great deal of such writing is naturally not religious, but when it is not it is often explicitly antireligious, understanding the relevance of transcendental issues but renouncing them in favor of a greater human freedom" (*The Great Code*, 25–26).

Chapter One. René Char

1. In Char's work the word "invent" often bears a negative inflection. He reaffirms, that is, the basic romantic opposition between "discovery" and "invention," the "organic" and the "mechanical," the "spontaneous" and the "conventional," as well as the basic romantic distrust of an excessive faith in technics and technique in every domain of life (see, for example, "The Inventors," M,

69–70, and "The Library is on Fire," PA, 149). But this is for him an existentially significant distinction that does not entail a poetics of spontaneous expression or self-expression: poetry is an "impersonalizing" work of cutting and carving (PA, 118), a labor of "hermetic workers" (M, 38), a studious making of discriminations by an inner "minutieuse" (MM, 128; PA, 112–13). It should be said, too, that while Char does now and then adopt a few Heideggerian terms, including "la Maison" or "the House" unfolded by poetic language, he is not obsessed with the question of technology. More frequent in his work are criticisms of avarice, conformity, and baseness. This marks a substantive difference with Heidegger. His major philosophical ally, if he has one, is Nietzsche, as Paul Veyne has persuasively shown in *René Char en ses poèmes*, 302–32, and passim. My understanding of Char owes a vast debt to Veyne's 500-page meditation on Char. Veyne's book, in turn, at times reads like an extraordinary unfolding of issues briefly sketched in Georges Mounin's still valuable early response to Char, first published in 1947, now available, along with several later essays, in his *La communication poétique*.

2. On Char's practice of meditation and experience of ecstasy, see Veyne's discussion in *René Char*, 223–44. Veyne writes: "It would sometimes happen that, when night came, René would bid farewell to a friend who was visiting, saying that the hour for his work had rung. His directed reverie was not the same thing as the composition of a poem (which occurred rather in a long session of fierce work, or, as he would say, of furious ascension, pen in hand); reverie involved following, with no particular intention, imaginative tracks, associations of ideas: the different meanings of the word 'chalk,' the lion as an animal and as a constellation, or the map of the sky and its mythology, as one sees from a different angle in *Aromatic Hunters*. In no case was reverie of this sort to take an intellectual turn or to try thinking clearly in the hope of thus expressing itself better. 'It wasn't necessary to embrace the heart of night. It was necessary that the dark be the power where the morning's dew is carved.' These disinterested reveries nourished the act of writing, which was itself highly conscious and voluntary. 'Night bears nourishment, daylight sharpens the nourished part'" (229). As Veyne's citations here show—they are from "Of an Unadorned Night" (PA, 168–69)—Char's practice of reverie does enter his poems. The night of reverie and spiritual voyage that he often evokes (PA, 189; NP, 101, 161–205) is akin to, though perhaps less tender than, the "growing and tender night," the "cool transparent night," the "hiding receiving night," the "mystical moist night-air" that Whitman is drawn to (*Leaves of Grass*, 43, 279, 281, 227).

3. For detailed and insightful discussions of this poem and the entire "Lascaux" sequence, see James Lawler, *René Char*, 51–80, and Elisabeth Bosch, "René Char, Georges Bataille et Lascaux." I've learned a great deal from these essays. A photograph of the painting to which Char's poem is probably a

response can be found in Norbert Aujoulat, *Lascaux: Movement, Space, and Time*, 180–81.

4. The experience of being as emanation is marvelously explored in a five-page meditation on Miró's painting that Char published in 1963 (RBS, 73–78). "An unlikely artist among the dislocations and injunctions of his epoch, Miró gives the latter what it lacks, or what it's looking for: a taste for sources and their taking flight. For in his painting is inscribed precisely that which a civilization in its old age no longer has. Our worn-away condition embraces it, undergoes its attraction. Narcissus in reverse. Our lucid heaviness is effaced. *Homo ludens* directs the game. Another epoch takes shape on all sides, and its plenitude is that of the first day, and its work, the first spark of time's childhood. Advent is without end" (74).

5. Crane, *The Complete Poems*, 160, and Éluard, *Poésie ininterrompue*, 40. On the surprising "impersonality" of many of Char's love poems—linked to the absence in these poems of the familiar "interiorization of the other" in love—see Eric's Marty's insightful discussion in *René Char*, 266–77.

6. Stendhal, *De l'amour*, 64; Shelley, *Poetry and Prose*, 504. "The press of my foot to the earth springs a hundred affections," Whitman says in "Song of Myself" (*Leaves of Grass*, 36). "Camus loves to walk with a supple step in a city street when, by the grace of youth, for a moment the street is entirely fortunate" (RBS, 94; cf. M, 78).

7. Given his heterosexual imagination, it is worth noting that Char, unlike some of his surrealist friends, was not homophobic. He was an open spirit, a free spirit. Advent or emanation, then, is for Char inward as well as outward. Its inward force is eros or enthusiasm. In words written in memory of one of his fallen companions in the Resistance, Roger Chaudon, he writes: "He was the one among us who had the gift of purifying every question through the exactly *just* substance of his response. He loved life as one loves it at forty years, with the eagle's gaze and the titmouse's exuberance. His generosity extended rather than hampered him. He believed that our ten fingers joined to the tenacity of our heart, to a measure of cunning as well, going forth to meet what evil there was (without being contaminated by it and, later, immediately tossing it aside like old junk), held against tyranny resources that we must not lose" (RBS, 22). Char goes on to underline that Chaudon was pessimistic about the course of history and the shape that European society was likely to take after the liberation. His generosity, Char suggests, came from another source. This question is again raised, from a different angle, in Char's "Are There Incompatibilities?" (RBS, 38–39). Georges Mounin, in the last chapter of his early book on Char, writes: "Char has the goodness of despair, unconditional, independent of every scientific or metaphysical justification" (167; cf. 175).

8. Wallace Stevens, *The Palm at the End of the Mind*, 135, 317. Serge Velay writes: "this 'insurgent order' [the poem as Char sees it] suggests a 'climate of

the hunt,' as if the reader, following the example of the poet, were invited on a *quest*. In the 'marvelous' space of the poem, the poet, 'the one who Begins,' 'intercessor' and 'ferryman,' not without cunning, calls the reader to an initiatory journey among the traces of a *passage*" (*René Char*, 103). In a late sequence, "Everyone Gone," Char writes: "Poetry masters the absurd. It's the summit of the absurd: the pitcher that, raised to the height of the loving mouth, fills it with desire and thirst, with distance and abandon. It's the inconstancy in fidelity. It connects the isolated" (ES, 56–57; cf. FM, 191). This is one of the basic contradictions that, for Char, poetry is always to hold to.

9. Eric Marty addresses these questions in a different but not unrelated way in *René Char*, 78–80, 142–43. "Perhaps eros," Forrest Gander writes, "is the fundamental condition of that escalation of meaning necessary to poetry, and of cognition itself. The father of Western logic, Socrates, claimed that he had only one real talent: to recognize at once the lover and the beloved" (*A Faithful Existence*, 8). It's good to see the word "escalation," with its roots in Diotima's ladder of eros, retrieved from its abuse by generals and strategists. Gander, particularly in his book *Science & Steepleflower*, is perhaps the contemporary American poet who is most resonantly "Charrian" in important respects: in the style that embodies at once incisiveness and tenderness; in the sheer intensity of perception; in the awakened eros of an encounter with the world at once exhilarating and wounding. In "Redness of the *Matinaux*" Char writes: "Go to the essential: are you not in need of young trees to replant your forest? / Intensity is silent. Its image is not. (I love that which dazzles me, then accentuates a darkness within me)" (M, 76).

10. On the tension in *Leaves of Hypnos* between a life in touch with the essential and a life hardened to the essential, see Jean-Claude Mathieu, *Poésie et résistance*, 237. There is currently no Georges de La Tour painting known as "The Prisoner." In searching for the painting that Char evokes, I discovered an online site where I learned that Char would have seen a Georges de La Tour painting with this title in a show in France in 1934–35 (see http://www.educnet.education.fr/louvre/ecriture/char2.htm). The painting, however, is now known to be titled "Job and his Wife" or "Job Mocked by his Wife." The second of these titles is rather misleading. A reproduction of the work can be found in Jacques Thuillier, *Georges de La Tour*, 227. As Thuillier's splendid discussion brings out, the painting, retitled, remains powerfully consonant with the response to it that Char expresses in *Leaves of Hypnos*. The emaciated Job is a prisoner of the world, bewildered, still hoping to find his way to understanding and recovery. Char, as it were, uncovers a trace of Job's defiance in La Tour's complex image. This history of reception raises intriguing questions that I haven't space to explore further here.

11. See Frye, *The Great Code*, 229–30. Jean-Claude Mathieu writes: "The notebook [*Leaves of Hypnos*] interiorizes 'fantastic friendship.' If the intimate

is the murmur of earth and night, it is also the network of friendly confidences, confiding gestures, that weave the common present of a collective conscience. This interval of intimacy, where the active being is momentarily relieved from the *idée fixe* of the struggle, is an enclave of freedom. Force of dialogue, resistance of the 'word of the highest silence,' word that the prisoner and the woman exchange at the heart of night: 'Gratitude to Georges de La Tour who overcame the hitlerian darkness with a dialogue between human beings'" (*Poésie et résistance*, 270). Greilsamer casts light on this issue, from a different angle, in *L'éclair au front*, 323–35, emphasizing the importance of a passage in "The Library is on Fire" that I cited in my introduction. Char, so often the solitary turning through the spaces of earth and night, writes in this passage: "Only my companion, she or he, can awaken me from my torpor, releasing poetry, launching me against the limits of the old desert so that I can overcome it. No other. Neither the heavens, nor a privileged place, nor the things by which we are shaken. / Torch, I dance only with a companion like this" (PA, 146). This torch is akin to the transpersonal fire of erotic beauty that the lover addresses in the last lines of "The Passage of Lyon": "Flame surpassing its destiny, which now thins me and now completes me, you brighten beside me this very moment, dauphine, salamander, and I am nothing to you" (FM, 128).

 12. Veyne, *René Char*, 35; cf. 245–47, 398. Char, it is true, is not quite as eccentric in this regard as Veyne suggests. Blanchot points out that Char is in a tradition of modern poets in whose work the question of poetry itself becomes central ("René Char," 105). Blanchot also emphasizes that Char's work makes clear the extent to which the poet is secondary to the work he writes, is invented by the poems he writes (104). This is a sound insight. Yet, lest it become unnecessarily mystical, one should add that it is not only true of the action of writing poems but of human action in general. As Sartre was emphasizing in the very years in which this first of Blanchot's essays on Char was written, we define ourselves and are defined by others above all through our acts. It is at this point that one can still seek to clarify the distinctive sense in which, for Char, the impersonal space of poetry promises to alter us.

 13. For an illuminating account of the prose poem as it emerges in the nineteenth century, see Donald Wesling, *The New Poetries*, 172–200. On Rimbaud's many portraits of the artist, see James Lawler, *Rimbaud's Theatre of the Self*.

 14. On the rhythm of expansion and contraction in Char's work, see Poulet, "René Char," and Richard, "René Char," especially 104–09. "Common Presence," an important early poem, concludes: "Let the dust swarm / None will detect your union" (MM, 143).

 15. See Mathieu, *Poésie et résistance*, 168. In the first volume of his study, *Traversée du surréalisme*, 286–321, Mathieu provides a ranging account of Char's initial turn to an aphoristic mode, drawing attention in particular to Char's agonistic relationship with Hugo. Virginia La Charité, in *The Poetics*

and Poetry of René Char, emphasizes the way the aphoristic sequences almost always involve a meditation on the poet's vocation. Mary Ann Caws, in the first chapter of *The Presence of René Char*, casts light on the interplay of *voix* and *voie*, voice and way, in these sequences.

16. Pascal, *Pensée*s, #186; Nietzsche, *Twilight of the Idols*, 35, 37, and *Thus Spoke Zarathustra*, 40; Mathieu, *Poésie et résistance*, 176, n. 32. Char recalls and re-tropes Pascal's reed at the end of a short essay on his experience in the Resistance (RBS, 23). Pippin's study of Nietzsche as a thinker in the tradition of the French moralists, based on a series of lectures given at the Collège de France, was originally published as *Nietzsche, moraliste français*. An expanded version of the work has been published as *Nietzsche, Psychology, and First Philosophy*. For an insightful discussion of Char's aphoristic mode that casts light on the literary backgrounds on which Char draws, see Kingma-Eijgendaal, "La poéticité de l'aphorisme chez René Char."

17. See Frye, *The Well-Tempered Critic*, 81–93. The practices addressed here, of course, appear not only in modernist but also in romantic and contemporary writing (Blake, Emerson, and Whitman, Novalis and Friedrich Schlegel, Baudelaire and Rimbaud, are all splendid aphorists). This is not the space to address the changes these practices have gone through in our own time, though I would make here a couple of general points. The first is that the practice of textual disjunction in our time has both a serious mode and a superficial mode. This is a simplification that sounds suspicious, perhaps, but it's hard even to begin a discussion of postmodern poetics without recognizing something like this distinction. As for the serious current of emphatic disjunction in our time, it's important to note that it tends to cast the whole question in terms of "reference" rather than, as in modernist and earlier forms of discontinuous writing, in terms of "meaning," and hence the first question to ask in this domain is why this question of reference has taken on such urgency at this historical moment. As for the things that are not serious, Frye notes that "discontinuous" writing is a form that has always invited parody, since there is a fine (or not so fine) line between the profound and the vapid "saying." On related questions in the field of contemporary painting, see Robert Pippin, *The Persistence of Subjectivity*, 305, n. 41.

18. Veyne, *René Char*, 246; Stevens, *The Palm at the End of the Mind*, 317, 354 (cf. 376); Mathieu, *Traversée du surréalisme*, 289, n. 49. In "A Primitive like an Orb" Stevens tends to imagine the giant of a fuller life as a masculine being and as a fictive projection. Char tends to imagine this giant as a woman, a feminine Presence, or a divine presence of Beauty, whom the poet seeks in love (see the late affirmations of this in ES, 135, 176). But there are surely variations on the masculine and the feminine throughout the work of both poets. Kingma-Eijgendaal, too, has underlined the way Char's aphoristic sequences become emblems or formal figures of Char's larger vision and journey: "Indeed,

not only the aphorisms, but Char's entire *oeuvre* constitutes a *Word as Archipelago* [the title of Char's major collection of 1962] in which figurative expressions, riddling antitheses, form conjunctions of abstract thought and concrete lyricism. Explicit statements, linked to one another even as they are dispersed across the work as a whole, refer to another form that remains implicit, namely, a reality that one cannot always know" ("La poéticité de l'aphorisme," 55). All of Char's poetry, in a sense, is an effort to bring to words what in the early poem "Common Presence" is called *la vie inexprimable*, inexpressible life, or life as élan and advent and occasional apparition (MM, 142–43). But there are times, he says, when he is not able to accomplish the task, not able to translate the Apparition he has loved into an elliptical pattern or galaxy: "Oh night, I could not *translate into galaxy* her Apparition that I intimately married in the pure time of flight. That immediate Sister turned the heart of day" (FM, 38, my emphasis). *Le poème pulvérisé*, the pulverized poem, is the refracted allusion to a call or presence that, in Rimbaud's phrase, has arrived from always, will depart everywhere. "What is it that we refract? The wings we do not have" (NP, 134). James Lawler writes: "Char shatters, that is to say, elaborates the image—Breton's 'unshatterable kernel of night'—composing a visionary ethic so much the more expressive for being found within the natural scene" (*René Char*, 95).

19. The brief poem just cited, "Rose of Oak," is a coda or an epilogue to *Leaves of Hypnos*. Char, in revising Nietzsche's dialectic of Dionysus and Apollo, perhaps draws on Heraclitus' identification of Dionysus and Hades. One of Heraclitus' fragments reads: "For if it were not to Dionysus that they made the procession and sang the hymn to the shameful parts, the deed would be most shameless; but Hades and Dionysus, for whom they rave and celebrate Lenaean rites, are the same" (Kirk, Raven, and Schofield, *The Presocratic Philosphers*, 209).

20. Veyne, *René Char*, 307. Eric Marty, in developing a "hermeticist" reading of Char, characterizes this paradoxical search thus: "If, on one side, the modernity of the twentieth century is based in a destruction of the work of art as an imposture, there runs parallel to this another adventure, quieter and more essential, not based in the spectacle of a derisory agony but anchored in the tragic asceticism of poetic hermeticism: the adventure undertaken by Rilke, Celan, Mandelstam, or Char. More vehemently than Hölderlin, Char named this moment of distress the 'brittle age.' [...] The brittle age is the world where poetry is no longer heard, a world governed by those who don't want to be the dupes of any revelation. The passage from the world of Poussin, a pacified space where belief was preserved, to the world of the negation of all revelation doesn't stir in Char a desire to restore lost values: it opens, rather, the imperative to explore the other side of a transparence now become anachronistic. The hermetic other side: where meaning is neither radiant nor cynically abandoned

but where, like the nocturnal flame, it rends us" (*René Char*, 142–43; cf. 78–80). If Kierkegaard's knight of faith, turning to the transcendent, is continually torn between doubt and joy, Char's tragic poet, turning to the open, is continually torn between wound and joy. There is a quieter side in Char, too, a meditative side, to which Veyne is deeply attentive throughout his book, and which is an important part of this tragic bearing. "Before Rimbaud," Char writes, "Heraclitus and a painter, Georges de la Tour, had constructed and shown that House among all houses which man is to inhabit: a dwelling at once for breath and for meditation" (RBS, 111).

21. See Stevens, *The Palm at the End of the Mind*, 241. Caws's sentences appear in her introduction to René Char, *Selected Poems*, ed. Mary Ann Caws and Tina Jolas, xv.

22. See Marty, *René Char*, 65–67. "Children and geniuses know that the bridge does not exist, only the water that lets itself be crossed" (RBS, 53).

23. C. D. Wright, *Cooling Time*, 84; Blake, "Introduction" to *Songs of Experience*. Maurice Blanchot, in an early essay on Char, suggests the way this sort of space, this open, is related to the traditional metaphysical question of the whole: "The search for the whole, in all its forms, is the poetic ambition par excellence, an ambition that embraces, as its condition, the impossibility of its accomplishment. [...] The poetic imagination attaches itself, not to things and persons as they are given, but to their lack, to what there is in them of something else, to the unknown that makes them infinite" (*La part du feu*, 108–9). From this perspective, a range of modern poets and philosophers can be seen as attempting to discover *the open* that traditional religious and metaphysical thought at once saw and concealed. This is the way metaphysics, the question of the whole, returns first in existentialist philosophy and later in certain currents of post-Heideggerian philosophy. Jean-Luc Nancy's recent *Dis-Enclosure: The Deconstruction of Christianity* is a particularly clear expression of this sort of thinking in our own moment. "Prayer," Nancy writes, "is primarily adoration: address, homage, recognition of the fact that its saying is deleted in going toward what it says (will never say). Homage, veneration, that is, simply the movement of 'transcendence' as [Michel] Deguy characterizes it, incessant trans-port without any 'landing having been reached' or transcendence without a transcendent (which can also be expressed as transcendence immanent to our immanence, homologous with and inherent to its plane itself)—constitutes the task of saying" (136). A limit to post-Heideggerian currents in general is that they have little to say about eros or the erotic turning of the soul. Here Nietzsche, Jaspers, and Camus, or Whitman, Oppen, and Char, are guides who go further. I think Nancy Kline Piore is right to say that when Blanchot, in his later essays on Char (in *L'Entretien infini*, 439–58), approaches Char in terms of his own thinking of *le neutre*, a rarefied elaboration of Heidegger's thinking of Being, he begins to lose Char (Kline Piori, *Lightning: The Poetry*

of René Char, 37–38). The later Blanchot, like Bataille, sets himself against the dominant existentialisms of the fifties and, so, against any straightforward Sartrean notion of engaged literature. Char, as his short piece "Are There Incompatibilities?" indicates (RBS, 38–39), is akin to Bataille and Blanchot in his resistance to Sartre's attempt to place literature wholly within the realm of practical politics. Yet Char is a romantic, naturalist, at times visionary writer in a certain existentialist tradition running from Nietzsche through Camus. He and Camus, indeed, share a reading of Nietzsche that is one important mark of the philosophical space they inhabit: a space different from *both* the space of Sartre *and* the space of Bataille or the later Blanchot. In the prefatory note to his wartime notebook, *Leaves of Hypnos*, Char affirms the resistant bearing of "a humanism aware of it duties" (FM, 85).

24. See Marty, *René Char*, 168–75, and Sereni, "Sur *Feuillets d'Hypnos*," especially 45–46. See, too, Giorgio Caproni, "Char comme source et invention de vie," 136–37. Caproni, an Italian poet of minimalist songs and a translator of Char, fought in the Italian Resistance. The two poems or fore-poems titled "Argument" in *Fureur et mystère*—the first one at the outset of the book, the second one at the outset of the volume *Le Poème pulvérisé*—read like condensed commentaries on the wider space in which *Formal Share* and *Leaves of Hypnos* resonate with one another. The first of these begins (it is the first line of the book): "Man flees suffocation" (FM, 19). It then evokes the *rapport-en-différence* of the individual who acts and the individual who writes, the resistance fighter "outside the imagination" and the meditative poet of "premonition." The second of these poems traces many of the walls that shut us off from genuine eros, freedom, encounter, and disclosure—not least importantly our conformism, our contempt for others and ourselves, our lack of generosity, our obsession with wealth—and then reaffirms the slope of poetry, the elsewhere here of *la vraie vie*. It thus brings together the metaphysical accent of *Formal Share* and the social accent of *Leaves of Hypnos* (FM, 169).

25. Greilsamer, *L'éclair au front*, 108.

Chapter Two. George Oppen

1. On the constructivist aesthetic of the objectivist tradition, see Altieri, "The Objectivist Tradition."

2. The last line cited here appears in Oppen, "Worksheets," *Iowa Review* 18.3, 6. Oppen's poetry, Randolph Chilton writes, "uniquely blends Heideggerian and objectivist concerns—concerns with objects of perception, and modes of perception, and with the intellectual context in which those objects must be placed" ("The Place of Being in the Poetry of George Oppen," 90). The Heideggerian dimension of Oppen's poetry is one of the major themes of Peter

Nicholls, *George Oppen and the Fate of Modernism*, and Susan Thackrey, *George Oppen: A Radical Practice*. Henry Weinfield, from a different point of view, emphasizes the importance in Oppen's work of a "poetic seeing" that goes well beyond the boundaries of an objectivist or empiricist framework (*The Music of Thought*, 199–206).

3. "The sustained music of [Oppen's] achievement [in "Of Being Numerous"]," Henry Weinfield writes, "is arrived at both through the depth and intensity of the thought process that unfolds and through the dialogue the poet carries on with a pantheon of other thinkers" (*The Music of Thought*, 40). A letter of Oppen's that seems to take place in the margins of "A Narrative" says a great deal about the relationship in his work between a meditative voice and a voice of serious conversation: "The new wave movies, the electronic music, or rather the music depending on hazard, the 'accidental' music, those of the paintings which are deliberately formless, the poetry which is automatic writing, more or less — they may indeed display the truth, the meaningless river which flows with ourselves and our talk. And it may be that this is what art will become, the narrative of nothing, or of the inhuman event of humans. But I ponder simple brutal self defense: if it is that river, that meaningless river in which we are, it is nevertheless talk by which we are alive. If we want to continue to invent life for ourselves and for our children and for our friends it might be worth one's whole effort to find the alternative, some seed of an alternative, to this art" (SL, 67). In a letter to William Bronk concerning the question of poet and audience, Oppen writes, "We (and you rightly mock this use of 'we') but *we* meaning those-who-have-been-alive-at-any-moment, have existed in the area of nihilism for a very long time. I think we can be interested only to know what may possibly lie beyond nihilism. For us? For anyone. For anyone who may be alive. [...] If we shout at them ['a general populace'], lecture them, is it not because we wish to converse? If we wish to converse is it not because of some hope? Is it true? or are we bothering a loose tooth, picking at incurable sores" (SL, 168).

4. Oppen, "Worksheets," *Sulfur* 26, 156.

5. Emerson, *Essays and Lectures*, 9; Thoreau echoes this approach to landscape in *Walden*, 76; Frank Lentricchia provides a critical account of this way of seeing in *Ariel and the Police*, 115–21. If there is no warranty-deed for the landscape itself, so there is no warranty-deed for the light itself, as Oppen suggests in the opening lines of a late love poem: "'The picturesque / common lot' the unwarranted light / Where everyone has been" (CP, 225–26). "The mind is capable not only of thinking," Oppen says in an interview, "but has an emotional root that forces it to look, to think, to see. The most tremendous and compelling emotion that we possess is the one that forces us to look, to know, if we can, to see. The difference between just the neuro-sensitivity of the eye and the act of seeing is one over which we have no control. It is a

tremendous emotional response, which fills us with the experience we describe as seeing, not with the experience of some twitching nerves in the eyeball. It can only be interpreted emotionally, and those who lack it I despair of" (IN, 186). In a letter addressing *Of Being Numerous*, Oppen says: "The book stays pretty close to that realistic point. Which has this oddity: it seems justified to call it a realistic or materialistic point, and quite as justifiable to refer to it as a metaphysical or even a religious point ---- that would be the value of the poems, maybe, insofar as they have a value: simply the sense of the 'size,' of the size of reality ---- something like that. An opening" (SL, 177). Olson speaks of size, "projective size," in his essay "Projective Verse" (*Selected Writings*, 25). A.R. Ammons speaks of "Scope" in "Corsons Inlet" (*Selected Poems*, 46). The fascination with continental scope was of great importance to the beat and countercultural imagination of these years, too, as Oppen suggests in the tenth poem of "A Narrative" (CP, 154–55).

6. "To walk up my stoop is unaccountable . . . I pause to consider if it really be," Whitman writes in "Song of Myself" (*Leaves of Grass: The First [1855] Edition*, 50), a line Oppen might well have written.

7. Henry Weinfield also draws attention to the allusion to Milton in both section 7 of "A Narrative" and in the essay "The Mind's Own Place" (*The Music of Thought*, 15, 26–27). While Weinfield reads the poem as a forceful reflection on the risk of solipsism, he is critical of the earlier essay, arguing that it is based in a reductive empiricism that evades the question taken seriously in the poem (27). My concern here is to suggest that there is a significant continuity between the 1963 essay and the 1965 poem. Yet the essay, I think, is likely to leave a contemporary reader uncomfortable in other ways. Oppen, perhaps inevitably, sees the social movements of the sixties through the lens of his particular experience of the Old Left in the thirties and forties. As Mary Oppen puts it in *Meaning a Life*: "If George and I had come from the working class we would probably never have joined the Communist Party—that was the nearly unanimous decision of the United States' working class. We searched for an escape from class" (151). Oppen entered politics as an individual of social and economic privilege. He seems always to have seen leftist politics in terms of an "ethic of altruism," as he puts it, or in terms of an effort on the part of the privileged to help or "rescue" the unprivileged. Members of the Old Left in America, given the social context of the time, the fragmentation of the working class, and their own commitments, may often have come to this sort of self-understanding. It is inadequate, in any case, to an understanding of the social movements of the sixties. Yet Oppen sees the civil rights movement through this lens, that is, he sees it largely in terms of white college kids lending support to the movement: he appears not to see the basis of the movement in the resistance, struggle, and self-assertion of black Americans themselves, in boycotts, sit-ins, protest movements, the formation of organizations

like the SCLC and SNCC, and many other activities. This strong tendency to see politics in terms of rescue or altruism, rather than in terms of liberation or liberatory self-shaping, may make it especially difficult for Oppen to find a connection between the horizons of politics and the horizons of poetry. But then, of course, for anyone, for all of us, this connection is always a difficulty, an open question.

8. Jane Hirshfield, *Nine Gates*, vii. In a letter Oppen writes: "Freedom of thought, freedom of style, freedom of emotion, which is openness to experience" (SL, 138). There is in this understanding of freedom a deep affinity with Char. Freedom is inseparable from openness to encounter.

9. DuPlessis, "George Oppen: 'What Do We Believe To Live With,'" 62. In the notes to Oppen's *Selected Letters*, DuPlessis very helpfully includes a sentence from a letter of Oppen's to an unidentified correspondent: "I ended ['Of Being Numerous'] with the word 'curious,' of which the root is *curia*: care, concern" (SL, 402–03, n. 6). Oppen's sounding of *curiosity* has affinities with Heidegger's account of *care* in *Being and Time*. A whole chapter of this work, titled "The Being of *Da-sein* as Care" (169–206), describes *care* as the primordial being of *da-sein*: a being always already ahead of itself, always already entangled in a world taken care of, always already concerned in its being about itself. In the experience of *angst*, Heidegger says, the primordial being of *da-sein* as care is revealed (171). Heidegger, too, is interested in the ancient meanings of *cura* (185).

10. Henry Weinfield has drawn attention to important thematic connections between Oppen's "Of Being Numerous" and Eliot's *The Waste Land* (*The Music of Thought*, 68–69). "Oppen," he says, "was more deeply influenced by Eliot than has perhaps been recognized, and he does not seem to have had the kind of animosity toward Eliot that Williams, for example, harbored; but though the 'wasteland' motif enters into the texture of his work, it does not pull it in a nostalgic (or reactionary) direction" (69). In "'The Air of Atrocity': 'Of Being Numerous' and the Vietnam War," John Lowney reads "Of Being Numerous" as a war poem, specifically, "a Vietnam War poem" (143). Kristin Prevallet, in "One Among Rubble: George Oppen and World War II," explores the place in Oppen's life and poetry of his experience of war.

11. The "bright light of shipwreck," at another point in the sequence, is associated with insanity and violence, specifically, the high-tech violence against the people of Vietnam: "Insanity in high places, / If it is true we must do these things / We must cut our throats // The fly in the bottle // Insane, the insane fly // Which, over the city / Is the bright light of shipwreck" (19). There are many other images of light in the poem: the "spot of light on the curb" associated with simple happiness (11), the shine of the things of an imagined simple social world close to nature (12), the "bright streets" of the city in which the anguished mind finds consolation (26), the "light of the closed pages" akin to the

"frightening light before sunrise" (28), the "dawn light" (29), the "blue bright sky" perceived from a yard (30), the "bright, bright skin" of a person loved and desired (32), the illumination of truthful speech (33), the light and lightness of the air (34), and the light of the setting sun that shines on the statue on top of the capitol in Whitman's letter cited in the last section of the poem (40). I had thought that Michael Davidson, in his notes to Oppen's *New Collected Poems*, had identified the source of the quoted words in "Image of the Engine," but in fact he does not. I'm not sure where I read this. Perhaps I'm mistaken. Oppen, in a letter to his sister written in 1960, cites other words that he recalls from his mother's suicide note (SL, 35). Camus writes of Char's poetry: "But I would have less admiration for the originality of this poetry if its inspiration were not, at the same time, so ancient. Char rightly lays claim to the tragic optimism of pre-Socratic Greece. From Empedocles to Nietzsche a secret has been passed from summit to summit, and after a long eclipse, Char once more takes up this hard and rare tradition. The fires of Etna smoulder beneath some of his unendurable phrases, the royal wind of Sils Maria irrigates his poems and makes them echo with the sound of clear and tumultuous waters. What Char calls 'wisdom with tear-filled eyes' is revived here, at the very height of our disasters" (*Lyrical and Critical Essays*, 322).

12. A little earlier in the sequence Oppen writes: "They develop / Argument in order to speak, they become / unreal, unreal, life loses / solidity, loses extent . . ." (13). Henry Weinfield notes the way the word "unreality" in this passage echoes the "Unreal City" passage at the end of the first part of *The Waste Land* (*The Music of Thought*, 68). If one sets this section of Oppen's sequence alongside section 17, section 4 of an earlier and much shorter version of the sequence, "A Language of New York" (CP, 116), "Guest Room" (CP, 107–10), and the sequence "A Narrative" (CP, 150–56), one can begin to unfold what Oppen has in mind with the words "real" and "unreal" here: the real involves solidity, extent or scope or depth, and a language of clarity (attention, disclosure) and respect (concern, conversation); the unreal involves ghostliness, narrowness or defensiveness, and a language of argument. "The distinction between the *full* and the *empty*," Gabriel Marcel once wrote, "seems to me more fundamental than that between the *one* and the *many*" ("On the Ontological Mystery," 12).

13. Weinfield, commenting on the lines I've just cited, says: "But even if Truth (in the sense of a Platonic form) does not exist, there can still be the possibility of *truthfulness*, which is something that presumably can be known—at least to the self, and at least insofar as it is able to gauge its own intentions. From this point of view, truthfulness would be one of 'the small nouns / Crying faith' that Oppen invokes so memorably in 'Psalm' (CP, 99). But if there are no eternal verities, if there is only the will to power, then why would one be 'afraid / To lie?' Oppen's unresolved syntax [in the section of "A Narrative" following the one I've cited] leaves the question open, but perhaps he is saying

that even in the absence of eternal verities (i.e., of God), to lie is to descend into an inferno of self-loathing" (*The Music of Thought*, 25).

14. David McAleavey, at the end of a ranging and illuminating reading of the whole book *Of Being Numerous*, underlines the importance of the "curiosity" of the woman in "Ballad" ("Clarity and Process: Oppen's *Of Being Numerous*," 403–04). "The final poem of the book," McAleavey writes, "offers us 'the real' itself in opening to us a possibility of humane sharing. If each solitary person is imaginatively active and accurately observant, then we can arrive at the condition of the lobsterman's wife that Oppen met on a small island in Maine" (403).

15. See Richard Elliott Friedman, *Who Wrote the Bible?*, 54–60, 237. I had thought that Friedman used the word "egg," but it appears that he does not; he speaks of a "bubble." This picture seems to have formed a part of ancient Near Eastern myth in general (see Kramer, *The Sumerians*, 112–13). I've included in the first map, alongside Oppen's language, the fourfold that Olson sketched in his 1965 talk at the Berkeley Poetry Conference: earth (orb), Imago Mundi, history (urb), Anima Mundi. Robert Creeley provides a brief account of these terms in his introduction to Olson's *Selected Writings*: "[Olson] also noted, as a usable context for that 'mapping' or measure of how one is where one is, these four terms. [...] By 'earth' is meant all that literal ground we walk on and its specific character, including water and sky; by 'Imago Mundi,' that way of seeing or view of existence evident in any particular circumstance of life; by 'history,' all the condition and accumulation of human acts and effects, as these exist; by 'Anima Mundi,' that which informs and quickens life in its own condition, the spirit—or what we speak of in saying, 'the *quick* and the dead.' I offer these simply as measure, for the relevance of what follows" (9–10). This fourfold is of great usefulness in measuring Olson's "The Kingfishers" in particular. In "George Oppen and the World in Common," a challenging and suggestive essay, John Peck draws attention to Oppen and Olson's shared concern with the common world of our lives, linking this concern to Hannah Arendt's concern with a rethinking of life in the *polis*. Peck argues that Oppen remains closer in his thought to the public sphere of a political ethic while Olson tends to turn toward an archetypal common world manifest to the body's vital awareness. By "archetypal," I think, Peck means something not far from what I have in this chapter called "metaphysical." Near the end of the essay he suggests that perhaps these two senses of the common could be brought together: "Oppen's expressed preference for Olson's shorter poems over the Maximus series is no surprise in view of the deeply differentiated senses of the common in their work. But these two concerns still meet in a concern for the construction of political space; and that means that the divisions between an archetypal and a traditionally political sense of the common (and by tradition I mean Arendt's 'Greek' understanding) remain fertile. Surely a dialectic exists between these

two senses of the common, whose articulation would benefit anyone awake to the mess we face" (86). My maps here are meant to suggest that both of these senses—and the tension between them—are in fact fully explored in Oppen's work itself. I should also note that the dialectic of the individual and the community, grounded in the fundamental loneliness of individuals who at the same time live together, a point of view I take to be essential to Oppen's work, is a point of view that Peck criticizes and that, he argues, Oppen's poetry criticizes. It is true, as he says, that political or social justice cannot be adequately addressed in terms of "fraternity" (or "fraternity and sorority") and "love." In a just society both my neighbor and I are treated justly even if we dislike or scorn each other. This marks one limit of any mythopoetic point of view. But the issue doesn't end there. For, as Freud says, social bodies do require some sort of libidinal or erotic or ideal attachments, however broad, vague, and plural, and the question is what the grounds and horizons of such attachments will be (one of the destructive ways in which such ties are formed, for example, is through the demonizing hatred of a common enemy). But here the issues at stake go far beyond the scope of this chapter.

16. See MacIntyre, *After Virtue*; Freud, *Civilization and Its Discontents*; Plato, *The Republic* and *The Symposium*; Emerson, *Essays and Lectures*, 385. I draw here in part on Christopher Gill's ranging introduction to his translation of *The Symposium*. Martha Nussbaum has argued that *The Symposium* shows the way an eros of transcendence leads to a failure of love for the particular individual (*The Fragility of Goodness*, 165–99). A. W. Price has countered that the dialogue evokes a dialectical path whereby two individuals, in the deepening of their love for each other, come to wider or "ascending" spiritual horizons (*Love and Friendship*, 15–54). I'm aware that my account above does not quite do justice to Freud, a naturalist whose sympathy for the measure of illness we all bear is profound, but I hope the larger point I want to make will emerge through these overdrawn lines. Axel Honneth, in an account of the way Freud sees the reflective self-understanding of the individual as a movement stirring the individual in pain to seek healing, notes that this relatively hopeful perspective toward the individual is "conspicuously opposed to the pessimism of his cultural theory" (*Pathologies of Reason*, 140). There is a similar rift in the older Oppen's picture of things. Of the contemporary world-economy shaping our lives, Niklas Luhmann writes: "Life may still take place in 'families' or similar communities, but it is dependent down to its last detail upon the market and upon organizations of professional work, of production and service, and hence upon transformations felt by the individual to be external and intractable. The integration of individual and society is becoming a matter of market forces and careers" (*Theories of Distinction*, 34). This is basically the account developed by the first generation of the Frankfurt School half a century ago. The difference is that Luhmann is neither a Hegelian Marxist, nor a romantic humanist, nor

a humanist of any sort, but a systems theorist. He thinks that our runaway systems will never again be grounded in reflective human concern; our best hope, he believes, is to find a way to manage the unmanageably proliferating systems. If Luhmann is right, the place in our lives of a poetry like Oppen's, or a poetry like Char's, or any existential poetry seeking to uncover or disclose basic conditions and orientations of our lives, seems to become a difficult question. I will return to this question in my conclusion.

17. This question is addressed in a letter from Oppen to his son-in-law, Alexander Mourelatos, a philosopher whose primary field of study is pre-Socratic philosophy. Apparently Oppen understood Mourelatos to have been subtly questioning an occasional blurring of the line between the ethical and the metaphysical in "Route." Oppen writes: "I enjoy the precision of your sentence, after you quote 'the sea anemone dreamed of something / filtering the seawater thru its body' [CP, 194] where you add: 'I suspect it would have interfered with its growth had it focussed its attention on the filtering process itself'/ The implication of 'suspect'   Acknowledged, yes. I move maybe too freely from metaphysical assertion to ---- the statement of how one can live a life. Freely, but --- a matter of trusting the emotions   since one must   And the title *Route*   and the autobiographical base of all the poems I think sufficiently acknowledges this   ? " (SL, 237). "I knew that I could not reconcile perfectly [...] the vertical and the horizontal sense of the redemption of life or the value of life," Oppen writes in a passage I cited above (see n. 4). DuPlessis emphasizes that Oppen "embraces his curiosity and his wariness" ("George Oppen," 62). Norman Finkelstein speaks of "the pervasive dialectic of doubt and commitment that [...] informs all of Oppen's poetry" ("The Dialectic of *This In Which*," 369).

18. I would guess that the peculiar exclamation "not by the dew on them!" is a critical allusion to the last lines of the penultimate canto of Stevens's "Sunday Morning," an unpersuasive canto. Jay Bernstein writes: "Instrumental rationality is in fact cognitively and rationally opaque because it limits reasoning to items that are good only as means, including the 'universal' means of profit, power, and order, thereby throwing into perpetual darkness the goodness or not of the actual ends of human action" (*Recovering Ethical Life*, 27). "The 'Marxism' of Discrete Series," Oppen writes in a letter, "is, was felt as, the struggle against the loss of the commonplace. [...] can make a touch of Marxism out of this: Love is love of the future   Without which not" (SL, 254). Oppen, intriguingly, thinks of the poetic line, too, as a place to "stand": "The process by which sometimes a line appears, I cannot trace. It happens. Given a line, one has a place to stand, and goes further--" (SL, 123). DuPlessis probes this last sentence with great insight in "George Oppen." Readers, I think, tend to read the lines concerning "that denial of death that paved the cities" as bearing a

negative implication. My sense, as I've suggested here, is that they bear a positive implication. This is an important question. But to spell out my reading requires some time and space: so I have placed the discussion in an extended note at the end of this chapter (see "A Note on Building and Seeing in Oppen").

19. Stevens, *The Palm at the End of the Mind*, 174. In an earlier section of the sequence Oppen recalls the talismanic Emersonian and Stevensian word *transparence*: "Clarity // In the sense of *transparence*, / I don't mean that much can be explained. // Clarity in the sense of silence" (22). My thanks to Youna Kwak for helping me to see (in a class discussion) the subtle turnings at the end of section 26.

20. However odd it may sound to place Frost and Oppen in the same space, Richard Poirier's account of the connection between poetry and love in Frost's work is of relevance to Oppen's vision in this respect: "Here as elsewhere Frost's Emersonism is grounded in certain basic actualities, especially the sexual relations of men and women, which Emerson himself tended to pass over with little more than citation [we needn't adopt the heterosexual restrictions of this insight, of course, only its emphasis on the erotics of life, vision, and language]. Within this sequence of three poems, 'A Dream Pang' looks ahead to the implications of a more considerable sequence of three poems, already mentioned, that includes 'The Most of It,' 'Never Again Would Bird's Song Be the Same,' and 'The Subverted Flower.' The implication, briefly noted also in 'The Vantage Point,' is that a man alone ('he thought he kept the universe alone') cannot see or hear anything in nature that confirms his existence as human. If he is alone, he cannot 'make' the world; he cannot reveal himself to it or in it; he becomes lost to it; it remains alien. He cannot make human sound" (*Robert Frost*, 71). Another way to look at this would be in terms of the debate between the romantic Adorno, concerned with the subject's relationship to non-identical material otherness, and the liberal Habermas, concerned with the subject's relationship to non-identical human others in dialogue. Perry Anderson and Peter Dews, in an interview with Habermas, suggest that this debate might be taken to involve less an opposition than a complementarity: "Can Adorno, in his evocations of reconciliation, justly be accused of surreptitiously employing categories of intersubjectivity from which he abstains philosophically, and can what he terms 'love toward things' be simply reformulated in terms of undistorted communication? [...] Would it not be plausible to suggest that there is a relation of complementarity—rather than of substitution—between Adorno's explorations of the subject-object relation and your own theory of communication?" (*Autonomy and Solidarity*, 153; cf. 166–69, 180, 197). Habermas, holding true to his liberalism, states that he finds the suggestion "a little too innocuous." Oppen, holding true to his romantic-existentialist bearing, explores this sort of complementarity.

21. DuPlessis, "George Oppen," 63. "Rather like Heidegger himself," Nicholls writes, "Oppen was often fascinated by a single phrase or sentence which seemed to promise illumination, and possibly access to another world of thought. [...] Much of Oppen's thinking thus entailed intensive consideration of what he called the 'seed phrases' [SL, 102] that he culled from favorite texts..." (*George Oppen*, 76–77). Heller makes a similar point in *Speaking the Estranged* (54–55, 91–92). As DuPlessis says, Oppen "turns on and returns to" such phrases, to the questions that such phrases bring with them. Mulling things over, turning things over and over in the mind, is the basic rhythm of his thought. There is an affinity, despite all the differences of style, between this approach to writing and Char's approach to writing (including his habit of finding his way through island-like aphorisms).

22. See Glück, *Proofs & Theories*, 30, and 78–82, pages that present an extraordinarily insightful account of Oppen's articulate pauses (my thanks to Chris Dombrowski for having drawn my attention to these pages many years ago now). "I write extremely slowly," Oppen says in an interview ("Poetry and Politics," 30). In Oppen's prosody, Weinfield says, there is "a conscious process of *deceleration*" (*Music of Thought*, 42). Charles Berntstein speaks of Oppen's hinge-like line-breaks ("Hinge Picture," 194). Oppen's notorious practice of revision—typing and retyping words, cutting words out, pasting words over words, till the page would come to resemble a sort of landscape—is a fascinating dimension of this art of searching: see Michael Davidson, "Palimtexts," 64–78, for an account of this practice. Oppen's "hovering" rhythms, DuPlessis says, "create three feelings in the reader: mental weightlessness, physical density or pressure, and a sense of the void" ("Objectivist Poetics and Political Vision," 144; cf. DuPlessis, "'Uncannily in the Open': In Light of Oppen," 216–23). A feature of Oppen's rhythmic texture that I haven't space to go into here, though it is of interest, is a strong bent toward iambic rhythms, particularly at moments of significant statement, so to speak, though also elsewhere. "There is a force of clarity, it is / Of what is not autonomous in us" (CP, 193).

23. For a suggestive reading of Oppen and Stevens together, from a perspective different from mine here, see Heller, "Oppen, Stevens, Wittgenstein: Reflections on the Lyrical and the Philosophical" in *Speaking the Estranged*, 64–81.

24. Jameson, "The Poetics of Totality" in *The Modernist Papers*, 3–44. DuPlessis, in "George Oppen," provides an illuminating account of what she calls Oppen's poetic of "dilemma," of articulating one position, and then an alternative, over and over, without coming to a resolution. He finds out as he goes.

25. For the passages from the daybooks cited here, see *Sulfur* 26, 150, and *Iowa Review* 18.3, 2. Mary Oppen and Dennis Young address the repetitions of Oppen's poetry in "Conversation with Mary Oppen," 31–32. "What gives the simple phrasing of the opening passage [in 'Of Being Numerous']

such resonance," Weinfield writes, "especially when we have worked our way through the poem a number of times, is the depth of the meditation in which it is embedded and out of which it emerges" (*Music of Thought*, 42). On the importance of silence in Oppen's work, see Glück, *Proofs & Theories*, 68–72, and Nicholls, *George Oppen*, 138–39, 160–61. Oppen writes in one of his daybooks: "I do not hear the rhythm as the poem forms — the beginning, the seed / of the poem — rather it is a shape, in fact a silence   The shape / silently forms as if 'above' me — the effort of the writing, the finding / of the cadence is the care not to shatter this presence — tho often it / must be shattered and only then restored" ("Worksheets" in *Conjunctions* 10, 200).

26. Oppen, in one of his daybooks, describes his late poetry as "written from the edge of despair, the edge of the void, a paean of praise to the world" (cited in Nicholls, *George Oppen*, 178). Weinfield finds a kind of mystical dialectic in this way of seeing: "The vision of ruin that Oppen shares with [William] Bronk, and that sometimes has the effect of estranging both poets from the quotidian, has a quasi-mystical origin in that it is connected to an influx of light" (*The Music of Thought*, 200). Everyone, I think, hears in Oppen's work the genuineness that Oppen himself always understood to be essential to serious poetry. In "The Mind's Own Place" he writes: "It is part of the function of poetry to serve as a test of truth. It is possible to say anything in abstract prose, but a great many things one believes or would like to believe or thinks he believes will not substantiate themselves in the concrete materials of the poem" (133). I have elsewhere briefly addressed this testimonial ideal so important to Oppen's work (*The Extravagant*, 304–07). Here I would like to respond to Peter Nicholls's claim that the passage from Oppen that I've just cited is "puzzling" (*George Oppen*, 54): since this will require a lengthy digression, however, I have placed the discussion in an extended note at the end of this chapter (see "A Note on Belief and Language in Oppen").

27. "All this is reportage," Oppen writes at two points in the sequence (10, 11), and it is a statement whose complex inflections are not easy to measure. "Reportage" is a word that circulated in the thirties, a word of Old Left political and artistic debates, referring to the sort of directly realistic and political writing that Oppen chose not to do when he chose, instead, to commit himself wholly to political activism. Now, over thirty years later, writing this poem that addresses historical and political and personal and metaphysical concerns all at once, he calls his writing, deeply based in his own life experience, "reportage." This leaves one thinking.

28. Perhaps a car was always an unsettling thing for Oppen. At the age of seventeen he was the driver in a fatal car wreck (see Nicholls, *George Oppen*, 5).

29. The hard *c* and *g* sounds accumulate with peculiar force from this point in the sequence through the end. On the transposition of a poem by St. John of the Cross in section 10, a poem translated by Mary Oppen, see Michael

Davidson's note in CP, 389–90. The earth is said to be at risk of crumbling in "The Translucent Mechanics": "what then   what spirit // Of the bent seas / Archangel // of the tide / brimming // in the moon-streak // comes in whose absence / earth crumbles" (CP, 228). In the next poem of "Some San Francisco Poems," the night itself is said to be crumbling: "We believe   we believe // Beyond the cable car streets / And the picture window // Lives the glittering crumbling night / Of obstructions and the stark structures // That carry wires over the mountain / One writes in the presence of something / Moving close to fear" (CP, 229).

30. See Adorno, *Minima Moralia*, 39; Borgmann, *Technology and the Character of Contemporary Life*, 169–82. Borgmann argues that deictic discourse, the characteristic disclosive language of art and other practices engaged with matters of ultimate concern, is essential to renewing the question of the good life in a society whose defining liberal and technological frames, for all their value in many other respects, are limited in their power to pose this question of farther or deeper horizons of care. "The word 'deictic' comes from Greek *deiknynai*, which means to show, to point out, to bring to light, to set before one, and then also to explain and to teach. Speakers of deictic discourse never finally warrant the validity of what they tell but point away from themselves to what finally matters; they speak essentially as witnesses. Enthusiasm gives deictic discourse the force of testimony. Sympathy requires that one testify not simply by setting out in some way what matters but by reaching out to the peculiar condition in which one finds the listener, by inviting the listener to search his or her experience and aspirations" (178). "Still, the statement, what statement one can make," Oppen says in a letter I cited at the outset of this chapter, "has value to me—O, has tremendous value, overwhelming value, as you know. There are things for each of us around which meaning gathers. The mission is to hold them, to be able to keep them in his mind, to try again and again to find the word, the syntax, the cadence of unfolding—I don't mean to promise redemption of course. A matter of being able to say what one is and where one is. And what matters" (SL, 160).

31. One of Oppen's great late poems explicitly mentions Job, "The Book of Job and a Draft of a Poem to Praise the Paths of the Living," and other late poems allude to the story. Peter Nicholls discusses Oppen's concern with this story in *George Oppen*, 162–93. Louise Glück writes: "I find, in Oppen, a sanity so profound as to be mysterious: this is a sound that has, for the most part, disappeared from poetry, possibly from thought" (*Proofs & Theories*, 81).

32. Heaney, "Crediting Poetry," 428. Oppen borrows the first two lines of the last stanza of Yeats's "The Stare's Nest By My Window" for one of the two epigraphs to *The Materials*. In fact, as has been often noted, he mis-cites the lines and, perhaps because he assumes that everyone of his era would recognize them, does not give the name of their author, though he gives the name of the

author of the other epigraph, Maritain. I would add here one last reflection on the final poem of "Route." The line about Cabeza de Vaca would seem to allude to the "spiritual despair" of those whom Cabeza de Vaca encountered in northern Mexico near the end of his 1528–36 journey from Florida to Mexico. During that part of the journey, according to his story, he was greeted as a miracle worker. Perhaps the line barely recalls, too, in a haunting way, the destruction of the peoples of the Mississippi Valley in the decades after Cabeza de Vaca and his companions had passed through the region. These peoples died of epidemics that "had been transmitted by coastal Indians infected by Spaniards visiting the coast" (Jared Diamond, *Guns, Germs, and Steel*, 211; cf. Robert Marks, *The Origins of the Modern World*, 76–77). Oppen's poem, after this line, turns to the history of Mexico and the disoriented response of the Aztecs to Cortés and the conquistadors. The tribes living under Aztec domination, unhappy and restless, tended to support the Spanish. But an unthinkable devastation and a vast despair would be consequences of the Spanish conquest and, later, the English conquest to the north. Again, then, the last poem of "Route" recalls the long catastrophe of imperial invasion from the sixteenth through the twentieth centuries, from North America to Vietnam, and perhaps from still further back in time. Adorno's bleak words on universal history in *Negative Dialectics*, published two years before Oppen's sequence, come to mind: "No universal history leads from savagery to humanitarianism, but there is one leading from the slingshot to the megaton bomb" (320). What, Oppen and Heaney ask, can we "credit" as a counter-reality in the face of this reality?

Conclusion

1. See DuPlessis, "George Oppen," 76.
2. I draw this familiar sketch from Stephen Gill, *William Wordsworth: A Life*.
3. M.H. Abrams, "English Romanticism: The Spirit of the Age." Harold Bloom's interpretation of this type of movement in the major English romantics, exuberantly set forth in "The Internalization of Quest-Romance," echoes that of Abrams while taking a Blakean or prophetic path. Bloom argues that the romantic quest ultimately demands a movement from a phase of organic energy, or the rebellion of the natural self, to a phase of imaginative energy, or the creative work of the spiritual self. It is plausible enough to read this as a sort of intra-psychic version of the familiar romantic passage from a youthful political radicalism to a later political disappointment accompanied by a faith in imaginative redemption. Yet the dialectic of critical negativity and transformative invention could be seen as relevant to politics as well as to poetry, not solely as a movement of disengagement and compensation, though,

in the light of Bloom's unsympathetic response to the sixties in *The Ringers in the Tower* and elsewhere, this would demand that one turn Bloom's larger vision against Bloom's local practice, as Mark Edmundson has done in a fine chapter in *Literature against Philosophy*. The dominant trend in recent studies of romanticism has been to repeat the basic story told by Abrams, now in a voice, not of imaginative sympathy, but of political criticism. In Jerome McGann's *The Romantic Ideology* and Marjorie Levinson's *Wordsworth's Great Period Poems*, for example, Wordsworth is taken to task for either his withdrawal from political struggles for the sake of a quietist care for his soul in its encounters with the natural world, or for an occlusion of the social realities of industrial capitalism, in particular the brutal dispossession of peasants, for the sake of a solipsistic poetry of inward transcendence. What Abrams interprets as a passage from political disillusion to spiritual recovery is characterized as a conservative political decision involving evasion and mystification. The basic issue, I take it, is whether one should primarily devote one's energies to political activism or to the practice of literature, and, if the latter choice is granted, whether one should primarily address in one's literary work (or literary criticism) social injustice and political conflict or existential and philosophical questions of the sort Wordsworth tends to address in his poems. These are immensely important questions. No one escapes them in practice. Yet I think they are more complex than critics like McGann and Levinson suggest. One of my intentions in this conclusion is to cast some light on the complexity of these questions, and on the deeper frameworks that condition this complexity in modern culture.

4. On Oppen's concern with family and fatherhood, see James Longenbach's thoughtful "A Test of Poetry," 32. Burton Hatlen understands Oppen's later work to be largely continuous with his earlier work ("Not Altogether Lone in a Lone Universe," 325–26, 331–32); Michael Heller takes the later work to be sharply discontinuous with the earlier work (*Speaking the Estranged*, 5–6); Peter Nicholls sees the later work as both continuous and discontinuous with the earlier work, characterizing Oppen's return to poetry as a "beginning again" (*George Oppen*, 4–29). My understanding of Oppen's path, in this respect, is akin to Nicholls's. A sort of "uneasy conscience" in culture does not really enter into our culture until the late nineteenth century, and only over the last century has it become widespread, in two major phases: first, from the twenties through the fifties, under the influence of marxist thought, the growth of working-class movements, the social crisis of the thirties, and the actual event or (in Perry Anderson's phrase) the "imaginative proximity" of revolution; second, from the fifties through our own time, under the influence of decolonization, the new social movements of the sixties and seventies, and the multiple political discourses emerging out of these movements.

5. I should make clear that in what follows my concern is with a cultural predicament of European and American modernity: I do not mean to present

an interpretative narrative of modernity in a broad sense. The predicament with which I am concerned, of course, is inseparable from those larger social and cultural changes that we take to be characteristic of modernity: the rise of the new sciences in the study of nature, the growth of large bureaucratic states backed by strong militaries of increasing technological sophistication, the extension and contestation over centuries of European colonialism, the development of early forms of political liberalism, the rise of democratic politics announced by the American and French revolutions, the emergence of a capitalist economy of production for profit, the industrial revolution or the shift to the use of fossil fuels for energy, the unfolding of new forms of individualism as well as new forms of class conflict, and a gradual secular and materialist reorientation of social life. These are among the prominent features of the whole context to which modern thinkers respond in one way or another. I do not here try to comprehend this whole. Nor do I address the range of contingencies—economic, military, geopolitical, cultural, ecological—at work in the emergence of early modernity in Europe and its settler colonies between the sixteenth and eighteenth centuries. That is yet another question. My claim, then, is not that Jewish, Christian, and Greek traditions simply presage European modernity: my claim is that—in the modern world as it emerges in Europe out of a range of contingent historical forces—these are the cultural resources that thinkers have naturally tended to draw upon and rearticulate in response to problems of social and individual life that are unfamiliar, or in some ways unprecedented, and at the same time not unrelated to older questions.

6. The primary texts at stake here are Hegel, *Phenomenology of Spirit* and *Philosophy of Right*, and Kierkegaard, *Fear and Trembling*, *Stages on Life's Way*, *Philosophical Fragments*, and *Concluding Unscientific Postscript*. My account of this debate has been enormously influenced by Alexandre Kojève, *Introduction à la lecture de Hegel*, Louis Mackey, *Kiekegaard: A Kind of Poet*, Charles Taylor, *Hegel and Modern Society* and *The Ethics of Authenticity*, Axel Honneth, *The Fragmented World of the Social* and *The Struggle for Recognition*, and, above all, Robert Pippin, *Idealism as Modernism* and *The Persistence of Subjectivity*. Readers of Sartre's *Search for a Method* will recognize that I have repeated Sartre's words here: "Hegel is right," "Kierkegaard is right," Sartre says (12). According to Sartre, Kierkegaard cogently criticizes Hegel's philosophical idealism in the name of the concretely existing individual irreducible to a moment of a conceptual system. Yet Marx cogently criticizes Hegel's philosophical idealism in the name of the material social reality of history and, so, at the same time critically situates Kierkegaard's bourgeois idealism. The battle of idealisms is comprehended and surpassed in Marx's dialectical understanding of historical life. Yet a version of atheistic or immanent existentialism remains necessary in our time, Sartre claims, because Marx's thought has been reduced to a dogmatic or undialectical approach to history. Existentialism thus remains a necessary

ideology in an age of insufficiently developed Marxism. This means, I gather, that existentialist philosophy would no longer be necessary in an age of sufficiently vital and capacious Marxist thought—presumably Marxist thought that had absorbed the existentialist anthropology of *need, transcendence*, and *project* that Sartre sketches in the last chapter of his book (171). Further, once the emancipation of humankind from the realm of necessity, scarcity, and injustice has been attained, there will emerge a new "philosophy of freedom" that, Sartre says, we cannot possibly imagine from our current position in history (34). There is much in this that I find suggestive. One of my major disagreements, however, could be put this way: I'm arguing here, in the discussion above, that the tension between Hegel and Kierkegaard, or between a sociological perspective and an existential perspective toward the life of the individual, could never be overcome in a world of any measure of freedom. — It is true that there are sophisticated Hegelian approaches that manage to embrace all that Kierkegaard or, in a secular key, Nietzsche or the pre-marxist Sartre have to teach and at the same time hold it within a many-sided Hegelian frame. Adorno (despite the anti-existentialist polemics), Gillian Rose, Jay Bernstein, and Charles Taylor, I think, could all be thought of in this way. Robert Pippin, to my mind, is the most brilliant contemporary philosopher able to take into his larger Hegelian picture of social freedom the whole range of existentialist insights spelled out in Kierkegaard, Nietzsche, and Sartre. I have in mind his essays in *Idealism as Modernism* and particularly in *The Persistence of Subjectivity* (both of which I have drawn on amply in my discussion here). My understanding is that Pippin would accept the statement that both Hegel and Kierkegaard are right, on one condition, namely, that it be recognized that this is ultimately to say that Hegel, read correctly, comprehended deeply, is right. Would this mean that Pippin wants to work out a relationship between Hegelianism and existentialism analogous to, though clearly different from, the relationship between Marxism and existentialism that Sartre wants to work out? I'm not sure. His recent *Hegel's Practical Philosophy*—a patient clarification of Hegel's social ethic—does not set for itself so sweeping an ambition. At any rate I will avoid this mountain for now. My concern is to show that versions of the Hegel-Kierkegaard debate, both sides of which are essential to our lives, have been played out again and again in modern culture.

    7. On the way modern philosophers tend to take death as the absolute limit to human life—rather than a divine being or a transcendent structure of forms—see Löwith, *From Hegel to Nietzsche*, 104–05, and Rosen, *The Mask of Enlightenment*, 124–25. Löwith and Rosen are both critical of this destruction of traditional metaphysics. In the wake of Kierkegaard, of course, there are also Jewish and Christian existentialist thinkers, who owe as much to Kierkegaard as do their atheistic counterparts. Jaspers, a Protestant, is perhaps the most Kierkegaardian of these. Marcel, a Catholic, voices a more "sacramentalist"

experience of our embeddedness in, our pre-reflective and inexhaustible participation in, what Marcel calls "the mystery of being." A mystery, for Marcel, is different from a problem (*Being and Having*, 116–21; "On the Ontological Mystery," 18–19). A problem is something we attempt to solve through technical or pragmatic efforts. A mystery is something we are caught up in, something we have to live in a certain way, something we lose insofar as we attempt simply to solve it. The analogy at work here, as in Martin Buber's *I and Thou*, is clearly the difference between an I-It relation of instrumental work and an I-Thou relationship of mutual engagement and dialogue. Marcel, again like Buber, would like to extend the latter to dimensions of our relationship to Being as a whole and ultimately to a divine source.

8. See Jaspers, *The Origin and Goal of History*; Nietzsche, *On the Genealogy of Morals*; Weber, *The Sociology of Religion*; Louis Dumont, "Le renoncement dans les religions de l'Inde" and *Essais sur l'individualisme*; Marcel Gauchet, *Le désenchantement du monde*; Charles Taylor, *Modern Social Imaginaries, Varieties of Religion Today*, and *A Secular Age*; Samir Amin, *Eurocentrism*; S.N. Eisenstadt, *The Origins and Diversity of Axial Age Civilizations*; Donald Harman Akenson, *Surpassing Wonder*; Karen Armstrong, *The Great Transformation*; William McNeil, *The Rise of the West*; Michael Mann, *The Sources of Social Power*. Rabbinic Judaism, if not a "world religion" in the sense that Hinduism, Buddhism, Christianity, and Islam are, is also a religion—a transformation of the prophetic tradition—that emerges in the second phase of the Axial Age. In my sketch above, I draw rather freely on all of the sources I've just named, though I borrow in particular from Dumont, Gauchet, Taylor, and Amin. I of course do not mean to suggest that all of these interpretations are the same or even compatible with one another. Their differences are an issue I hope to address elsewhere. My concern here, again, is, first, to clarify the background of the debate between Hegel and Kierkegaard or, more broadly, between modern sociological and modern existential pictures of freedom, and second, related to this concern, to clarify the picture of spiritual freedom that was invented in Jewish, Greek, and Christian metaphysics and that continues to influence a modern culture which largely defines itself in opposition to metaphysics.

9. This is perhaps the place to make clear that Axial Age redefinitions of the good can be understood to involve, not only an ascetic antithesis to natural conceptions of the good, as Charles Taylor has emphasized, but also a spiritual deepening or "extension" of natural conceptions of the good, as Northrop Frye has emphasized: "the metaphorical or 'spiritual' direction," Frye says, "is thought of as fulfilling the physical need in another dimension of existence: it may require sublimation, but it does not cut off or abandon its physical roots" (*Words with Power*, 45; cf. 115–16, 224–25). Frye's approach, I think, is a characteristically modern or "Feuerbachian" way of translating Axial Age orientations into the generally naturalist frameworks of the modern world (cf. Paul

Ricoeur's reading of The Song of Songs in *Penser la Bible*, 411–57). This has been an important romantic project throughout modern culture.

10. See Emerson, *Essays and Lectures*, 475.

11. Coleridge, *Biographia Literaria*, 173. M. H. Abrams illuminates this dimension of romanticism in great depth in *Natural Supernaturalism*. Fredric Jameson, in *Valences of the Dialectic*, 204–05, 330–31, emphasizes the way Lukács draws together Schiller, Marx, and Weber. Axel Honneth, in *Pathologies of Reason*, 56–62, provides an insightful account of the influence of Lukács on Adorno and Benjamin in particular.

12. See Pierre Manent, *Histoire intellectuelle du libéralisme*, 143–72 (146 for the citation—a thought that Manent attributes to Allan Bloom—and 160–62 for the account of the indeterminacy of the nature to which Rousseau appeals in his critique of society). A similar point is made by Auerbach in his brief but illuminating account of Rousseau in *Mimesis*, 466–67. Emerson sees the issue clearly from his decidedly idealist perspective: "The critics who complain of the sickly separation of the beauty of nature from the thing to be done," he says, "must consider that our hunting of the picturesque is inseparable from our protest against false society. Man is fallen; nature is erect, and serves as a differential thermometer, detecting the presence or absence of the divine sentiment in man. By fault of our dulness and selfishness, we are looking up to nature, but when we are convalescent, nature will look up to us. We see the foaming brook with compunction: if our own life flowed with the right energy, we should shame the brook" (*Essays and Lectures*, 546). The great romantic writers, significantly, tend to speak of intimations, hints, traces, glimpses, promises, "hallucinations come to daze the corner of the eye" (Stevens): natural presence is felt to be a force of awakening, beckoning, calling. It is never fully itself, never fully there, but always, as Emerson says, "still elsewhere" (553). It has therefore been named and conceived in a range of guises across the modern period: Nature, Being, the Open Road, the abandoned streets and places of an older city, the dislocative negativity of time itself, the "anywhere out of the world" of Baudelaire and Kafka, or all the internal correlatives of these, including imagination, reverie, the unconscious, sheer restless expectation without a clear horizon, the voyage in the open dark of all the negative a-theologies of the last sixty years. Elsewhere I've tried to provide a sketch of this history and to suggest the limitations of its most recent phase (*The Extravagant*, 162–74, 273–85). Here, in a study based in two poets who belong in some sense to the whole tradition of existentialist thought, I would like to keep my attention turned to understandings of Nature or Being that have perhaps had a greater continuity across time.

13. See Pierre Hadot, *Qu'est-ce que la philosophie antique?* See, too, Jan Patocka's account of Democritus, and of the likeness between Democritus' path of care for the self and Plato's path of care for the self, despite all the immense

differences, in *Plato and Europe*, 71–90. Perhaps one could say that, as modern Newtonian and post-Newtonian science reconceives Nature in mathematical terms, and as modern technological society treats Nature as blank material to be exploited, modern culture at the same time seeks to approach Nature or Being as a whole by reworking two ancient models of the world: the biblical model of a Creation ultimately caught up in a history of suffering and redemption, and the Greek model of a Cosmos, an eternal bedrock pattern of things, that abides through all change. These are two of the four ancient pictures of the world, *le monde*, described in Rémi Brague's fascinating *La Sagesse du monde* (the other two are the atomist model and the gnostic anti-cosmic model). They were brought together, Brague shows, in the picture of the medieval synthesis.

14. William Barrett, in his still valuable study, *Irrational Man*, provides an incisive and suggestive account of the Hebrew roots of modern existentialist philosophies (73–79). Elsewhere in the book he underlines that the figure of Socrates does amply complicate this picture of origins (4–5, 86–87).

15. Virgil, *The Georgics*, Book II, 475–89. "But if some chill in the blood about the heart": this is not a modern romantic voice: Epicureans took the "heart" to be the literal site of "reason" (see Lucretius, *The Nature of Things*, III.136–144). Rousseau's *Reveries* is an early romantic version of a stance of this sort that would become widespread in modern culture: the stance of one who is neither a Socrates of philosophical virtue nor a Cato of civic virtue—the two ideals of human achievement evoked in Rousseau's political writings—but a poetic solitary given to reverie, to roving meditation (see Victor Gourevitch's introduction to his edition of *The Discourses and Other Early Political Writings*, ix–x). My discussion here is indebted to important themes in Paul Alpers's sweeping, subtle, immensely illuminating *What Is Pastoral?* Alpers draws a clear distinction between the pastoral tradition, with its representation of shepherds or their social likenesses as emblematically human speakers, and the romantic poetry of nature, in which pastoral is assimilated to romance and a prophetic horizon (the greatest speculative voice of this approach, he notes, is Northrop Frye's). Yet he also, in turning to seventeenth-century poems like Marvell's "The Garden," traces the replacement of shepherds by what he calls "pastoral speakers" of an aristocratic or courtly type. This opens the way to a path that would later arrive at the romantic solitary and all the transformations of the genre that then take place. Empson's *Some Versions of Pastoral* provides a thought-provoking study of the class issues at stake in both traditional and modern pastoral. His chapter on "the cult of independence" is relevant to the questions I've tried to address here from a different angle. From Virgil to Wordsworth and beyond, further, the pastoral and the elegy are intimately intertwined: the meditation on the green world is often a meditation on evening, twilight, autumn, loss, sorrow. It's as though the promise found in pastoral emerged in the very space of the grief explored in pastoral. This is a complex

question. For a deeply suggestive reflection on the elegiac dimension of the poetry of nature in the modern world, see Geoffrey Hartman, *The Fateful Question of Culture*, 66–77.

16. See Hadot, *Qu'est-ce que la philosophie antique?* 265–352, and *Exercices spirituels et philosophie antique*, 19–98; E. R. Dodds, *The Greeks and the Irrational*, 135–78; Michael Morgan, *Platonic Piety*; Geoffrey Harpham, *The Ascetic Imperative in Culture and Criticism*; Gavin Flood, *The Ascetic Self*. In an interview Hadot acknowledges the importance to his formation as a young scholar—hence to his approach to ancient philosophy—of the existentialist philosophies so prominent in the middle of the last century (*La philosophie comme manière de vivre*, 203–08). Unfortunately, to my knowledge, he has nowhere given this connection the extended engagement it invites. He also neglects a question that has long preoccupied historians of Hellenistic philosophy, namely, the nearly complete collapse in this period of an interest in political philosophy (for an overview of approaches to this question, see Isaiah Berlin, "The Birth of Greek Individualism"). Foucault, as is well known, borrows themes from Hadot's work in the last two volumes of *The History of Sexuality*. Hadot has expressed a measured criticism of the way Foucault, in his view, risks turning the ancient philosophical care for the self into a "new form of dandyism" (*Exercises spirituels*, 331; *La philosophie comme manière de vivre*, 215). Here, again, an engagement with modern existentialist thought, in particular with Kierkegaard's picture of stages of existence, would be rewarding. The later Foucault's turn to the question of concrete self-formation, the later Lyotard's turn to Heideggerian questions of authenticity, and the later Derrida's turn to a sort of decisionist ethic, taken together, raise interesting questions: post-structuralist thinkers, in their old age, seem at least in part to return to the existentialist themes that they had begun by so sharply opposing. One could add that the two thinkers who have by far exerted the greatest influence on the entire field of post-structuralist thought, Nietzsche and Heidegger, are generally included in any history of existentialist philosophy. The ramifications of existentialist currents in modern philosophy extend far.

17. See Charles Taylor, *A Secular Age*, 90–145 (112 for the citation). The classic studies with which Taylor's work is in conversation would include Weber, *The Protestant Ethic and the Spirit of Capitalism*, Horkheimer and Adorno, *Dialectic of Enlightenment*, and Foucault, *Discipline and Punish* and the first volume of *The History of Sexuality*.

18. For searching accounts of these trends in the contemporary world, see Richard Sennett, *The Corrosion of Character* and *The New Capitalism*, Zygmunt Bauman, *Liquid Modernity*, Nicole Aubert, *Le culte de l'urgence*, and Gilles Lipovetsky, *Les temps hypermodernes*. Sennett is particularly careful to underline that a clear acknowledgment of these problematic trends need not involve any nostalgia for the bad old days. On the spreading slums of the contemporary

world, see Mike Davis, *Planet of Slums*. J. M. Bernstein, in *Recovering Ethical Life*, has developed a suggestive philosophical approach to this contemporary condition. His approach, as I would paraphrase it, involves three initial steps: first, the domination of the individual by society, as Adorno puts it, has developed in our time to such an extent that the dominant classes are in some ways as dominated as the subordinate classes (this does not mean that domination is experienced in the same way among different classes); second, the instrumental habit of thought driven by the logic of capitalist productivity is the overwhelming imperative at work in the life of everyone in this society, for the economic, having become an autonomous social sphere in the eighteenth century, has since expanded and returned to re-colonize, as Habermas puts it, every domain of social life; and third, this imperative increasingly undermines any alternative bearings or horizons of thought, say, those of enduring Axial Age traditions, or Kantian humanism, or romantic humanism, or existentialist humanism, or marxist humanism, or what have you. The hypertrophy of economic reason tends to erode the power of the modern ideal of moral autonomy or spiritual independence: contemporary social structures, demanding instrumental performance at all costs, lend only spurious support to the ideal. This is one thing Sennett means when he speaks of the way contemporary society tends to corrode character. Bernstein's philosophical account of this reality and Senett's concrete sociological account, in fact, are close to one another in important respects. Both emphasize that the process is tendential, not complete; if it were complete, we could not even see it, not even talk about it (see *Recovering Ethical Life*, 23). For a skeptical response to this whole question, see Fredric Jameson, *Valences of the Dialectic*, 281–82. Jameson, hardly a postmodern cheerleader, has said that we would do well to abandon this older picture of the self (a self he likens, alas, to the private railroad car of a bygone era). Our task, he argues, is to conceptualize more clearly than we have the new kinds of flattened, dispersive, multiplied subjectivities that characterize our time.

19. See Erich Fromm, *The Sane Society*, 144; Thomas Frank, *The Conquest of Cool*; Jean Baudrillard, *Simulations*; Fredric Jameson, *Postmodernism, or, The Cultural Logic of Late Capitalism*; and Zaki Laïdi, *Le sacre du présent*. Nicole Aubert, *Le culte de l'urgence*, 324–42, drawing on Laïdi, speaks of the contemporary erasure of eternity beneath intensity. Northrop Frye, from a Blakean point of view, speaks of eternity as a visionary deepening of the here and now (*The Great Code*, 130). Elsewhere he describes the "primitive" in literature in terms that recall the passage from Fromm I've cited: "Poetry is continually bringing us back to the starting-point, not necessarily of time, but of social attitude" (*The Critical Path*, 89). *Primitive*, significantly, is the title of Oppen's last book. The word seems to have meant for him something akin to the return to basic questions that Fromm describes in the passage I've cited (see Nicholls, *George Oppen*, 127–28). The primitive, in this sense, is what we do not see when we are

"glassed in" the overprotected car or the corporate tower. "I find the contemporary substitution of society for the cosmos captive and deadly," Charles Olson writes in a letter of 1959 (*Selected Writings*, 29), speaking in a voice akin to the voice of Camus in *The Rebel* and in his debate with Sartre in the early fifties: a debate that repeats, in the immanent frame of a romantic existentialist and a post-existentialist marxist, the earlier debate between Kierkegaard and Hegel. Sartre is generally thought to have won this debate, at the level of argumentation or polemic, if not necessarily at the level of the issues (see David Sherman's thoughtful discussion of this in *Camus*, 174–84).

20. See Jameson, *Marxism and Form*, 372–73, and Marcel, "On the Ontological Mystery," 23–24. The passage of Jameson's could be compared with Merleau-Ponty's description, in phenomenological rather than historicist terms, of a "hyperdialectic" (*The Visible and the Invisible*, 94–95). The passage of Marcel's could be compared with Ricoeur's account, in both existentialist and hermeneutic terms, of the work of reflection in retrieving the self out of opacity and dispersion ("The Hermeneutics of Symbols and Philosophical Reflection," 328–30).

21. See Horkheimer and Adorno, *Dialectic of Enlightenment*, 100, 135, 166–67. This book is infamous for its mandarin and entirely unnuanced attack on mass culture, or on what today is usually called popular culture, a slippage that elides a basic point that Horkheimer and Adorno want to make. In this respect the book carries a certain modernist stance to an extreme. In our time, as is often said, the boundaries between high and popular culture are far more blurred. In our time, in fact, as Fredric Jameson has said, the boundaries between any cultural domain at all and the economic domain have largely collapsed (see "Notes on Globalization as a Philosophical Issue"). Today, then, it is perhaps most useful to read Horkheimer and Adorno's critique as an account of the threats to any and every sphere of thought in our world, and *a fortiori* to the realm of high culture, academic and non-academic.

22. For the poem from which I've cited here, see Brock-Broido, *Trouble in Mind*, 67. Oppen writes in a late letter: "my respect for Rilke [is] so great that I tend to hear him whenever a sufficient depth is reached" (SL, 314). Mary Ann Caws emphasizes Rilke's resonance in Char's work in a long thread running throughout the footnotes of her *The Presence of René Char* (see especially 100, n. 6, 150, n. 9, and 159, n. 16). She also cites a number of suggestive passages from Heidegger on the disclosive force of wonder (283, n. 11). Rilke is a poet in whose work all is seen as sheer transience, the weather of elegy, and at the same time as sheer wonder, the weather of encounter. In Rilke, elegy is hymn, hymn is elegy, and in both Char and Oppen, for all their differences from Rilke, there is a deep sounding of this paradox (a paradox so important to religious experience). They are in the dark, again and again; at fortunate moments, again and again, they are taken up in wonder, the wonder of response to what is there, of

response to the whole, of response to another in love. The last of Rilke's *Sonnets to Orpheus* is like a spirit in the margins of all of Char's and Oppen's work: it is at once a meditation on death, a meditation on the whole, a meditation on loss and recovery, a meditation on transience, and a meditation on the life of encounter.

23. I draw here on Norman Finkelstein's insightful reading of "Guest Room" in "The Dialectic of *This In Which*," 360–63.

24. See Rosen, *The Mask of Enlightenment*, 177–89. In this section of his book, a careful reading of Zarathustra'a affirmative stance, Rosen does not speak of a dimension of hysteria. He has written of Nietzsche—and of the relationship between Nietzsche and Plato—in many places. I've not been able to locate the source of the particular characterization of Zarathustra's laughter that I recall above. Walter Kaufmann interprets Nietzsche's will to power as a rearticulation of the Eros of Plato's *Symposium* (*Nietzsche*, 211–56). He also emphasizes Nietzsche's antagonistic admiration for Socrates, suggesting that *Ecce Homo* be read as Nietzsche's *Apology* (391–411).

25. Louise Glück, *Proofs & Theories*, 133–34.

BIBLIOGRAPHY

Abrams, M.H. "English Romanticism: The Spirit of the Age." In *Romanticism and Consciousness*, edited by Harold Bloom. New York: Norton, 1970. 90–118.

———. *Natural Supernaturalism: Tradition and Revolution in Romantic Literature*. New York: Norton, 1971.

Adorno, Theodor. *Metaphysics: Concepts and Problems*. Edited by Rolf Tiedemann and translated by Edmund Jephcott. Stanford: Stanford University Press, 2001.

———. *Minima Moralia*. Translated by E.F.N. Jephcott. London: Verso, 1974.

———. *Negative Dialectics*. Translated by E.B. Ashton. New York: Continuum, 1973.

Akenson, Donald Harman. *Surpassing Wonder: The Invention of the Bible and the Talmuds*. Chicago: University of Chicago Press, 1998.

Alpers, Paul. *What Is Pastoral?* Chicago: University of Chicago Press, 1996.

Altieri, Charles. "The Objectivist Tradition." In DuPlessis and Quartermain, *The Objectivist Nexus*, 25–36.

Amin, Samir. *Eurocentrism*. Translated by Russell Moore. New York: Monthly Review Press, 1989.

Ammons, A.R. *The Selected Poems*. Expanded ed. New York: Norton, 1986.

Annas, Julia. *An Introduction to Plato's "Republic."* Oxford: Clarendon, 1981.

Armstrong, Karen. *The Great Transformation: The Beginnings of our Religious Traditions*. New York: Knopf, 2006.

Aubert, Nicole. *Le culte de l'urgence*. Paris: Flammarion, 2003.

Auerbach, Erich. [1946.] *Mimesis: The Representation of Reality in Western Literature*. Translated by Willard R. Trask with a new introduction by Edward Said. Princeton: Princeton University Press, 2003.

Aujoulat, Norbert. *Lascaux: Movement, Space, and Time*. New York: Harry N. Abrams, Inc., 2005.

Baker, Robert. *The Extravagant: Crossings of Modern Poetry and Modern Philosophy*. Notre Dame, IN: University of Notre Dame Press, 2005.

Barrett, William. *Irrational Man: A Study in Existential Philosophy*. New York: Anchor, 1958.
Baudrillard, Jean. *Simulations*. Translated by Paul Foss, Paul Patton, and Philip Beitchman. New York: Semiotext (e), 1983.
Bauman, Zygmunt. *Liquid Modernity*. Cambridge: Polity Press, 2000.
Becker, Ernest. *The Denial of Death*. New York: Simon & Schuster, 1973.
Berlin, Isaiah. "The Birth of Greek Individualism." In *Liberty*, edited by Henry Hart. New York: Oxford University Press, 2002. 287–321.
Bernstein, Charles. "Hinge Picture." In *Speeches and Poems*. Chicago: University of Chicago Press, 1999. 192–96.
Bernstein, Jay. *Adorno: Disenchantment and Ethics*. New York: Cambridge University Press, 2001.
———. *Recovering Ethical Life: Jürgen Habermas and the Future of Critical Theory*. London: Routledge, 1995.
Bishop, Elizabeth. *The Complete Poems*. New York: Farrar, Straus, Giroux, 1979.
Blake, William. *The Complete Poetry and Prose*. Newly revised ed. Edited by David Erdman with commentary by Harold Bloom. New York: Doubleday, 1988.
Blanchot, Maurice. "René Char." *La part du feu*. Paris: Gallimard, 1949. 103–14.
———. "René Char et la pensée du neutre." *L'entretien infini*. Paris: Gallimard, 1969. 439–50.
Bloom, Harold. "The Internalization of Quest-Romance." In *The Ringers in the Tower: Studies in the Romantic Tradition*. Chicago: University of Chicago Press, 1971. 13–35.
Borgmann, Albert. *Technology and the Character of Contemporary Life: A Philosophical Inquiry*. Chicago: University of Chicago Press, 1984.
Bosch, Elizabeth. "René Char, Georges Bataille, et Lascaux." In Kingma-Eijgendaal and Smith, *Lectures de René Char*, 98–117.
Brague, Rémi. *La Sagesse du monde: Histoire de l'expérience humaine de l'univers*. Paris: Fayard, 1999.
Brock-Broido, Lucie. *Trouble in Mind*. New York: Knopf, 2004.
Buber, Martin. *I and Thou*. Translated and with prologue by Walter Kaufmann. New York: Touchstone, 1970.
Camus, Albert. *The Myth of Sisyphus and Other Essays*. Translated by Justin O'Brien. New York: Random House, 1983.
———. *The Rebel*. Translated by Anthony Bower. New York: Random House, 1991.
———. "René Char." In *Lyrical and Critical Essays*, edited by Philip Thody and translated by Ellen Conroy Kennedy. New York: Random House, 1970. 321–25.

Camus, Albert, and René Char. *Correspondance: 1946–1959*. Edited by Franck Planeile. Paris: Gallimard, 2007.
Caproni, Giorgio. "Char comme source et invention de vie." In Fourcade, *René Char*, 134–38.
Caws, Mary Ann. *The Presence of René Char*. Princeton: Princeton University Press, 1976.
Chilton, Randolph. "The Place of Being in the Poetry of George Oppen." In Hatlen, *George Oppen*, 89–112.
Claudel, Paul. *Art Poétique*. Paris: Gallimard/Folio, 1984.
Coleridge, Samuel Taylor. *Biographia Literaria with Aesthetic Essays*. Edited by John Shawcross. 2 vols. London: Oxford University Press, 1967.
Crane, Hart. *The Complete Poems*. Edited by Marc Simon and with an introduction by Harold Bloom. New York: Liveright, 2000.
Cronin, Anthony. *Samuel Beckett: The Last Modernist*. New York: Da Capo Press, 1999.
Davidson, Michael. "Palimptexts: George Oppen, Susan Howe, and the Material Text." In *Ghostlier Demarcations: Modern Poetry and the Material Word*. Berkeley: University of California Press, 1997. 64–93.
Davis, Mike. *Planet of Slums*. London: Verso, 2006.
Diamond, Jared. *Guns, Germs, and Steel: The Fate of Human Societies*. New York: Norton, 2005.
Dodds, E. R. *The Greeks and the Irrational*. Berkeley: University of California Press, 1951.
Dumont, Louis. *Essais sur l'individualisme: Une perspective anthropologique sur l'idéologie moderne*. Paris: Seuil, 1983.
———. *Homo aequalis I. Genèse et épanouissement de l'idéologie économique*. Paris: Gallimard, 1985.
———. *Homo aequalis II. L'idéologie allemande: France–Allemagne et retour*. Paris: Gallimard, 1991.
———. "Le renoncement dans les religions de l'Inde." In *Homo hierarchicus: Le système des castes et ses implications*. Paris: Gallimard, 1966. 324–50.
DuPlessis, Rachel Blau. "George Oppen: 'What Do We Believe to Live With.'" *Ironwood* 5 (1975): 62–77.
———. "Objectivist Poetics and Political Vision." In Hatlen, *George Oppen*, 123–48.
———. "'Uncannily in the Open': In the Light of Oppen." In Shoemaker, *Thinking Poetics*, 203–27.
DuPlessis, Rachel Blau, and Peter Quartermain, eds. *The Objectivist Nexus: Essays in Cultural Poetics*. Tuscaloosa: University of Alabama Press, 1999.
Edmundson, Mark. *Literature against Philosophy, Plato to Derrida: A Defence of Poetry*. New York: Cambridge University Press, 1995.

Eisenstadt, S.N., ed. *The Origins and Diversity of Axial Age Civilizations.* Albany: State University of New York Press, 1986.
Eliot, T.S. *The Complete Poems and Plays.* New York: Harcourt Brace, 1967.
Éluard, Paul. *Poésie ininterrompue.* Paris: Gallimard, 1946.
Emerson, Ralph Waldo. *Essays and Lectures.* Edited by Joel Porte. New York: Library of America, 1983.
Empson, William. *Some Versions of Pastoral.* New York: Penguin, 1935.
Finkelstein, Norman. "The Dialectic of *This In Which*." In Hatlen, *George Oppen*, 359–74.
Flood, Gavin. *The Ascetic Self: Subjectivity, Memory, and Tradition.* New York: Cambridge University Press, 2004.
Foucault, Michel. *Discipline and Punish: The Birth of the Prison.* Translated by Alan Sheridan. New York: Random House, 1977.
———. *The History of Sexuality.* Translated by Robert Hurley. 3 vols. New York: Random House, 1978, 1985, 1986.
Fourcade, Dominique. "Essai d'introduction." In Fourcade, *René Char*, 19–30.
———, ed. *René Char.* Special edition of *L'Herne* 15 (1971).
Frank, Thomas. *The Conquest of Cool: Business Culture, Counterculture, and the Rise of Hip Consumerism.* Chicago: University of Chicago Press, 1998.
Fredman, Stephen. "'And All Now Is War': George Oppen, Charles Olson, and the Problem of Literary Generations." In DuPlessis and Quartermain, *The Objectivist Nexus*, 286–93.
Freud, Sigmund. *Civilization and Its Discontents.* Edited and translated by James Strachey, with a biographical introduction by Peter Gay. New York: Norton, 1989.
Friedman, Richard Elliott. *Who Wrote the Bible?* 2nd edition. New York: Harper Collins, 1997.
Fromm, Erich. *The Sane Society.* New York: Henry Holt, 1955.
Frye, Northrop. *The Critical Path: An Essay on the Social Context of Literary Criticism.* Bloomington: Indiana University Press, 1971.
———. *The Great Code: The Bible and Literature.* New York: Harcourt Brace Jovanovich, 1982.
———. *The Well-Tempered Critic.* Bloomington: Indian University Press, 1963.
———. *Words with Power: Being a Second Study of the Bible and Literature.* New York: Harcourt Brace Jovanovich, 1990.
Gander, Forrest. *A Faithful Existence: Reading, Memory, and Transcendence.* Washington, DC: Shoemaker & Hoard, 2005.
———. *Science & Steepleflower.* New York: New Directions, 1998.
Gauchet, Marcel. *L'Avènement de la démocratie I. La révolution moderne.* Paris: Gallimard, 2007.
———. *L'Avènement de la démocratie II. La crise du libéralisme.* Paris: Gallimard, 2007.

———. *La condition historique: Entretiens avec François Azouvi et Sylvain Piron.* Paris: Gallimard, 2003.

———. *Le désenchantement du monde: Une histoire politique de la religion.* Paris: Gallimard, 1985.

Gill, Stephen. *William Wordsworth: A Life.* Oxford: Oxford University Press, 1990.

Glück, Louise. *Proofs & Theories: Essays on Poetry.* New York: Ecco Press, 1994.

Greilsamer, Laurent. *L'éclair au front: la vie de René Char.* Paris: Fayard, 2004.

Habermas, Jürgen. *Autonomy and Solidarity: Interviews with Jürgen Habermas.* Revised ed. With an introduction by Peter Dews. London: Verso, 1992.

Hadot, Pierre. *Exercises spirituels et philosophie antique?* Revised and enlarged ed. With a foreword by Arnold I. Davidson. Paris: Albin Michel, 2002.

———. *The Inner Citadel: The Meditations of Marcus Aurelius.* Translated by Michael Chase. Cambridge, MA: Harvard University Press, 1998.

———. *La philosophie comme manière de vivre: Entretiens avec Jeannie Carlier et Arnold I. Davidson.* Paris: Albin Michel, 2001.

———. *Qu'est-ce que la philosophie antique?* Paris: Gallimard, 1995.

Harpham, Geoffrey Galt. *The Ascetic Imperative in Culture and Criticism.* Chicago: University of Chicago Press, 1987.

Hartman, Geoffrey. *The Fateful Question of Culture.* New York: Columbia University Press, 1997.

Hatlen, Burton, ed. *George Oppen: Man and Poet.* Orono, ME: National Poetry Foundation, 1981.

———. "'Not Altogether Alone in a Lone Universe.'" In Hatlen, *George Oppen*, 325–58.

Heaney, Seamus. "Crediting Poetry." In *Opened Ground*, 415–30.

———. *Opened Ground: Selected Poems 1966–1996.* New York: Farrar Straus Giroux, 1998.

Hegel, G.W.F. *Elements of the Philosophy of Right.* Edited by Allen W. Wood and translated by H.B. Nisbet. New York: Cambridge University Press, 1991.

———. *Phenomenology of Spirit.* Translated by A. V. Miller with an analysis of the text and a foreword by J. N. Findlay. New York: Oxford University Press, 1977.

Heidegger, Martin. *Being and Time.* Translated by Joan Stambaugh. Albany: State University of New York Press, 1996.

———. *Pathmarks.* Edited and translated by William McNeill. New York: Cambridge University Press, 1998.

———. *Poetry, Language, Thought.* Translated and with an introduction by Albert Hofstadter. New York: Harper and Row, 1971.

Heller, Michael. *Speaking the Estranged: Essays on the Work of George Oppen.* Cambridge: Salt, 2008.

Hill, Geoffrey. *Collected Critical Writings*. Edited by Kenneth Haynes. Oxford: Oxford University Press, 2008.
Hirshfield, Jane. *Nine Gates: Entering the Mind of Poetry*. New York: Harper Collins, 1997.
Honneth, Axel. *The Fragmented World of the Social: Essays in Social and Political Philosophy*. Edited by Charles W. Wright. With multiple translators. Albany: State University of New York Press, 1995.
———. *Pathologies of Reason: On the Legacy of Critical Theory*. Translated by James Ingram. New York: Columbia University Press, 2009.
———. *The Struggle for Recognition: The Moral Grammar of Social Conflicts*. Translated by Joel Anderson. Cambridge, MA: MIT Press, 1995.
Horkheimer, Max, and Theodor W. Adorno. *Dialectic of Enlightenment: Philosophical Fragments*. Edited by Gunzelin Schmid Noerr and translated by Edmund Jephcott. Stanford: Stanford University Press, 2002.
Jameson, Fredric. *Marxism and Form: Twentieth-Century Dialectical Theories of Literature*. Princeton: Princeton University Press, 1971.
———. "Notes on Globalization as a Philosophical Issue." In *Cultures of Globalization*, edited by Fredric Jameson and Masao Miyoshi. Durham, NC: Duke University Press, 1998. 54–77.
———. "The Poetics of Totality." In *The Modernist Papers*. London: Verso, 2007. 3–44.
———. *Postmodernism, or, The Cultural Logic of Late Capitalism*. Durham, NC: Duke University Press, 1991.
———. *Valences of the Dialectic*. London: Verso, 2009.
Jaspers, Karl. *The Origin and Goal of History*. New Haven: Yale University Press, 1953.
———. *Reason and Existenz*. Translated and with an introducton by William Earle. Milwaukee: Marquette University Press, 1997.
———. *Way to Wisdom: An Introduction to Philosophy*. Translated by Ralph Manheim. New Haven: Yale University Press, 1954.
Kant, Immanuel. *Critique of Practical Reason*. Edited and translated by Mary Gregor, with an introduction by Andrews Reath. New York: Cambridge University Press, 1997.
Kaufman, Walter. *Critique of Religion and Philosophy*. Princeton: Princeton University Press, 1958.
———. *Nietzsche: Philosopher, Psychologist, Anti-Christ*. 4th ed. Princeton: Princeton University Press, 1974.
Kenner, Hugh. "Disconnected Numerousness." *Ironwood* 32 (1985): 205–11.
Kierkegaard, Soren. *Concluding Unscientific Postscript*. Translated by David F. Swenson and Walter Lowrie. Princeton: Princeton University Press, 1968.

———. *Fear and Trembling* and *Repetiton*. Edited and translated by Howard V. Hong and Edna H. Hong. Princeton: Princeton University Press, 1983.

———. *Philosophical Fragments* and *Johannes Climacus*. Edited and translated by Howard V. Hong and Edna H. Hong. Princeton: Princeton University Press, 1985.

———. *Stages on Life's Way*. Edited and translated by Howard V. Hong and Edna H. Hong. Princeton: Princeton University Press, 1988.

Kingma-Eijgendaal, Tineke. "La poéticité de l'aphorisme chez René Char: quelques exemples." In Kingma-Eijgendaal and Smith, *Lectures de René Char*. 43–58.

Kingma-Eijgendaal, Tineke, and Paul Smith, eds. *Lectures de René Char*. Groningue: C.R.I.N, 1992.

Kirk, G. S., J. E. Raven, and M. Schofield, eds. *The Presocratic Philosophers*. 2nd ed. New York: Cambridge University Press, 1983.

Kojève, Alexandre. *Introduction à la lecture de Hegel*. Ed. Raymond Queneau. Paris: Gallimard, 1947.

Kramer, Samuel Noah. *The Sumerians: Their History, Culture, and Character*. Chicago: University of Chicago Press, 1963.

La Charité, Virginia. *The Poetics and the Poetry of René Char*. Chapel Hill: University of North Carolina Press, 1968.

Laïdi, Zaki. *Le sacre du présent*. Paris: Flammarion, 2000.

Lawler, James. *René Char: The Myth and the Poem*. Princeton: Princeton University Press, 1978.

———. *Rimbaud's Theatre of the Self*. Cambridge, MA: Harvard University Press, 1992.

Lentricchia, Frank. *Ariel and the Police*. Madison: University of Wisconsin Press, 1988.

Levinson, Marjorie. *Wordsworth's Great Period Poems*. New York: Cambridge University Press, 1986.

Lipovetsky, Gilles. *Les temps hypermodernes*. Paris: Bernard Grasset, 2004.

Longenbach, James. "A Test of Poetry." *The Nation* 286.5 (February 2008): 29–32.

Löwith, Karl. *From Hegel to Nietzsche: The Revolution in Nineteenth-Century Thought*. Trans. David E. Green with a foreword by Hans-Georg Gadamer. New York: Columbia University Press, 1991.

Lowney, John. "'The Air of Atrocity': 'Of Being Numerous' and the Vietnam War." In Shoemaker, *Thinking Poetics*, 143–59.

Lucretius. *The Nature of Things*. Translated by Frank O. Copley. New York: Norton, 1977.

Luhmann, Niklas. *Observations on Modernity*. Trans. William Whobrey. Stanford: Stanford University Press, 1998.

———. *Theories of Distinction: Redescribing the Descriptions of Modernity*. Edited and with an introduction by William Rasch. Translated by Joseph O'Neil, Elliott Schreiber, Kerstin Behnke, and William Whobrey. Stanford: Stanford University Press 2002.
Lukács, Georg. *History and Class Consciousness: Studies in Marxist Dialectics*. Translated by Rodney Livingstone. Cambridge, MA: MIT Press, 1988.
MacIntyre. Alasdair. *After Virtue*. 2nd ed. Notre Dame, IN: University of Notre Dame Press, 1984.
Mackey, Louis. *Kierkegaard: A Kind of Poet*. Philadelphia: University of Pennsylvania Press, 1971.
Manent, Pierre. *La cité de l'homme*. Paris: Fayard, 1994.
———. *Histoire intellectuelle du libéralisme*. Paris: Hachette, 1997.
Mann, Michael. *The Sources of Social Power*. Vol. 1. *A History of Power from the Beginning to A.D. 1760*. New York: Cambridge University Press, 1986.
Marcel, Gabriel. *Being and Having: An Existentialist Diary*. New York: Harper, 1965.
———. *The Existential Background to Human Dignity*. Cambridge, MA: Harvard University Press, 1963.
———. "On the Ontological Mystery." In *The Philosophy of Existence*. Translated by Many Harari. New York: Citadel Press, 1995. 9–46.
Marks, Robert. *The Origins of the Modern World: A Global and Ecological Narrative from the Fifteenth to the Twenty-first Century*. 2nd ed. New York: Rowman and Littlefield, 2007.
Marty, Eric. *René Char*. Paris: Seuil, 1990.
Marx, Karl. *Capital*. Vol. 1. Translated by Ben Fowkes with an introduction by Ernest Mandel. New York: Penguin, 1990.
———. *The Economic and Philosophic Manuscripts of 1844*. Edited and with an introduction by Dirk J. Struik. Translated by Martin Milligan. New York: International Publishers, 1964.
Mathieu, Jean-Claude. *La poésie de René Char I. Traversée du surréalisme*. Paris: José Corti, 1988.
———. *La poésie de René Char II. Poésie et résistance*. Paris: José Corti, 1990.
McAleavey, David. "Clarity and Process: Oppen's *Of Being Numerous*." In Hatlen, *George Oppen*, 381–406.
McGann, Jerome. *The Romantic Ideology: A Critical Investigation*. Chicago: University of Chicago Press, 1983.
McNeil, William. *The Rise of the West: A History of the Human Community*. With a retrospective essay. Chicago: University of Chicago Press, 1991 [1963].
Merleau-Ponty. *The Visible and the Invisible*. Edited by Claude Lefort. Translated by Alphonso Lingis. Evanston: Northwestern University Press, 1968.
Mill, John Stuart. *On Liberty*. Edited and with an introduction by Gertrude Himmelfarb. New York: Penguin, 1985.

Morgan, Michael L. *Platonic Piety: Philosophy and Ritual in Fourth-Century Athens*. New Haven: Yale University Press, 1990.
Mottram, Eric. "The Political Responsibilities of the Poet." In Hatlen, *George Oppen*, 149–68.
Mounin, George. *La communication poétique*. Précédé de *Avez-vous lu Char?* Paris: Gallimard, 1969.
Nancy, Jean-Luc. *Dis-Enclosure: The Deconstruction of Christianity*. Translated by Bettina Bergo, Gabriel Malenfant, and Michael B. Smith. New York: Fordham University Press, 1988.
Nicholls, Peter. *George Oppen and the Fate of Modernism*. New York: Oxford University Press, 2007.
Nietzsche, Friedrich. *On the Genealogy of Morals* and *Ecce Homo*. Translated and with commentary by Walter Kaufmann. New York: Random House, 1967.
———. *Thus Spoke Zarathustra*. Translated and with a preface by Walter Kaufmann. New York: Penguin, 1978.
———. *Twilight of the Idols* and *The Anti-Christ*. Translated by R. J. Hollingdale with an introduction by Michael Tanner. New York: Penguin, 1990.
Nussbaum, Martha. *The Fragility of Goodness: Luck and Ethics in Greek Tragedy and Philosophy*. Updated ed. New York: Cambridge University Press, 2001.
Olson, Charles. *Selected Writings*. Edited and with an introduction by Robert Creeley. New York: New Directions, 1966.
Oppen, George. "The Mind's Own Place." *Kulchur* 3.10 (1963): 2–8.
———. "Worksheets." *Conjunctions* 10 (1987): 186–208.
———. "Worksheets." *Iowa Review* 18.3 (1988): 1–17.
———. "Worksheets." *Sulfur* 26 (1990): 135–49.
Oppen, George, and Mary Oppen. "Poetry and Politics: An Interview with George and Mary Oppen." With Burton Hatlen and Tom Mandel. In Hatlen, *George Oppen*, 23–50.
Oppen, Mary. "Conversation with Mary Oppen." With Dennis Young. *Iowa Review* 18.3 (1988): 18–47.
———. *Meaning a Life: An Autobiography*. Santa Rosa: Black Sparrow, 1990.
Pascal, Blaise. *Pensées*. Edited by Michel Le Guern. Paris: Gallimard/Folio, 2004.
Patocka, Jan. *Plato and Europe*. Translated by Peter Lom. Stanford: Stanford University Press, 2002.
Peck, John. "George Oppen and the World in Common." In Hatlen, *George Oppen*, 63–88.
Piore, Nancy Kline. *Lightning: The Poetry of René Char*. Boston: Northeastern University Press, 1981.
Pippin, Robert. *Hegel's Practical Philosophy: Rational Agency as Ethical Life*. New York: Cambridge University Press, 2008.

———. *Idealism as Modernism: Hegelian Variations*. New York: Cambridge University Press, 1997.

———. *Nietzsche, moraliste français: la conception nietzshéene d'une psychologie philosophique*. Translated from English by Isabelle Wienand with a preface by Marc Fumaroli. Paris: Odile Jacob, 2006.

———. *Nietzsche, Psychology, and First Philosophy*. Chicago: University of Chicago Press, 2010.

———. "On 'Becoming Who One Is' (and Failing): Proust's Problematic Selves." In *The Persistence Of Subjectivity*. 307–38.

———. *The Persistence of Subjectivity: On the Kantian Aftermath*. New York: Cambridge University Press, 2005.

Plato. *Phaedo*. Translated and with an introduction by David Gallop. New York: Oxford University Press, 1993.

———. *Phaedrus* and *Letters VII and VIII*. Translated and with introductions by Walter Hamilton. New York: Penguin, 1973.

———. *The Republic*. Edited by G. R. F. Ferrari. Translated and with a preface by Tom Griffith. New York: Cambridge University Press, 2000.

———. *The Symposium*. Translated and with an introduction by Christopher Gill. New York: Penguin, 1999.

Poirier, Richard. *Robert Frost: The Work of Knowing*. New York: Oxford University Press, 1977.

Poulet, Georges. "René Char." In *Le point de départ*. Paris: Plon, 1964. 92–108.

Prevallet, Kristin. "One Among the Rubble: George Oppen and World War II." In Shoemaker, *Thinking Poetics*, 131–42.

Price, A.W. *Love and Friendship in Plato and Aristotle*. Oxford: Clarendon Press, 1989.

Richard, Jean-Pierre. "René Char." In *Onze études sur la poésie moderne*. Paris: Seuil, 1964. 81–127.

Ricoeur, Paul. "The Hermeneutics of Symbols and Philosophical Reflection: II." Translated by Charles Freilich. In *The Conflict of Interpretations*, edited by Don Ihde. Evanston: Northwestern University Press, 1974. 315–34.

———. "La métaphore nuptiale." In André LaCocque and Paul Ricoeur, *Penser la Bible*. Paris: Seuil, 1998. 411–57.

Rilke, Rainer Maria. *Ahead of All Parting: The Selected Poetry*. Edited and translated by Stephen Mitchell. New York: The Modern Library, 1995.

Rimbaud, Arthur. *Oeuvres*. Rev. ed. Edited by Suzanne Bernard and André Guyaux. Paris: Classiques Garnier, 1991.

Rosen, Stanley. *The Elusiveness of the Orindary: Studies in the Possibility of Philosophy*. New Haven: Yale University Press, 2002.

———. *The Limits of Analysis*. New York: Basic Books, 1980. Reprint ed. South Bend, IN: St. Augustine's Press, 2000.

———. *The Mask of Enlightenment: Nietzsche's "Zarathustra."* New York: Cambridge University Press, 1995.
Rousseau, Jean-Jacques. *The Discourses and Other Early Political Writings.* Edited and translated by Victor Gourevitch. New York: Cambridge University Press, 1997.
———. *Emile or On Education.* Translated and with an introduction and notes by Allan Bloom. New York: Basic Books, 1979.
———. *The Reveries of a Solitary Walker.* Translated and with a preface, notes, and an interpretative essay by Charles Butterworth. New York: Harper, 1979.
———. *The Social Contract and Other Later Political Writings.* Edited and translated by Victor Gourevitch. New York: Cambridge University Press, 1997.
Sartre, Jean-Paul. *Being and Nothingness.* Translated and with an introduction by Hazel E. Barnes. New York: Washington Square, 1966.
———. *Search for a Method.* Translated by Hazel E. Barnes. New York: Random House, 1968.
Schiller, Friedrich. *Letters on the Aesthetic Education of Man.* Translated by Elizabeth M. Wilkinson and L. A. Willoughby. London: Oxford University Press, 1967.
———. *Naïve and Sentimental Poetry.* Translated by Julius A. Elias. New York: Frederick Ungar Publishing Co., 1966.
Sennett, Richard. *The Corrosion of Character: The Personal Consequences of Work in the New Capitalism.* New York: Norton, 1998.
———. *The Culture of the New Capitalism.* New Haven: Yale University Press, 2006.
Sereni, Vittorio. "Sur *Feuillets d'Hypnos.*" In Fourcade, *René Char*, 45–49.
Shelley, Percy Bysshe. "On Love." In *Shelley's Poetry and Prose*, edited by Donald H. Reiman and Neil Fraistat. 2nd ed. New York: Norton, 2002. 503–04.
Sherman, David. *Camus.* Oxford: Blackwell, 2009.
Shoemaker, Steve, ed. *Thinking Poetics: Essays on George Oppen.* Tuscaloosa: University of Alabama Press, 2009.
Stendhal. *De l'amour.* Paris: Flammarion, 1965.
Stevens, Wallace. *The Necessary Angel.* New York: Random House, 1951.
———. *The Palm at the End of the Mind.* Edited by Holly Stevens. New York: Random House, 1971.
Taylor, Charles. *The Ethics of Authenticity.* Cambridge, MA: Harvard University Press, 1991.
———. *Hegel and Modern Society.* New York: Cambridge University Press, 1979.
———. *Modern Social Imaginaries.* Durham, NC: Duke University Press, 2004.
———. *A Secular Age.* Cambridge, MA: Harvard University Press, 2007.

———. *Varieties of Religion Today: William James Revisited*. Cambridge, MA: Harvard University Press, 2002.
Thackrey, Susan. *George Oppen: A Radical Practice*. San Francisco: O Books, 2001.
Thoreau, Henry David. *Walden*. Edited and with an introduction by Stephen Fender. New York: Oxford University Press, 1997.
Thuillier, Jacques. *Georges de la Tour*. Translated by Fabia Claris. Paris: Flammarion, 1993.
Tocqueville, Alexis. *De la démocratie en Amérique*. With a preface by André Jardin. 2 vols. Paris: Gallimard/Folio, 1986.
Velay, Serge. *René Char: qui êtes-vous?* Lyon: La Manufacture, 1987.
Veyne, Paul. *René Char en ses poèmes*. Paris: Gallimard, 1990.
Virgil. *The Eclogues*. Translated and with an introduction by Guy Lee. New York: Penguin, 1984.
———. *The Georgics*. Translated and with an introduction by L. P. Wilkinson. New York: Penguin, 1982.
Weber, Max. *The Protestant Ethic and the Spirit of Capitalism*. Translated by Talcott Parsons with an introduction by Anthony Giddens. London: Routledge, 1992.
———. *The Sociology of Religion*. Translated by Ephraim Fischoff with an introduction by Talcott Parsons and a new foreword by Ann Swidler. Boston: Beacon Press, 1991.
Weinfield, Henry. *The Music of Thought in the Poetry of George Oppen and William Bronk*. Iowa City: University of Iowa Press, 2009.
Wesling, Donald. *The New Poetries: Poetic Form since Coleridge and Wordsworth*. London and Toronto: Associated University Press, 1985.
Whitman, Walt. *Leaves of Grass and Other Writings*. Edited by Michael Moon. New York: Norton, 2002.
———. *Leaves of Grass: The First (1855) Edition*. Edited and with an introduction by Malcom Cowley. New York: Penguin, 1959.
Williams, William Carlos. *The Collected Poems*. Edited by A. Walton Litz and Christopher MacGowan. 2 vols. New York: New Directions, 1986.
———. *Paterson*. New York: New Directions, 1963.
Wordsworth, William. *The Major Works*. Edited by Stephen Gill. New York: Oxford University Press, 1984.
Wright, C. D. *Cooling Time: An American Poetry Vigil*. Port Townsend, WA: Copper Canyon, 2005.
Yeats, William Butler. *The Collected Poems*. Revised 2nd ed. Edited by Richard J. Finneran. New York: Scribner, 1996.

INDEX

Abrams, M. H., 123–24, 197n.3
  Natural Supernaturalism, 202n.11
Adorno, Theodor, 154, 193n.20, 199n.6, 202n.11
  Dialectic of Enlightenment, 143, 144–46, 147, 164, 204n.17, 206n.21
  Minima Moralia, 105
  Negative Dialectics, 196n.32
  on openness and metaphysics, 176n.2
  on societal domination of individual, 204n.18
  on universal history, 196n.32
Akenson, Donald Harman:
  Surpassing Wonder, 201n.8
Akhmatova, Anna, 7, 109
alienation, 4, 6, 59, 71, 86, 112, 132, 157
Alpers, Paul, 150
  What Is Pastoral?, 203n.15
Altieri, Charles, 35
American revolution, 129, 138, 198n.5
Amin, Samir, 136–37
  Eurocentrism, 201n.8
Ammons, A. R., 186n.5
Anderson, Perry, 193n.20, 198n.4
Annas, Julie, 175n.1
aphorisms, 34, 35, 36–41, 42, 46–54, 181n.15, 182nn.16–18

Arendt, Hannah, 190n.15
Armstrong, Karen, 136
  The Great Transformation, 201n.8
asceticism, 19, 137, 148, 151–58, 167, 168, 201n.9
Ashbery, John, 29
atheism, 71, 133, 139, 141, 199n.6, 200n.7
Aubert, Nicole, 155
  Le culte de l'urgence, 204n.18, 205n.19
Auerbach, Erich
  Mimesis, 176n.3, 202n.12
  on realist novels, 176n.3
Axial Age, 136–38, 169, 170, 201n.8, 204n.18
  ascetic discipline in, 137, 151–53, 159, 167, 201n.9
  the good in, 105, 137–38, 144–45, 159, 166, 201n.9
  vs. modernity, 138, 139, 145, 152–53, 155–58, 162–63
  spiritual freedom in, 137–39, 140, 142, 145, 148–49, 155, 162, 167
  transcendent horizon in, 137, 141, 151, 159
Aztecs: Spanish conquest of, 95, 196n.32

Bacon, Sir Francis, 145

Balzac, Honoré de: *Le Père Goriot*, 176n.3
Barrett, William: *Irrational Man*, 203n.14
Bataille, Georges, 184n.23
Baudelaire, Charles, 34, 182n.17, 202n.12
Baudrillard, Jean
  on Nature, 159
  Simulations, 205n.19
Bauman, Zygmunt: *Liquid Modernity*, 204n.18
Becker, Ernest: *The Denial of Death*, 114
Being, 179n.4, 202n.12
  Heidegger on, 3, 56, 99, 100, 134, 184n.23
  Marcel on, 162, 200n.7
  Merleau-Ponty on, 134
  and Oppen, 64, 72, 76, 77, 81, 95, 99, 100, 128, 156, 167, 185n.2
  as the whole, 4, 134–35, 141–42, 148–49, 165, 167, 200n.7, 202n.13
Benjamin, Walter, 202n.11
Berlin, Isaiah, 204n.16
Bernstein, Charles, 194n.22
Bernstein, Jay, 84, 192n.18, 199n.6
  Recovering Ethical Life, 204n.18
Bertrand, Aloysius, 34
Bishop, Elizabeth: "At the Fishhouses," 115–16
Blake, William, 124, 142, 143, 147, 168, 170, 182n.17
  vs. Char, 9, 15, 16, 22, 33, 39, 40, 46, 52, 53, 128
  on doors of perception, 96
  on exuberance, 33
  fury of, 15, 16
  on Los, 22, 122, 125
  vs. Oppen, 75, 87, 96, 122, 128
  on Orc, 15, 22, 122, 125
  on Urizen, 122

Blanchot, Maurice, 181n.12, 184n.23
Bloom, Allan, 202n.12
Bloom, Harold
  "The Internalization of Quest-Romance," 197n.3
  The Ringers in the Tower, 197n.3
Borgmann, Albert: on deictic discourse, 105, 196n.30
Bosch, Elisabeth, 21–22, 178n.3
Brague, Rémi: *La Sagesse du monde*, 202n.13
Braque, Georges, 9
Breton, André, 15, 124, 182n.18
Brock-Broido, Lucie, 166
Bronk, William, 186n.3, 195n.26
Buber, Martin: *I and Thou*, 200n.7
Buddhism, 136, 137

Cabeza de Vaca, Álvar Núñez, 95, 106, 107, 196n.32
Camus, Albert, 179n.6
  on Char, 71, 188n.11
  vs. Char, 125–26, 184n.23
  The Rebel, 205n.19
  relationship with Char, 9, 12, 125–26
  and Sartre, 5, 205n.19
  on whole of nature, 134, 149
capitalism, 78, 153–55, 159, 197n.5, 204n.18
  Marx on, 6, 143–44, 145
Caproni, Giorgio, 185n.24
Cavell, Stanley, 73
Caws, Mary Ann, 32, 44–45, 206n.22
Celan, Paul, 7, 12, 176n.4, 183n.20
Césaire, Aimé, 7
Char, René
  on Apollo and Pluto, 41, 42
  and archipelagoes, 34, 40, 93, 164
  on beauty, 23, 25, 26, 31, 33–34, 42, 49, 51, 53, 125, 134, 163, 182n.18

vs. Blake, 9, 15, 16, 22, 33, 39, 40, 46, 52, 53, 128
vs. Camus, 125–26, 184n.23
and clairvoyance, 16, 52, 53, 119, 165
on climbing/ascending, 19
on contemporaneity, 29
and death, 11, 18, 43
and departure, 18, 35
and disclosure, 185n.24
early life, 8, 52, 126
and emanation, 179n.4, 179n.7
on encounters, 16, 19, 20, 24, 25, 32, 35, 42, 46, 51, 63, 185n.24
and enthusiasm, 22, 23–24, 25, 26, 32, 33, 35, 179n.7
and eros, 7, 8, 9, 13–14, 16, 23–27, 28–29, 32–33, 35, 42, 45–46, 53, 166–68, 170–71, 171, 179n.5, 179n.7, 180n.9, 182n.18, 184n.23, 185n.24, 206n.22
on the essential, 30, 180n.9, 180n.10
as existentialist, 10, 12, 71, 121, 128, 156, 162–63, 176n.4, 184n.23, 191n.16
on fury (*fureur*) 15–16, 22, 42, 52, 125
vs. Gander, 180n.9
on health of misfortune, 171
vs. Heidegger, 177n.1
on Heraclitus, 37, 38, 43, 49, 183nn.19–20
and history, 29, 46, 50–51, 128
and hope, 22, 23, 42, 49, 51, 165, 171
on human condition, 50, 51, 53
and human freedom, 12, 17, 44–45, 49, 50, 51, 52, 53–54, 71, 121, 164, 165–66, 185n.24, 188n.8
and the hunt, 20–22, 26–29, 167, 179n.8
as Hypnos, 47–48

on imagination, 53, 164
individualism of, 9–10
on justice, 51
and Lascaux cave paintings, 20, 21–22, 25, 28, 178n.3
and La Tour's "Prisoner," 31, 49–50, 180nn.10–11
on life as inexpressible, 182n.18
and meditation, 20, 24, 42, 44, 121, 125, 163, 164–65, 178n.2, 181n.15, 183n.20, 206n.22
and metaphysics, 6–7, 46, 47, 50, 121, 125, 128, 163, 165, 185n.24
on Miró, 179n.4
on mystery (*mystère*), 15, 22, 44, 52, 125
vs. Nietzsche, 12, 37–38, 42, 43–44, 177n.1, 183n.19
and openness, 31–32, 44, 49, 71, 168, 184n.23, 188n.8
vs. Oppen, 6–7, 10–14, 71, 92, 121, 122, 126, 128, 134, 156, 162–68, 170–71, 176n.4, 188n.8, 191n.16, 194n.21, 206n.22
pessimism of, 38, 43, 50, 53, 71, 171
vs. Petrarch, 26
vs. Plato, 45–46
on poetry, 16, 19, 22, 23–24, 25, 26–27, 32–34, 36, 37, 39, 40–42, 43, 47, 51, 125, 126, 134, 165, 168, 177n.1, 179n.8, 181n.12, 181n.15, 183n.20, 185n.24
and politics, 9, 124, 125–26
on premonition, 22, 164, 185n.24
relationship with Camus, 9, 12, 125–26
relationship with Éluard, 8, 9
relationship with Péret, 52
Resistance experience, 8–9, 10, 11, 14, 16, 17, 20, 22, 30, 36, 37, 46–47, 48, 50–51, 52, 53, 124–25, 126, 179n.7

Char, René (*continued*)
  vs. Rilke, 206n.22
  on Rimbaud, 41–42, 53, 128
  vs. Rimbaud, 8, 9, 15, 17, 22, 23, 29, 34–35, 39, 40, 53, 124, 165, 182n.18
  and romanticism, 19–20, 26, 34, 42–43, 177n.1
  vs. Shelley, 40, 52, 166
  and spaciousness, 44–46, 51, 52
  vs. Stevens, 17, 27, 28, 30, 31, 33, 40–41, 44, 182n.18
  and surrealism, 7, 8, 9, 12, 16, 36–37, 45, 52–53, 124, 126, 179n.7
  on Time, 19, 42
  and tragedy, 42, 43, 71, 169, 170–71, 183n.20
  and transcendence, 42–43, 45–46
  on Transparence/Transparents, 16, 17–19, 28, 32, 51, 163
  and value, 121, 134, 168
  and vision, 7, 8, 10, 14, 15, 19–20, 22, 24, 26, 29, 31, 32, 37, 39–40, 42, 46, 51, 52, 53, 165, 171
  vs. Whitman, 33, 40, 44, 128, 178n.2
  and the whole, 7, 13, 71, 121, 134, 165, 167, 170–71, 206n.22
  and the wolf, 27, 29
  and wonder, 11, 71, 166, 167, 206n.22
  vs. Wordsworth, 9, 17, 122, 125, 128
Char, René, works of
  "The Absent One," 16, 35, 48
  aphorisms, 34, 35, 36–41, 42, 46–47, 125, 181n.15, 182n.18, 194n.21
  "Are There Incompatibilities?," 179n.7, 184n.23
  "Argument" (*Fureur et mystère*), 185n.24
  "Argument" (*Le Poème pulvérisé*), 185n.24
  "The Black Stags," 20–24, 25
  "Calendar," 44–45
  "Common Presence," 182n.18
  "Companions in the Garden," 19, 32
  "The Crystal Wheat-Ear Sheds in the Grasses its Transparent Harvest," 17, 19, 25, 35
  "During the Journey," 23
  "The Effacement of the Poplar," 31
  "Enchantment in the Fox Den," 25
  "Everyone Gone," 45, 179n.8
  "The Fatal Partner," 28, 35
  First Mill, 36–37
  "The First Moments," 25
  Formal Share, 15, 37, 46–54, 125, 185n.24
  "From Moment to Moment," 17, 19
  Fureur et mystère (FM), 16, 17, 18, 22, 23, 24, 25, 26, 28, 31, 32, 33, 36, 37, 38, 40, 41, 42–43, 44–45, 47–48, 50, 51, 52, 53, 125, 165, 166–67, 179n.8, 180n.11, 182n.18, 185n.24
  "I Inhabit Pain," 32, 40
  "The Inventors," 177n.1
  "Invitation," 32–33
  Leaves of Hypnos/Feuillets d'Hypnos (FH), 9, 19, 20, 25, 29–31, 37, 46–54, 125, 168, 171, 180n.10, 180n.11, 183n.19, 184n.23
  "Lettera amorosa," 24–25
  "The Library is on Fire," 32, 36, 177n.1, 180n.11
  "Long Live," 36
  "Lord," 35
  Les Mantinaux (M), 17, 28, 32, 36, 51, 163, 177n.1, 180n.9

Le Marteau sans maitre (MM), 15, 177n.1, 181n.14
"Muttering," 27–29, 35
"Notwithstanding," 45
Le Nu perdu (NP), 22, 28, 31, 40, 51, 178n.2, 182n.18
The Nuptial Face, 31
Oeuvres Complètes (OC), 16, 18
"Of an Unadorned Night," 36, 178n.2
parable in, 17, 35, 44–45
La Parole en archipel (PA), 14, 19, 22, 23, 24, 25, 27, 29, 32, 33, 36, 38, 39, 40, 43, 91, 95, 154, 156, 163, 165, 171, 177n.1, 178n.2, 180n.11
"La passe de Lyon," 29, 180n.11
Le Poème pulvérisé, 9, 34, 125, 182n.18, 185n.24
prose poems, 34–36, 46, 125
"The Raised Scythe" (PA, 184), 14
"Redness of the *Matinaux*," 17, 180n.9
"Renewal," 25
Recherche de la base et du sommet (RBS), 8, 9, 12, 15, 16, 29, 31, 40, 41–43, 47, 50, 53, 171, 179n.4, 179nn.6–7, 182n.16, 183n.20, 184n.20, 184n.23
"Restore to Them," 19, 44
"Rose of Oak," 183n.19
"The Shark and the Gull," 35
"So That Nothing Be Changed," 25
The Sovereign Conversation, 32
"The Struck Adolescent," 32
Substantial Allies, 32
"That Smoke Which Carried Us...," 36
They Alone Remain, 46, 125
"Threshold," 18, 35, 44
To a Tense Serenity, 171

The Transparents, 17
Word as Archipelago, 182n.18
Chateaubriand, François-René, 34
Chaudon, Roger, 48, 179n.7
Chilton, Randolph, 185n.2
Chomsky, Noam: *Year 501: The Conquest Continues*, 107
Christianity, 38, 46, 53, 124, 136
  ascetic discipline in, 151
  Jesus, 4, 35, 129
  spiritual freedom in, 129, 130–31, 137, 138, 141
  transcendence in, 118, 129–32, 133, 134, 137
  See also Kierkegaard, Søren
civil rights movement, 187n.7
Claudel, Paul: *Art Poétique*, 1
Coleridge, Samuel Taylor, 90, 124
  on the poet, 142
  relationship with Wordsworth, 123
  "The Rime of the Ancient Mariner," 123
communism
  Char's attitudes regarding, 9, 124
  Oppen's attitudes regarding, 10–11, 64, 126–27, 187n.7
  Stalinism, 127, 144
Confucianism, 136
consumer culture, 78, 154–55
counter-cultures, 154, 158
Crane, Hart, 24, 115
Creeley, Robert, 190n.15

Davidson, Michael, 188n.11, 194n.22
Davis, Mike, 155, 204n.18
death, 66, 130, 152, 166, 170, 206n.22
  and Char, 11, 18, 43
  denial of, 83, 85, 86, 110–13, 192n18
  and existentialism, 134, 149, 161, 200n.7
  Freud on, 79

death (*continued*)
  and Oppen, 11, 73–74, 76, 77, 83, 85, 86, 94, 110–13, 114–15, 168–69, 192n.18
  and the self, 7, 134, 141
Deguy, Michel, 184n.23
Dembo, Louis: interview with Oppen, 55, 63, 73–74, 87, 88, 96, 126, 168, 176n.4
Democritus, 202n.13
Derrida, Jacques, 204n.16
Descartes, René, 145, 153, 156
de Staël, Nicolas, 9
Dews, Peter, 193n.20
Dombrowski, Chris, 194n.22
Donne, John, 74
Dostoevsky, Fyodor, 147
Dumont, Louis, 136, 137
  Essais sur l'individualisme, 201n.8
  "Le renoncement dans les religions de l'Inde," 201n.8
DuPlessis, Rachel Blau
  on Oppen, 66, 88, 90–91, 111, 122, 127, 176n.4, 188n.9, 192nn.17–18, 194nn.21–22, 194n.24
  on value, 66, 78, 88
Durkheim, Émile, 166

Edmundson, Mark: *Literature against Philosophy*, 197n.3
Eisenstadt, S. N.: *The Origins and Diversity of the Axial Age Civilizations*, 201n.8
Eliot, T. S.
  vs. Oppen, 67–68, 188n.10
  The Waste Land, 67–68, 188n.10, 189n.12
Éluard, Paul, 8, 9, 24, 165, 166
Emerson, Ralph Waldo, 81, 84, 100, 169, 182n.17
  "Compensation," 149
  on expansive vision, 60–62
  individualism of, 119
  Nature, 60–62
  on Nature, 202n.12
  on the spiritual, 139
  "Spiritual Laws," 119
Empson, William: *Some Versions of Pastoral*, 203n.15
Engels, Friedrich, 5
Enlightenment, the, 154
Epicureanism, 148, 150, 151, 203n.15
eros
  and Char, 7, 8, 9, 13–14, 16, 23–27, 28–29, 32–33, 35, 42, 45–46, 53, 166–68, 170–71, 171, 179n.5, 179n.7, 180n.9, 182n.18, 184n.23, 185n.24, 206n.22
  Freud on, 67, 79, 81
  and Oppen, 7, 13–14, 67, 74, 76, 77, 78–82, 85, 109, 166, 166–68, 170–71, 171, 184n.23, 206n.22
  Oppen and eros, 57, 60, 66, 72, 87–88, 95
  Plato on, 24, 25, 31, 67, 80, 167–68, 170, 180n.9, 191n.16, 207n.24
  and poetry, 24–26
  as source of vision and companionship, 14, 71, 88, 109, 168
existentialism, 44, 52, 59, 204n.16, 204n.18
  atheistic existentialism, 71, 133, 139, 141, 199n.6, 200n.7
  authenticity in, 117–18, 133–34, 139, 140, 149, 156
  and Char, 10, 12, 71, 121, 128, 156, 162–63, 176n.4, 184n.23, 191n.16
  and death, 134, 149, 161, 200n.7
  existential phenomenology, 7, 12, 56, 58, 62, 66, 111, 113, 156, 157–58, 166, 206n.20
  Hebrew roots of, 203n.14
  vs. modern poetry, 4, 7

Nature/Being in, 134–35, 141–42, 149, 156, 165
and Oppen, 10, 12, 71, 78, 81, 95, 111, 113, 121, 128, 156, 162–63, 176n.4, 191n.16, 193n.20
relationship to Marxism, 199n.6
vs. romanticism, 4, 6, 134–35, 155–56, 167
vs. sociology, 4–6, 176n.3, 201n.8
spiritual freedom in, 133–34, 140, 151, 155, 167
and the whole, 3–4, 160
and wonder, 166

fascism, 47, 50, 144
Feuerbach, Ludwig, 129
Finkelstein, Norman, 192n.17, 207n.23
Foucault, Michel, 154, 155
  Discipline and Punish, 204n.17
  The History of Sexuality, 204nn.16–17
Fourcade, Dominique, 176n.4
France
  Popular Front in, 8
  Revolution, 2, 122–23, 129, 138, 176n.3, 198n.5
  Vichy regime, 8
Frank, Thomas: *The Conquest of Cool,* 158
Frankfurt School, 130, 143, 158, 191n.16
Fredman, Stephen: "And All Now Is War," 176n.4
freedom, human, 3, 4, 6, 7, 10
  and Char, 12, 17, 44–45, 49, 50, 51, 52, 53–54, 71, 121, 164, 165–66, 185n.24, 188n.8
  and Oppen, 12, 59, 71, 73, 111, 121, 164, 165–66, 188n.8
  See also social freedom; spiritual freedom

Freud, Sigmund, 152, 190n.15, 191n.16
  on civilization, 79
  on death-instinct, 79
  on eros, 67, 79, 81
  vs. Oppen, 79–81
  on repression, 144
  on sublimation, 79–81
Friedman, Richard Elliott, 75, 190n.15
Fromm, Erich, 157–58, 163, 164
  The Sane Society, 158
Frost, Robert, 193n.20
Frye, Northrop, 32–33, 203n.15
  on Axial Age, 201n.9
  on discontinuous prose, 38–39, 182n.17
  on eternity, 205n.19
  on existential writing, 176n.4
  on poetry, 205n.19
  on wisdom writing, 38–39, 93

Gadamer, Hans-Georg, 74
Gander, Forrest, 180n.9
Gauchet, Marcel, 136, 137, 176n.2
  Le désenchantement du monde, 201n.8
Genesis creation stories, 75, 202n.13
Gill, Christopher, 191n.16
Gill, Stephen: *William Wordsworth,* 197n.2
Girard, René, 75, 166
Glück, Louise, 89, 172–73, 194n.22, 194n.25, 196n.31
Great Depression, 10–11, 126
Greilsamer, Laurence, 26, 53, 176n.4, 180n.11

Habermas, Jürgen, 193n.20
  on dialogue, 71
  on social life, 204n.18

Hadot, Pierre, 148, 151–52, 162, 175n.1, 204n.16
Hartman, Geoffrey: *The Fateful Question of Culture*, 203n.15
Hatlen, Burton, 176n.4
  "Not Altogether Lone in a Lone Universe," 112–13, 198n.4
  on Oppen, 112–13, 114, 115
  "Poetry and Politics," 115
Heaney, Seamus, 109, 121, 128, 196n.32
  "Station Island," 128
Hegel, G. W. F., 3, 52, 81, 142, 144, 176n.2, 176n.4
  on absolute spirit, 159
  on Christianity and secular modernity, 129
  vs. Kant, 5, 139–42
  vs. Kierkegaard, 5–6, 128–35, 139, 141, 161, 199n.6, 201n.8, 205n.19
  Marx on, 6, 199n.6
  Phenomenology of Spirit, 199n.6
  Philosophy of Right, 199n.6
  on recollection, 161
  on religion, philosophy, and art, 159
  on the romantic, 131–32
  on the self, 71, 132, 138
  on social freedom, 6, 128–30, 132–33, 160
  on the unhappy consciousness, 129, 131, 132–33
Heidegger, Martin, 5, 66, 204n.16
  on Being, 3, 56, 99, 100, 134, 184n.23
  Being and Time, 99, 111, 188n.9
  on care, 188n.9
  on conformity, 133
  on death, 134
  on human being/*da-sein*, 3, 188n.9
  vs. Oppen, 12, 111, 112, 185n.2, 188n.9, 194n.31
  on presencing, 23
  on technology, 177n.1
  on wonder, 206n.22
Hellenistic philosophy, 129, 136, 148, 149, 151, 152, 204n.16
Heller, Michael, 110, 194n.21, 194n.23
Heraclitus, 37, 38, 43, 49, 183nn.19–20
Hernández, Miguel, 7
Hill, Geoffrey, 26
  Collected Critical Writings, 119
Hinduism, 136
Hirshfield, Jane, 66
historicism, 3, 71, 158, 176n.3
historicist sociology, 6, 133, 160
history
  and Char, 29, 46, 50–51, 128
  and metaphysics, 2–3, 4, 6–7, 13, 121, 128
  in modernity, 2–3
  and Oppen, 64, 95, 106–8, 109, 128
Hobbes, Thomas, 78, 138, 145
Hölderlin, Friedrich, 183n.20
Honneth, Axel, 129–30, 191n.16
  The Fragmented World of the Social, 199n.6
  Pathologies of Reason, 202n.11
  The Struggle for Recognition, 199n.6
Horkheimer, Max: *Dialectic of Enlightenment*, 143, 144–46, 147, 164, 204n.17, 206n.21
House Un-American Activities Committee, 11, 126
Hugo, Victor, 38, 181n.15

irony, 29
Islam, 136

Jameson, Fredric
  on cultural and economic domains, 206n.21
  on dialectical thinking, 160–61, 206n.20
  on modernist nominalism, 92
  on Nature, 159
  Postmodernism, 205n.19
  on the self, 204n.18
  Valences of the Dialectic, 202n.11, 204n.18
Jaspers, Karl, 184n.23, 200n.7
  on the Axial Age, 136
  The Origin and Goal of History, 201n.8
  on the whole, 176n.2
Job, 86, 108, 180n.10, 196n.31
John of the Cross, St., 97, 195n.29
Joyce, James, 38, 108

Kafka, Franz, 202n.12
Kant, Immanuel, 156, 169, 204n.18
  vs. Hegel, 5, 139–42
  on modern culture, 159
  on moral autonomy, 139–41, 142
  on moral freedom, 139–41
  on practical postulates, 140–42
  on reason, 108, 139–40
Kaufman, Walter, 175n.1, 207n.24
Kenner, Hugh: "Disconnected Numerousness," 114
Kierkegaard, Søren, 147, 176n.4
  on authenticity, 117, 118
  on Christianity, 133, 139
  Concluding Unscientific Postscript, 5, 199n.6
  on faith, 130–31, 133, 141, 183n.20
  Fear and Trembling, 199n.6
  on Hegel, 5, 6
  vs. Hegel, 5–6, 128–35, 135–36, 139, 141, 161, 199n.6, 201n.8, 205n.19

  on the individual, 3, 5, 6, 129, 130–31, 133–34, 141, 155, 161–62, 199n.6
  negative theology of, 3
  Philosophical Fragments, 5, 199n.6
  The Present Age, 5
  on self-deception, 131, 132
  The Sickness unto Death, 5
  on spiritual freedom, 128–29, 130–31, 132, 160
  on stages of existence, 130–31, 155, 204n.16
  Stages on Life's Way, 199n.6
  on truth, 72
Kingma-Eijgendaal, 182n.16, 182n.18
Kline Piore, Nancy, 184n.23
Kojève, Alexandre: *Introduction à la lecture de Hegel*, 199n.6
Kwak, Youna, 193n.19

La Charité, Virginia, 181n.15
Laïdi, Zaki: *Le sacre du présent*, 205n.19
La Rouchefoucauld, François de, 38
La Tour, George de, 183n.20
  "The Prisoner," 31, 49–50, 180nn.10–11
Lautréamont, Comte de, 124
Lawler, James: *René Char*, 178n.3, 182n.18
Leibniz, Gottfried Wilhelm, 176n.4
Lentricchia, Frank: *Ariel and the Police*, 186n.5
Levinson, Marjorie: *Wordsworth's Great Period Poems*, 197n.3
Lipovetsky, Gilles: *Les temps hypermodernes*, 204n.18
Locke, John, 78, 138, 145, 156
Lorca, Federico Garcia, 7
love. *See* eros

Löwith, Karl, 134, 200n.7
Lowney, John, 188n.10
Lucretius, 151, 203n.15
Luhmann, Niklas, 191n.16
Lukács, Georg, 5, 202n.11
  History and Class Consciousness, 142–43
  on reification, 142–43
Luther, Martin, 176n.4
Lyotard, Jean-François, 204n.16

MacIntyre, Alasdair, 78
Mackey, Louis: *Kierkegaard*, 199n.6
Mallarmé, Stéphane, 34
Mandelstam, Osip, 7, 183n.20
Manent, Pierre, 147, 176n.1, 202n.12
Mann, Michael: *The Sources of Social Power*, 201n.8
Marcel, Gabriel, 66, 100
  on being, 162, 200n.7
  on the full and the empty, 189n.12
  on recollection, 161–62, 206n.20
Marcuse, Herbert: *Eros and Civilization*, 158
Marty, Eric, 45, 50, 179n.5, 180n.9, 183n.20
Marvell, Andrew: "The Garden," 203n.15
Marx, Karl, 81, 125, 129, 154, 202n.11
  on capitalism, 6, 143–44, 145
  on class conflict, 6
  on commodification, 142
  The Communist Manifesto, 5
  The German Ideology, 5
  on Hegel, 6, 199n.6
  on history, 199n.6
  on ideology, 6
  on organization of work, 143–44
  Paris Manuscripts, 5
  on work with others, 71
Marxism, 160–61, 176n.4, 192n.18, 198n.4, 199n.6, 204n.18

Mathieu, Jean-Claude: on Char, 29–30, 37, 38, 40, 176n.4, 180n.11, 181n.15
McAleavey, David, 190n.14
  "Clarity and Process," 114
McGann, Jerome: *The Romantic Ideology*, 197n.3
McNeil, William: *The Rise of the West*, 201n.8
Mead, George Herbert, 130
Melville, Herman, 86, 115
Merleau-Ponty, Maurice, 12, 66, 149
  on Being and the self, 134
  on philosophy and wonder, 1
  The Visible and the Invisible, 1, 206n.20
metaphysics, 1–4
  and Char, 6–7, 46, 47, 50, 121, 125, 128, 163, 165, 185n.24
  and history, 2–3, 4, 6–7, 13, 121, 128
  and Nietzsche, 43–44
  and Oppen, 6–7, 64, 75, 81, 95, 103, 104–5, 115, 121, 121–22, 127, 128, 163, 165, 192n.17
  See also whole, the
Mill, John Stuart: *On Liberty*, 5
Milton, John: Satan, 62
Miró, Joan, 179n.4
modernity, 127–28, 142, 143–44, 145–48, 152–58, 198n.5
  ascetic discipline of, 153–55
  vs. Axial Age, 138, 139, 145, 152–53, 155–58, 162–63
  Fromm on, 157–58
  routine in, 157–58, 160
modern poetry, 55–56, 92
  vs. existentialism, 4, 7
modern realist novels, 176n.3
Montaigne, Michel de, 148
Montale, Eugenio, 7, 40
Moore, Marianne, 115
Moss, Thylias, 172

Mottram, Eric, 176n.4
Mounin, Georges, 179n.7
   La communication poétique, 177n.1
Mourelatos, Alexander, 192n.17

Nancy, Jean-Luc: *Dis-Enclosure,*
   184n.23
nature
   Camus on, 134, 149
   Emerson on, 202n.12
   Jameson on, 159
   in romanticism, 134–35, 141–43,
      145, 146–49, 154, 155–56, 165,
      202n.12, 203n.15
   and Rousseau, 146–49
   as the whole, 4, 7, 134–35, 141–42,
      147, 148–49, 150–51, 154, 167,
      200n.7, 202n.13
Neoplatonism, 136
Neruda, Pablo, 7
Newtonian science, 135, 202n.13
Nicholls, Peter, 195n.26
   George Oppen and the Fate of
      Modernism, 185n.2, 205n.19
   on Oppen, 110, 113, 117, 118,
      176n.4, 185n.2, 194n.21, 196n.31,
      198n.4, 205n.19
Nietzsche, Friedrich, 117, 136, 145,
   147, 182n.16, 184n.23, 199n.6,
   204n.16
   on *amor fati,* 134, 149, 170
   aphorisms of, 37–38
   The Birth of Tragedy, 169
   vs. Char, 12, 37–38, 42, 43–44,
      177n.1, 183n.19
   on death of God, 133
   Ecce Homo, 207n.24
   on eternal recurrence, 3
   on human freedom, 133
   and metaphysics, 43–44
   on naturalism, 138
   On the Genealogy of Morals, 201n.8
   vs. Oppen, 71
   on Plato, 169
   vs. Plato, 207n.24
   on religion and suffering, 166
   Twilight of the Idols, 37
   on will to power, 29, 78, 143,
      207n.24
   Zarathustra, 134, 152, 169–70,
      207n.24
nihilism, 51, 79, 143, 169–70, 186n.3
Novalis, 182n.17
Nussbaum, Martha, 191n.16

Olson, Charles, 12, 61, 176n.4,
   186n.5
   "The Kingfishers," 190n.15
Oppen, George
   and beauty, 72
   and Being, 64, 72, 76, 77, 81, 95, 99,
      100, 128, 156, 167, 185n.2
   on belief, 117–19
   on benevolence of the real,
      99–100, 102, 107, 108
   vs. Blake, 75, 87, 96, 122, 128
   on built world, 61, 69, 79, 84–85,
      95, 96–98, 102, 103, 111–12, 114
   and care, 67, 72, 73, 74, 76, 77, 82,
      86, 87–88, 108, 167
   vs. Char, 6–7, 10–14, 71, 92, 121,
      122, 126, 128, 134, 156, 162–68,
      170–71, 176n.4, 188n.8, 191n.16,
      194n.21, 206n.22
   and choice, 78, 81
   and clarity, 14, 15, 20, 37, 44, 57, 64,
      65, 66, 71, 76, 77, 86–87, 88–89,
      93, 95, 96, 100, 102, 166, 171,
      189n.12, 193n.19, 194n.22
   and companionship, 63, 70, 71, 76,
      77, 80–81, 87, 88, 95, 109, 146,
      168
   and conversation, 57, 167, 186n.3
   and covenant, 76, 77, 79

Oppen, George (*continued*)
- on curiosity, 64, 67, 73–74, 76, 77, 93, 108, 188n.9
- and death, 11, 73–74, 76, 77, 83, 85, 86, 94, 110–13, 114–15, 168–69, 192n.18
- during Depression, 10–11
- and despair, 95, 96
- and dialogical openness, 57, 58
- and disclosure, 56, 58, 76, 92, 95, 99, 100, 102, 107, 164
- early life, 10, 126
- vs. Eliot, 67–68, 188n.10
- vs. Emerson, 60–62, 84, 119, 193n.19
- and eros, 7, 13–14, 57, 60, 66, 67, 72, 74, 76, 77, 78–81, 85, 87–88, 95, 109, 166, 166–68, 170–71, 184n.23, 206n.22
- and ethics, 64
- as exile in Mexico, 11
- as existentialist, 10, 12, 71, 78, 81, 95, 111, 113, 121, 128, 156, 162–63, 176n.4, 191n.16, 193n.20
- vs. Freud, 79–80
- vs. Frost, 193n.20
- on the future, 82, 85
- vs. Heidegger, 12, 111, 112, 185n.2, 188n.9, 194n.31
- vs. Hill, 119
- and history, 64, 95, 106–8, 109, 128
- on horizontal dimension of life, 59, 64, 67–68, 74, 75, 76, 78, 80–82, 86, 99, 103, 104–5, 121–22, 128, 192n.17
- and human freedom, 12, 59, 71, 73, 111, 121, 164, 165–66, 188n.8
- interview with Dembo, 55, 63, 73–74, 87, 88, 96, 126, 168, 176n.4
- on limitation, 84, 88–89
- and love, 57, 60, 66, 80–81, 82, 87–88, 95
- and luck, 107–8
- on Marxism, 111–12, 113, 115
- on meaning, 164
- and meditation, 56–57, 58, 67, 86, 88, 91, 92–93, 95, 103, 109, 113, 121–22, 127, 163, 164–65, 186n.3, 206n.22
- and metaphysics, 6–7, 64, 75, 81, 95, 103, 104–5, 115, 121, 121–22, 127, 128, 163, 165, 192n.17
- vs. Milton, 62–63
- on the mind, 62–66, 71, 72, 81–82, 83–84, 86–87, 92–93, 100, 108, 113, 127, 128, 151, 164, 166
- on natural world, 61, 84, 86, 100, 112, 113, 114–15, 135
- vs. Nietzsche, 71
- as objectivist, 7, 12, 55–56, 91–92, 185n.2
- on Old Left vs. New Left, 103–4, 105, 108, 187n.7
- vs. Olson, 190n.15
- and openness, 71, 73–74, 81, 87–88, 99, 102, 108, 111, 113, 151, 165–66, 168, 169, 188n.8
- on Père-Lachaise cemetery, 78–79
- pessimism of, 71, 73–74, 79, 171
- on place, 30–31, 87, 134, 166
- on poetry, 10, 55–58, 61, 63, 64, 71–72, 73–74, 82, 84, 86, 88, 95, 96, 104, 117, 118–19, 127, 186n.3, 194n.25, 195n.26
- on politics, 10–11, 63, 64, 94, 103–5, 108, 111–12, 126–27, 187n.7
- practice of revision, 194n.22
- and purpose of life, 104–5

on reportage, 195n.27
and rescue, 59, 66, 69, 71, 76, 77, 82, 84
and respect, 20, 57, 65, 66, 71, 76, 77, 189n.12
on Rilke, 206n.22
vs. Rimbaud, 128
and romanticism, 58, 59–61, 87, 103, 111, 112, 113, 125, 193n.20
and sanity, 102
on self with others, 58, 59, 71
and shipwreck images, 59, 69–71, 74, 93–94, 96, 97, 188n.11
on solitary self, 58–59, 69, 70, 71, 73, 86, 190n.15
vs. Stevens, 61, 65, 86, 87, 91, 94, 100, 115, 193n.19, 194n.23
and surrealism, 99
vs. Thoreau, 100
on time, 169
and tragedy, 71, 94, 102, 170–71
and truthfulness, 72–73, 76, 77, 88, 117, 164, 189n.13
and value, 64, 66, 68, 72, 73, 75, 76, 78, 79–80, 81, 87–88, 105, 109, 121, 134, 165, 168, 192n.17
on vertical dimension of life, 59–60, 64, 74, 76, 81–82, 86, 99, 103, 104–5, 109, 128, 165–66, 192n.17
and vision, 7, 60–62, 63, 67, 71, 76, 77, 80–81, 87–88, 102–3, 109, 171, 185n.2, 186n.5
on what matters, 157, 168
vs. Whitman, 58, 59–60, 61, 64, 69, 73, 84, 87–88, 99, 100, 128, 186n.6
and the whole, 7, 10, 13, 61, 64, 71, 72, 100, 102, 105, 106, 107–8, 111, 113, 121, 128, 151, 161, 165, 167, 170–71, 206n.22

vs. Williams, 56, 58, 67, 71, 88, 89, 102, 188n.10
and wonder, 10, 11, 61, 66, 69–70, 71, 72, 76, 80, 87, 93, 108, 109, 113, 127, 151, 165–66, 166, 167, 171, 206n.22
vs. Wordsworth, 57, 87, 122, 126, 127, 128
vs. Yeats, 106, 109, 196n.32
Oppen, George, works of
"Anniversary Poem," 87
"Ballad," 74, 190n.14
"Blood from a Stone," 68, 84, 111, 115
"The Book of Job and a Draft of a Poem to Praise the Paths of the Living," 85, 111, 196n.31
"Chartres," 85, 111
"The Crowded Countries of the Bomb," 107
"Disasters," 87
Discrete Series, 11, 96, 111, 192n.18
earlier vs. later, 198n.4
"Eclogue," 61
"Eros," 78–79, 84–85, 111
expansiveness in, 93–94
"Giovanni's *Rape of the Sabine Women* at Wildenstein's," 102
"Guest Room," 69–70, 100–101, 168, 169, 189n.12, 207n.23
"The Hills," 60
"Image of the Engine," 70, 85, 188n.11
"The Impossible Poem," 101–2
language in, 62, 69, 88–94, 97
"A Language of New York," 189n.12
"Leviathan," 57
The Materials, 11, 57, 58, 60, 112, 196n.32

Oppen, George, works of (*continued*)
"The Mind's Own Place," 62, 63, 64, 112, 117–18, 164, 187n.7, 195n.26
"Myself I Sing," 58–59
Myth of the Blaze, 88
"A Narrative," 62–63, 65–66, 74, 81–82, 86, 87, 98, 100, 111, 115, 157, 186n.3, 186n.5, 187n.7, 189nn.12–13
"Of Being Numerous," 55, 58–59, 64, 67–74, 82–86, 87, 88, 89–90, 91, 92, 94, 96, 98, 100, 101, 107, 110–16, 156, 186n.3, 186n.5, 188nn.9–11, 189nn.12–13, 192n.18, 194n.25
Of Being Numerous, 66, 67, 74, 103, 187n.5, 190n.14
"Of This All Things," 87
"The Poem," 97
Primitive, 205n.19
"Psalm," 56, 189n.13
repetition in, 90–92, 115, 194n.25
"Route," 56, 68, 81, 85, 86, 87, 92, 94–109, 121–22, 169, 171, 192n.17, 195n.27, 195n.29, 196n.32
"Sara in Her Father's Arms," 112
Seascape: Needle's Eye, 122
"Some San Francisco Poems," 122, 171, 195n.29
and "stand," 85, 111, 192n.18
This in Which, 85
"The Translucent Mechanics," 195n.29
"World, World," 101
Oppen, Mary, 176n.4, 187n.7, 194n.25
Orphism, 152

Pascal, Blaise, 38, 176n.4, 182n.16
pastoral, 149–51, 155–56, 203n.15
Patocka, Jan, 202n.13
Peck, John, 190n.15

on Oppen, 112, 113
Péret, Benjamin, 52
Perse, Saint-John, 39
Pippin, Robert
on Hegel and Kierkegaard, 199n.6
Hegel's Practical Philosophy, 199n.6
Idealism as Modernism, 199n.6
on Nietzsche and French moralists, 38, 182n.16
The Persistence of Subjectivity, 199n.6
on the self, 117–18, 132, 139
Plato, 136, 152, 189n.13
on the cave, 137, 151
vs. Democritus, 202n.13
on Eros, 24, 25, 31, 67, 80, 167–68, 170, 180n.9, 191n.16, 207n.24
on the good, 45–46, 57, 134, 167–68, 169
on justice, 175n.1
vs. Nietzsche, 207n.24
Phaedo, 134, 170
Phaedrus, 93, 175n.1
Republic, 80, 167, 170
on the soul, 169, 170, 202n.13
Symposium, 24, 25, 31, 32, 67, 80, 167–68, 180n.9, 191n.16, 207n.24
on thinking, 57
on written word, 93
poetry
Char on, 16, 19, 22, 23–24, 25, 26–27, 32–34, 36, 37, 39, 40–42, 43, 47, 51, 125, 126, 134, 165, 168, 177n.1, 179n.8, 181n.12, 181n.15, 183n.20, 185n.24
and eros, 24–26
Oppen on, 10, 55–58, 61, 63, 64, 71–72, 73–74, 82, 84, 86, 88, 95, 96, 104, 117, 118–19, 127, 186n.3, 194n.25, 195n.26
vs. philosophy, 2, 4

Stevens on, 91
and vision, 2, 4, 22, 24, 26
Poirier, Richard, 193n.20
popular culture, 206n.21
postmodernism, 182n.17
post-structuralism, 204n.16
Pound, Ezra, 10, 55, 118, 126, 176n.4
   The Cantos, 68
Poussin, Nicolas, 183n.20
pre-Socratics, 38, 43, 92, 188n.11, 192n.17
   See also Heraclitus
Prevallet, Kristin, 188n.10
Price, A. W., 191n.16
prose poems, 34–36, 46, 125, 181n.13
Protestantism, 153–54
Proust, Marcel, 147
Pythagoreanism, 152

Rabbinic Judaism, 201n.8
Rabelais, François, 38
reification, 142–43, 158, 160, 164
Renaissance, the, 154
Ricoeur, Paul, 201n.9, 206n.20
Rilke, Rainer Maria, 40, 183n.20, 206n.22
   Duino Elegies, 166
   Sonnets to Orpheus, 166
Rimbaud, Arthur, 125, 182n.17
   vs. Char, 8, 9, 15–16, 17, 22, 23, 29, 34–35, 39, 40, 53
   Char on, 41–42, 53, 128
   on *éclosion,* 23
   fury of, 15
   Illuminations, 35
   on Prince and Génie, 22
   prose poems of, 34
   A Season in Hell, 16
romanticism, 52, 91, 99, 115, 122, 158, 197n.3, 204n.18
   and Char, 19–20, 26, 34, 42–43, 177n.1

vs. existentialism, 4, 6, 134–35, 155–56, 167
and Kierkegaard, 130, 131
Nature/Being in, 134–35, 141–43, 145, 146–49, 154, 155–56, 165, 202n.12, 203n.15
and Oppen, 58, 59–61, 87, 103, 111, 112, 113, 125, 193n.20
Rose, Gillian, 199n.6
Rosen, Stanley, 2, 170, 175n.1, 200n.7, 207n.24
Roudaut, Jean, 176n.4
Rousseau, Jean-Jacques, 53, 169
   Emile, 148
   First Discourse, 148
   on modernity, 146–47, 202n.12
   and Nature, 146–49
   Reveries, 148, 203n.15
   Second Discourse, 148
   on the self, 146–48
   The Social Contract, 147
Rukeyser, Muriel, 7

Sandburg, Carl, 115
Sartre, Jean-Paul, 117, 176n.4
   on action, 181n.12
   on bad faith, 133–34
   and Camus, 5, 205n.19
   on consciousness, 3
   on contingency, 3
   on engaged literature, 12–13, 184n.23
   on Hegel and Kierkegaard, 199n.6
   Search for a Method, 199n.6
satire, 38
Schiller, Friedrich, 52, 143, 144, 146, 147, 202n.11
   Letters on the Aesthetic Education of Man, 142
   on pastoral, 149
Schlegel, Friedrich, 182n.17

self, the
  as alienated, 4, 6, 59, 86, 112, 157
  and death, 7, 134, 141
  as fragmented, 142–43, 145, 147, 156, 161–62
  Hegel on, 71, 132, 138
self-preservation, 78, 79
Sennet, Richard
  The Corrosion of Character, 204n.18
  The New Capitalism, 204n.18
Sereni, Vitorrio, 50
Shelley, Percy Bysshe, 29, 167
  vs. Char, 40, 52, 166
  "On Love," 25
Sherman, David: on Sartre-Camus debate, 206n.19
Smith, Adam, 145
Snyder, Gary, 115
social freedom
  Hegel on, 6, 128–30, 132–33, 160
  vs. spiritual freedom, 128–34, 137–40, 201n.8
sociology
  vs. existentialism, 4–6, 176n.3, 201n.8
  historicist sociology, 6, 133, 160
Socrates, 4, 111, 170, 180n.9, 203n.14, 207n.24
  in *Phaedrus,* 93, 134, 175n.1
  in *Symposium,* 14, 80, 167
Spanish Civil War, 8
spiritual freedom, 170, 201n.8
  in Axial Age, 137–39, 140, 142, 145, 148–49, 155, 162, 167, 201n.8
  in Christianity, 129, 130–31, 138
  in existentialism, 133–34, 140, 151, 155, 167
  Kant on moral freedom, 139–41
  Kierkegaard on, 128–29, 130–31, 132, 160
  relationship to the whole, 141–42, 145, 149, 151, 152, 159, 166
  vs. social freedom, 128–34, 137–40, 201n.8
Stalinism, 127, 144
Stendhal
  on beauty, 25
  Le Rouge et le Noir, 176n.3
Stevens, Wallace, 9, 202n.12
  vs. Char, 17, 27, 28, 30, 31, 33, 40–41, 44, 182n.18
  "Chocorua to its Neighbor," 40, 44
  on imaginative force, 115
  on nobility, 33
  vs. Oppen, 61, 65, 86, 87, 91, 94, 100, 115, 193n.19, 194n.23
  on poetry, 91
  "A Primitive like an Orb," 40–41, 182n.18
  repetitions in works of, 91
  "The River of Rivers in Connecticut," 17
  "Sunday Morning," 192n.18
Stoicism, 138, 148, 149

Taoism, 136
Taylor, Charles
  on Axial Age, 136, 137–38, 201n.9
  The Ethics of Authenticity, 199n.6
  on Great Reform, 153–54
  Hegel and Modern Society, 199n.6
  Modern Social Imaginaries, 201n.8
  A Secular Age, 201n.8, 204n.17
  Varieties of Religion Today, 201n.8
technology, 145, 153, 159, 163, 177n.1
Thackrey, Susan: *George Oppen,* 185n.2
Thomas, St., 176n.4
Thoreau, Henry David, 53, 100, 115, 148, 186n.5
Thuillier, Jacques, 180n.10

Tocqueville, Alexis de, 5, 147
tragedy
    and Char, 42, 43, 71, 169, 170–71, 183n.20
    and Oppen, 71, 94, 102, 170–71

Vallejo, César, 7
value
    and Char, 121, 134, 168
    and deictic discourse, 196n.30
    DuPlessis on, 66, 78, 88
    the good, 2, 7, 32, 34, 45, 45–46, 57, 63, 64, 76, 87, 121, 134, 137, 159, 167–68, 169, 196n.30, 201n.9
    and Oppen, 64, 66, 68, 72, 73, 75, 76, 78, 79–80, 81, 87–88, 105, 109, 121, 134, 165, 168, 192n.17
    Plato on the good, 45–46, 57, 134, 167–68, 169
Velay, Serge, 179n.8
Verlaine, Paul, 8
Veyne, Paul
    on Char, 10, 20, 33–34, 39–40, 43–44, 50, 177n.1, 178n.2, 181n.12, 183n.20
    on Nietzsche, 43–44, 177n.1
    René Char en ses poèmes, 177n.1
Vietnam War, 68, 95, 105, 106–7, 108, 188nn.10–11
Virgil, 149, 151
    The Georgics, 150–51, 203n.15
vision
    and Char, 7, 8, 10, 14, 15, 19–20, 22, 24, 26, 29, 31, 32, 37, 39–40, 42, 46, 51, 52, 53, 165, 171
    expansive vision, 60–61
    and Oppen, 7, 60–62, 63, 67, 71, 76, 77, 80–81, 87–88, 102–3, 109, 171, 185n.2, 186n.5
    and poetry, 2, 4, 22, 24, 26
    of the whole, 3, 4, 61, 175n.1

Weber, Max, 129, 136, 145, 155, 202n.11
    The Protestant Ethic and the Spirit of Capitalism, 204n.17
    on Protestant ethnic and capitalism, 153–54
    on rationalization, 142, 143
    The Sociology of Religion, 201n.8
Weinfield, Henry: on Oppen, 110, 112, 114, 185n.2, 186n.3, 187n.7, 188n.10, 189n.12, 194n.22, 194n.25, 195n.26
Wesling, Donald: *The New Poetries*, 181n.13
Whitman, Walt, 115, 182n.17, 184n.23, 188n.11
    vs. Char, 33, 40, 44, 128, 178n.2
    vs. Oppen, 58, 59–60, 61, 64, 69, 73, 84, 87–88, 99, 100, 128, 186n.6
    "Song of Myself," 179n.6, 187n.6
whole, the
    Blanchot on, 184n.23
    and Char, 7, 13, 71, 121, 134, 165, 167, 170–71, 206n.22
    as fragmented in modernity, 143, 145, 159–60
    Jaspers on, 176n.2
    and Kant's practical postulates, 140–42
    Nature/Being as, 4, 7, 134–35, 141–42, 147, 148–49, 150–51, 154, 165, 167, 200n.7, 202n.13
    and Oppen, 7, 10, 13, 61, 64, 71, 72, 100, 102, 105, 106, 107–8, 111, 113, 121, 128, 151, 161, 165, 167, 170–71, 206n.22
    in philosophy, 1, 2–4, 156, 160
    relationship to spiritual freedom, 141–42, 145, 149, 151, 152, 159, 166

whole, the (*continued*)
   vs. social world, 129, 161
   vision of, 3, 4, 61, 175n.1
Williams, William Carlos, 10, 55, 115
   "Asphodel," 58, 88
   vs. Oppen, 56, 58, 67, 71, 88, 89, 102, 188n.10
   Paterson, 67–68, 71, 92
   Spring and All, 67
wonder
   and Char, 11, 71, 166, 167, 206n.22
   Heidegger on, 206n.22
   and Oppen, 10, 11, 61, 66, 69–70, 71, 72, 76, 80, 87, 93, 108, 109, 113, 127, 151, 165–66, 166, 167, 171, 206n.22
   as origin of philosophy, 1–2
Wordsworth, William, 53, 109, 203n.15
   vs. Char, 9, 17, 122, 125, 128
   criticisms of, 197n.3
   early life, 122–23, 125, 126
   and French Revolution, 122–23, 124
   and human suffering, 123, 124
   Lyrical Ballads, 123
   "Michael," 124
   and natural world, 123, 124, 142, 148
   vs. Oppen, 57, 87, 122, 126, 127, 128
   pastoral in, 150
   The Prelude, 123, 124
   relationship with Coleridge, 123
   "Tintern Abbey," 123, 146
World War I, 68
World War II, 68, 95, 144
   See also Char, René, Resistance experience
Wright, C. D., 46, 172

Yeats, William Butler
   vs. Char, 35
   vs. Oppen, 106, 109, 196n.32
   "The Stare's Nest By My Window," 109, 121, 196n.32
Young, Dennis, 194n.25

Zervos, Yvonne, 34
Zimet, Julian, 114
Zoroastrianism, 136
Zukofsky, Louis, 10, 55

ROBERT BAKER

is associate professor of English at the University of Montana.

www.ingramcontent.com/pod-product-compliance
Lightning Source LLC
Chambersburg PA
CBHW050349230426
43663CB00010B/2055